AF870682

From the Global to the Local

From the Global to the Local: How International Rights Reach Bangladesh's Children develops a unique perspective on human rights governance in developing countries, where the state often lacks the required resources, capacities and expertise for implementing rights. Considering how rights that have been agreed upon in the global arena of world politics are locally implemented, this book then specifically explores how they reach the local children of Bangladesh's urban slums and poor rural areas.

Andrea Schapper combines an analytical framework grounded in international relations scholarship on global governance with empirical field research methods that have their basis in sociology and anthropology. Utilizing this methodology, the book examines three principles that represent a global consensus on children's rights (the protection of children from the worst forms of child labor, providing them with primary education, and delivering basic health care services to them) to illuminate the need for local and contextual solutions to transnational issues.

Exploring such concerns with vigor, this book fills a gap in the study of human rights implementation and protection and will thus be of immense interest to students of Law, of International Relations and of Development Studies.

Andrea Schapper is an Assistant Professor at the Technische Universität Darmstadt.

Law, Development and Globalization

Series Editor—Julio Faundez

University of Warwick

During the past decades, a substantial transformation of law and legal institutions in developing countries has taken place. Whether prompted by market-based policies or the international human rights movement, by the relentless advance of the process of globalization or the successive waves of democratization, no area of law has been left untouched. The aim of this series is to promote cross-disciplinary dialogue and cooperation among scholars and development practitioners interested in understanding the theoretical and practical implications of the momentous legal changes taking place in developing countries.

Titles in the series:

State Violence and Human Rights: State Officials in the South
Andrew M. Jefferson and Steffen Jensen (eds.)

The Political Economy of Government Auditing: Financial Governance and the Rule of Law in Latin America and Beyond
Carlos Santiso

Global Perspectives on the Rule of Law
James J. Heckman, Robert L. Nelson and Lee Cabatingan (eds.)

Marginalized Communities and Access to Justice
Yash Ghai and Jill Cottrell (eds.)

Law in the Pursuit of Development: Principles into Practice?
Amanda Perry-Kessaris (ed.)

Governance Through Development: Poverty Reduction Strategies and the Disciplining of Third World States
Celine Tan

Lawyers and the Rule of Law in an Era of Globalization
Yves Dezalay and Bryant Garth (eds.)

Policing and Human Rights: The Meaning of Violence and Justice in the Everyday Policing of Johannesburg
Julia Hornberger

Gender, Justice and Legal Pluralities: Latin American and African Perspectives
Rachel Sieder and John McNeish

Justice and Security Reform: Development Agencies and Informal Institutions in Sierra Leone
Lisa Denney

Lawyers and the Construction of Transnational Justice
Yves Dezalay and Bryant Garth (eds.)

Social Movements, Law and the Politics of Land Reform
George Meszaros

From the Global to the Local: How International Rights Reach Bangladesh's Children
Andrea Schapper

Forthcoming titles in the series:

Multinational Integration, Cultural Identity and Regional Self-Government, Comparative Experiences for Tibet
Roberto Toniatti and Jens Woelk

Governing Refugees
Kirsten McConnachie

Law and Society in Latin America
Cesar Rodriguez Garavito

From the Global to the Local: How International Rights Reach Bangladesh's Children

Andrea Schapper

Routledge
Taylor & Francis Group
LONDON AND NEW YORK

First published 2014
by Routledge
2 Park Square, Milton Park, Abingdon, Oxon, OX14 4RN

Simultaneously published in the USA and Canada
by Routledge
711 Third Avenue, New York, NY 10017
A GlassHouse Book
Routledge is an imprint of the Taylor & Francis Group, an informa business

© 2014 Andrea Schapper

The right of Andrea Schapper to be identified as author of this work has been asserted by her in accordance with sections 77 and 78 of the Copyright, Designs and Patents Act 1988.

All rights reserved. No part of this book may be reprinted or reproduced or utilised in any form or by any electronic, mechanical, or other means, now known or hereafter invented, including photocopying and recording, or in any information storage or retrieval system, without permission in writing from the publishers.

Trademark notice: Product or corporate names may be trademarks or registered trademarks, and are used only for identification and explanation without intent to infringe.

British Library Cataloguing in Publication Data
A catalogue record for this book is available from the British Library

Library of Congress Cataloging-in-Publication Data
A catalog record has been requested for this book

ISBN: 978-0-415-66186-7 (hbk)
ISBN: 978-0-203-40994-7 (ebk)

Typeset in Garamond by
Servis Filmsetting Ltd, Stockport, Cheshire

Contents

Tables

Figures

List of Abbreviations

ADB	Asian Development Bank
AL	Awami League
BANBEIS	Bangladesh Bureau of Educational Information and Statistics
BBS	Bangladesh Bureau of Statistics
BDSC	Bangladesh Development Service Centre
BDT	Bangladesh Taka
BEHTRUWC	Basic Education for Hard to Reach Urban Working Children
BGMEA	Bangladesh Garments Manufacturers and Exporters Association
BGMEA/ILO/UNICEF	Bangladesh Garment Sector Projects
BILS	Bangladesh Institute of Labour Studies
BINP	Bangladesh Integrated Nutrition Programme
BNFE	Bureau of Non-formal Education
BNP	Bangladesh National Party
BRAC	Bangladesh Rural Advancement Committee
CCT	Conditional Cash Transfers
CDI	Child Development Index
CIDA	Canadian International Development Agency
CLEP	Child Labour Elimination Project
CLMIS	Child Labour Monitoring Information System
CMC	Center Management Committee
CPI	Corruption Perception Index
CRC	UN Convention on the Rights of the Child
CTA	Chief Technical Advisor
C138	ILO Minimum Age Convention
C182	ILO Worst Forms of Child Labour Convention
DAM	Dhaka Ahsania Mission
DFID	UK Department for International Development
ECOSOC	Economic and Social Council
EFA	Education for All

EHCL	Eradication of Hazardous Child Labour Project
ESDO	Eco-Social Development Organization
ESP	Essential Services Package
EU	European Union
FFE	Food for Education Programs
FSSP	Female Secondary Stipend Program
GSS	Gono Shahajjo Sangstha
GTZ	Deutsche Gesellschaft für Technische Zusammenarbeit
HDI	Human Development Index
HPSP	Health and Population Sector Programme
ICCD	Intensive Child Collection Drive
ICCPR	International Covenant on Civil and Political Rights
ICESCR	International Covenant on Economic, Social and Cultural Rights
IGA	Income Generating Activities
ILO	International Labour Organization
ILO/IPEC USDoL	Preventing and Eliminating the Worst Forms of Child Labour in Selected Formal and Informal Sectors in Bangladesh, Project funded by the United States Department of Labor
ILO/IPEC Net	Prevention and Elimination of Selected Worst Forms of Child Labour in the Informal Economy in Dhaka City, Project funded by the Government of the Netherlands
IMF	International Monetary Fund
IO	International Organization
IPEC	International Programme on the Elimination of Child Labour
IR	International Relations
IREWOC	Foundation for International Research on Working Children
ISPI	Italian Social Partners Initiative
JSK	Jano Seba Kendra
JTAG	Joint Technical Advisory Group
LO/FTF	Danish Trade Union Council
MDG	Millennium Development Goal
MLG	Multi-level Governance
MoLE	Ministry of Labour and Employment
MoPME	Ministry of Primary and Mass Education
MoU	Memorandum of Understanding
MPC	Multi Purpose Center
MWCA	Ministry of Women and Children Affairs

NCLS	National Child Labour Survey
NFE	Non-formal Education
NGO	Non-governmental Organization
NHP	National Health Policy
NORAD	Norwegian Agency for Development Cooperation
NPA	National Plan of Action
NSC	National Steering Committee
OHCHR	Office of the High Commissioner for Human Rights
PEDP	Primary Education Development Program
PESP	Primary Education Stipend Project
PIU	Project Implementation Unit
PPP	Public-Private Partnership
PRSP	Poverty Reduction Strategy Paper
QCA	Qualitative Comparative Analysis
RIC	Resource Integration Centre
R190	Worst forms of Child Labour Recommendation
SDT	Skills Development Training
SEE	Social and Economic Empowerment Program
SHE	Safety, Health and Environment Committees
SIBL	Social Investment Bank Limited
SIDA	Swedish International Development Agency
SMC	School Management Committee
TBP	National Time Bound Programme
UCEP	Underprivileged Children's Educational Programs
UDHR	Universal Declaration of Human Rights
UIA	Union of International Associations
UIE	Urban Informal Economy
UN	United Nations
UNDP	United Nations Development Program
UNICEF	United Nations International Children's Emergency Fund
USA	United States of America
USAID	United States Agency for International Development
USDoL	United States Department of Labor
WFP	World Food Program
WIP	Workplace Improvement Program

Acknowledgements

Compiling this book has been a long and exciting journey. It led me from Bremen where I started off with first research preparations, to Geneva for data collection at the International Labour Organization (ILD), to Bangladesh for intensive field research, to Cornell University in the United States of America for analyzing my data and discussing first results with South Asia experts, and back to Bremen for writing up my doctoral thesis. In Darmstadt, I finally found time to prepare this book format of my research.

Many close friends and colleagues have accompanied me part of this way or even through the entire journey. Both of my supervisors, Prof. Dr. Peter Mayer and Prof. Dr. Eva Senghaas-Knobloch, have seen this project being born and growing and they helped me to keep it alive. I am more than grateful for their advice, their support, their intellectual food and their critique. In Bremen, I also appreciate the work of Werner Dressel who supported me during my time at BIGSSS and helped me to secure funds for my research trips. In addition, I would like to thank Eva Senghaas-Knobloch, Peter Mayer, Alaka Basu, Susanne Tönsmann, Tine Hanrieder and Stephanie Vogel for reading and commenting on earlier drafts of this book. Without my friends from Bremen, this journey would not have had a home to return to. Dörte Dinger was a fun office mate – always in the mood for competition at the kicker table and a cigarette at five in the afternoon in front of the BIGSSS building. I want to thank Benedikt Rogge, Oskar Marg, Sigrid Kannengießer, Stefanie Henneke and Christian Reisinger for being there, for distracting me from work every once in a while and for making grey Bremen days colorful.

In the course of field research in Bangladesh, Ronald Berghuys, Jamal Chowdhury and Sharfuddin Khan have been of invaluable help. I would like to thank them for opening doors, for securing access to key informants and for their critical reflections on the children's rights situation in Bangladesh. At ILO headquarters, Bharati Pflug, Patricia Tagle and Klaus Günther provided me with access to the *International Programme on the Elimination of Child Labour* databases and a temporary working place in Geneva.

During my time at Cornell University, Prof. Ann Blackburn, Prof. Alaka Basu, Sreemati Mukherjee and Prof. Shelley Feldman shared their views on

South Asia and Bangladesh with me. These discussions truly enhanced my perspective towards the regional context. Prof. Daniel Gold hosted me at Cornell's South Asia Program and I want to thank him for providing me with this unique opportunity.

In Hannover, my in-between home, I would like to thank Nicole Ansorge for a place to stay and an open ear to my sorrows. Moreover, I am grateful to Tony Bünger for excellent cooking, wonderful talks at the kitchen table and for opening the door to my new home. Cooking, talking and living with him indeed were so wonderful that I fell in love with him.

In Darmstadt, I am grateful to Markus Lederer for his advice, his friendly temper and his patience with me, although I kept revising this book for a considerable amount of working time. During this time, I had lots of support from Routledge, particularly from Rebekah Jenkins and Colin Perrin. Also, I very much appreciate the helpful comments by the series editor, Julio Faundez, and the three anonymous reviewers of the book manuscript.

I want to thank my parents, Angelika and Helmut Schapper, for simply trusting in me and the ways I chose. My sisters, Christine, Teresa and Juliane, have always been there for a fun time and a good laugh back home. Special thanks to my oldest sister Tine who has taken good care of me when I came back from Bangladesh with unidentified diseases and who sent me survival packages during final write-up phases. Furthermore, my aunt Renate Rath and her husband Karl have always encouraged me with their strong interest in my work.

This book is dedicated to Barbara Fischer who left our family too early and too suddenly and who we still miss sorely.

Chapter 1

Introduction

> [...] if [human] rights don't have meaning locally they will have little meaning elsewhere.
>
> (Robinson 2002)

Wandering through the urban slums of Dhaka in Bangladesh – well aware of the fact that the government has ratified the most relevant international children's rights treaties – makes one speculate whether these rights solely exist on paper. In addition to desperate living conditions children have to face in many of these areas, even the most basic child protection and essential social services are lacking. A Chief Technical Advisor (CTA) of the International Labour Organization (ILO) in Dhaka summarizes the situation of Bangladesh's slum children with the following words: "They are surviving in an urban jungle. The notion that they have certain rights is very often simply not there. And this is, of course, sustained [...] by overall society".[1]

Rights denial, he claims, goes hand in hand with fighting for survival in the poverty context of an urban slum in one of South Asia's overcrowded megacities, and it is anchored in children's communities, in the entire society.

Facing such a setting of poverty and neglect makes one wonder how global rights can initiate local change in the lives of these children. If children's rights – as a consequence of ratification – indeed constituted a governmental commitment, why do some of these children still work in inhumane, indecent, and hazardous circumstances, deprived of basic education and primary health provisions? What has to happen for global norms to make an impact on the local level regarding the rights situation of the ones they are made for, the children in the slums of Bangladesh and elsewhere in the world?

Human rights practitioners explain the discrepancy between increasing rights ratification rates and a stagnating rights situation on the ground with key gaps in implementation, particularly at the local level (OHCHR 2006a). The former UN High Commissioner for Human Rights, Mary Robinson,

1 Interview Ronald E. Berghuys, ILO/IPEC Chief Technical Advisor, 19 May 2008.

suggests that human rights have to gain meaning among the people at the grassroots (Robinson 2002). They are best protected if they become rooted in the local context (UN 2004: 239). Does this prove to be true for children's rights as well? And how exactly do these rights trickle down from the global to the local? How can children at the local level benefit in one way or another from entitlements granted to them in the international arenas of world politics? What exactly is it that – following ratification – improves the situation of those for whom these rights are made?

1.1 Embedding the problem into International Relations scholarship

International Relations (IR) scholarship points to the importance of implementation processes that a state government has to initiate following ratification. In socialization research, norm implementation is grasped as the reflective adoption of rules by collective actors (Schimmelfennig 2002: 408). The theoretical literature on compliance highlights employing measures for making international treaties effective in national legislation (compare Jacobsen and Brown Weiss 2000: 4–5). And the Spiral Model of Human Rights Change understands human rights implementation as a socialization process that leads governments, as well as political and societal elites, to internalize standards of appropriate behavior from the international community (Risse, Jetschke and Schmitz 2002: 19). Examining theoretical treatise in IR research, however, leads to a deepening of the question at hand. What if implementation processes, according to these conceptions, have been pursued and basic principles of international children's rights conventions are anchored in national legislation and policies, but the situation for the children on the ground still has not changed comprehensively?

This study departs from a status quo that reflects exactly this empirical puzzle; global children's rights are ratified and nationally implemented, but they have not yet resulted in a comprehensive change of the rights situation of children at the grassroots. Analyzing the case of children's rights in Bangladesh, this book explores what has been termed a *local children's rights implementation* process. It proceeds from a situation in which children's rights have been ratified and transferred into national legislation and domestic policies by Bangladesh's government, and it explores ways that change the rights situation for the local target group, i.e. the children from remote rural areas and urban slums of Bangladesh. Local change is understood as an improvement of the rights situation of children. Hence, this study considers observations that reflect children's rights change and traces the rights implementation process from the endpoint to the beginning in order to identify what has initiated this change. Knowing more about that helps to single out what is needed for those local children who have not yet been reached by global rights.

This study is limited to investigating three major children's rights. These are (1) the right to protection from the worst forms of child labor, (2) the right to education, and (3) the right to basic health care. The results of this book reveal that a *local implementation process* requires the establishment of a local infrastructure, managing institutions, and the initiation of regulative mechanisms that foster children's rights through the delivery of social services. In Bangladesh, this process is managed by local non-governmental organizations (NGOs) and local governmental actors whose representatives directly interact with the rights-holders. *Local NGOs* is a term used for non-state actors who are particularly recognized in certain areas like urban slums or poor rural parts of Bangladesh. They might be well-known in major cities, such as Chittagong and Sylhet, or solely in one or two of the urban slums of Dhaka, Hazaribagh or Lalbagh. Usually, they are very small and sometimes hardly known NGOs with strong communal ties that have access and influence not granted to others. The results from the case study in Bangladesh reveal that these NGOs cooperate in *multilevel actor partnerships* that include the national government, the domestic private sector, and/or international organizations (IOs). These forms of partnerships operate across several levels and comprise actors of international, national, and local arenas. Some of their particularities are yet new to IR scholarship, such as their *multi-level* composition, their hierarchical character and the specific responsibilities that actors at each level take. In this book, it will be shown that both, their structure and their functioning, differ from what has so far been elaborated in research on global policy networks (Reinicke and Deng 1999), public private partnerships (Börzel and Risse 2005; Beisheim, Liese and Ulbert 2007; Huckel, Rieth and Zimmer 2007) and multipartite inclusive institutions (Rittberger 2009).

Altogether, two dominant departures characterize the research endeavor presented in this book. The first entails a move beyond the focus on the national towards the sub-national, highlighting interrelatedness between the global, national, and local levels. The second suggests reconsidering the exclusively governmental responsibility in a rights implementation process towards cooperation between different governmental and non-governmental actors at various levels. This implies a shift from the emphasis on the *norm addressee* towards the *norm target*. In the case of children's rights, the norm addressee remains the state government but the norm targets are the children, their families, potential employers, and entire communities. All of the norm targets together protect and provide for children's rights. Therefore, this project can be situated into governance research. The case study conducted here is a *governance case study on the implementation of children's rights in Bangladesh*. Governance research accounts for considering an extended vertical dimension in a regulatory system and allows for integrating all activities between the global and the local sphere. On the other hand, it also emphasizes an extended horizontal governance dimension with the involvement of civil society and private business actors in regulation (Bache 2012: 630; Bache and Flinders 2004: 35, compare also Benz 2009: 16). Hence, it provides an appropriately broadened analytical framework for discovering the local implementation process of international children's rights.

1.2 Specifying questions, objectives and arguments of this book

The main research question under investigation in this book is: *How can global children's rights norms reach their local rights-holders?* Of interest is not how state governments are encouraged to ratify international children's rights treaties or how they decide to implement them within domestic legislative acts and policies. More important is what has to happen *after the ratification process* to make these rights come alive for the children. And even more relevant is what needs to be arranged after *national implementation*, if these rights have still not reached the children at the grassroots level. Raising these questions goes hand in hand with a perspective change. It is not only the addressee of children's rights treaties, i.e. the state government, which is in the focus of the analysis. The emphasis is on the children, the norm targets, themselves. One overall objective of this book is to explore how global rights can be called into life for the children of Bangladesh to generate hypotheses on what is required for a *local rights implementation* process to evolve. Knowing more about that leads to a reconsideration of how children's rights and human rights implementation, in general, are understood in IR scholarship. Whereas the government bears the main responsibility for the international treaties it ratifies, reaching out to societal rights-holders requires the initiation of protective and provisional measures that the government might not always be capable of delivering. In cases like these, for instance in weak state contexts in which the government bears the monopoly of state power but faces serious limitations in exercising its functions pertinent to the rule of law, legitimacy and providing welfare services (see Schneckener 2007: 107–9), state agents can cooperate in multi-level actor partnerships. In such – often developmental – contexts like in Bangladesh, the government temporarily institutionalizes with IOs, private business actors, and local NGOs to guarantee child protection and the delivery of social services. In these multi-level actor partnerships, different actor types of various regulatory levels bale their strengths to compensate for governmental implementation deficits. Of importance is that the societal targets are directly being addressed by the local actors in these partnerships – governmental or non-governmental ones – who communicate with them, make them aware of their entitlements and enable them to claim their rights. Therefore, these local NGOs (or governmental actors) serve as transmitting agents between international (governmental) organizations, the government and the rights-holders within society. In the end, it is exactly this reconsideration – this perspective change towards norm compliance among society –

that helps to find solutions for the empirical puzzle, the discrepancy between rights ratification and continued rights denial.

1.3 Methodological proceedings

This endeavor has been pursued by conducting an in-depth case study on the realization of children's rights in Bangladesh. The South-Asian country is a typical and politically significant case that represents the discrepancy delineated above. Its government belonged to the first in the world that ratified the *UN Convention on the Rights of the Child* (CRC), which officially entered into force in 1990. Shortly after its adoption at the International Labour Conference, Bangladesh's government also legally committed to the 1999 *ILO Worst Forms of Child Labour Convention* (C182). These two conventions belong to the so-called targeted treaties, which means that they embrace civil and political as well as economic, social, and cultural rights (Alston 2005: 789). Both types of children's rights are investigated in this book, taking account of the interdependent and mutually reinforcing character of human rights.

Three major principles derived from these children's rights conventions were selected for the empirical analysis. These are (1) the protection of children from the worst forms of child labor and engagement in hazardous occupations, mainly derived from the C182, (2) children's right to basic education, and (3) primary health care services predominantly corresponding to the CRC. Following ratification, the government of Bangladesh has reformed and harmonized national legislation and policies in accordance with both international treaties. As a consequence, the three rights under investigation became anchored in constitutional law with the right to education and the right to health and nutrition being considered fundamental principles of state policy (The Constitution of the People's Republic of Bangladesh: Article 15.1, 16–18). Furthermore, the 2006 Bangladesh *Labour Code* explicitly prohibits child labor, calls for protection of adolescents from hazardous work and stipulates a national minimum age for admission to employment of 14 years. The latter even constitutes a provision of the *ILO Minimum Age Convention*, which has not yet been ratified by Bangladesh's government, but is nevertheless being implemented in legislative acts. In addition to changes in national law, a bulk of domestic policies promoting the three rights considered here became initiated in Bangladesh. Many of them carry the stamp of external influence from donor countries or international agencies, such as the IMF's *Poverty Reduction Strategy Paper* and the *National Plan of Action for Children*, a follow-up requirement for national governments which have ratified the CRC. Yet, all of these policies, including the recently adopted *National Child Labour Elimination Policy* which contains obligatory regulations set forth in the C182, promote the provisions of the conventions that the government of Bangladesh has committed itself to.

Despite these legislative and political developments, change could only be observed in some of Bangladesh's communities and not in others. It was exactly these area-based changes, however, that made Bangladesh a significant case for further in-depth exploration. In other words, Bangladesh reflected the empirical puzzle of interest and, at the same time, recorded punctual progressive developments in its children's rights situation. The latter became visible through considerably increased school enrollment rates, gender parity in primary education, declining child labor figures and a health situation that improved in certain respects, e.g. relating to children's vaccination coverage. Hence, the idea behind an appropriate research design was to put the cart before the horse. If improvements are to be observed in certain communities, where do they come from and what exactly causes them? Under what conditions can outcomes like these be achieved, what can we learn from them, and in which way can they be transformed to broad-based and sustainable change?

In order to search for answers to these questions, the expected outcome of a local implementation process had to be defined. Implementation measures that have been formulated in both international conventions served as a compass in this regard. According to them, very simple indicators – focusing the societal norm targets – for the three interdependent children's rights were determined. Hence, a successful outcome, in the sense of Underdal's (2004: 34) dimension of effectiveness was to be observed if at least one of the following indicators proved to be true (1) a number of children could be withdrawn from the worst forms of child labor and/or the hazards of a number of their workplaces could be removed, (2) a number of children could be provided with non-formal education and/or vocational skills training, and (3) a number of children could be supplied with basic health care services. All policy and program activities that – following ratification – met one or more of these indicators were taken into the pool of within-case observations. The exact numbers of children profiting from such policy programs has not been quantified to enhance the variety of initiatives considered for the empirical analysis. However, the respective initiative had to target at least the number of an entire school class – which are between 30 and 100 students in Bangladesh – at the minimum.

This proceeding led to a Y-centered or outcome-oriented research design (Ganghof 2005) that comparatively analyzed seven transnational, national, and local projects fostering children's rights in one way or another. The data pool comprised the following policy programs:

- the governmental *Food for Education* (FFE) programs,
- the governmental *Eradication of Hazardous Child Labour* (EHCL) project,
- the non-governmental *Child Labour Elimination Project* (CLEP),
- UNICEF's *Basic Education for Hard to Reach Urban Working Children* (BEHTRUWC) project,

- the ILO/IPEC *Preventing and Eliminating the Worst Forms of Child Labour in Selected Formal and Informal Sectors in Bangladesh* (ILO/IPEC USDoL) project,
- the ILO/IPEC *Prevention and Elimination of Selected Worst Forms of Child Labour in the Informal Economy in Dhaka City* (ILO/IPEC Net) project
- and the Bangladesh *Garment Sector Projects*, a cooperative undertaking of the ILO, UNICEF, and the Bangladesh Garments Manufacturers and Exporters Association (BGMEA).

These within-cases displayed minimal variance on the outcome variable and maximal variance on the case characteristics (van Evera 1997: 57–8). Hence, several comparative proceedings, including a structured–focused comparison and a Qualitative Comparative Analysis (QCA), would point to certain common benchmarks that constitute necessary factors for the implementation outcome.

A broad range of data collected within and beyond Bangladesh's borders was utilized for the comparative analysis. They ranged from various kinds of primary and secondary documents, transcripts of problem-centered expert interviews (Witzel 2000) and an expert focus group to detailed notes from field observation (Whyte 1984) and grassroots level research in Bangladesh. The overall evaluative method selected for the data analysis was a process-tracing (George and Bennett 2005; Checkel 2005a), which implied a structured–focused comparison (George and Bennett 2005: 86–9), a content analysis (Atkinson and Coffey 1997; Prior 2004), and a crisp-set QCA (Ragin 1989; Rihoux and Ragin 2009). A comparative lens dominated the entire investigation and focused on guiding principles, such as the local infrastructure established, institutions launched, actor partnerships at stake, and relevant configurations of regulative mechanisms representing necessary conditions for the local implementation outcome.

1.4 Some words on multi-disciplinary research

Special about the research conducted for this book was that it combined field research methods originating from sociology and anthropology, such as conducting problem-centered interviews and field observation at the grassroots, with research questions and theoretical assumptions based in IR and political science. Considering the research question at hand, this seemed to be appropriate for several reasons. First of all, in this book concerns regarding responsibilities are being raised. Who is responsible for children's rights implementation? What happens if a state government ratifies legal treaties and does not lack political willingness but capacities, resources and expertise to realize pertinent entitlements for the rights-holders? Can other non-state actors or particular actor partnerships compensate governmental deficits in such weak state contexts? Second, the book will provide some answers on regulatory mechanisms that need to be installed to achieve children's rights compliance among society in such contexts. Which strategies can be pursued to convince children to refrain from hazardous labor and regularly attend school although their families face severe poverty? Third, in this book norm research is being developed. Norms are made in the global arenas of IOs; how they trickle down to the local sphere is a central question of their effectiveness. But how can this effectiveness be achieved? Are material or immaterial factors needed to foster norm implementation? Fourth, this book tackles sustainability issues. What happens if externally funded policy projects terminate; will rights-related social services still be provided? Is the state government going to continue what has been initiated by IOs and local NGOs? What happens to the norm targets after they have participated in such programs? All of these four aspects and pertinent questions raised in this book have their disciplinary grounding in IR and Political Science.

At the same time, the book leaves international and national spheres which are the most familiar to IR scholars and puts an emphasis on individual rights-holders at the local level – yet a skeleton in the closet of IR scholarship. Therefore, I have utilized anthropological field research methods that are useful for analyzing grassroots phenomena and small-scale social units (Merry 2006a: 28–9). During my field research in Bangladesh, I have identified the policy projects mentioned above as sites in which global, national and local processes are reflected in the social reality of children, their families and entire communities (compare Merry 2006a: 29). With my comparison of norm implementation in these seven cases, I will engage in what anthropologists call multi-sited ethnography (Marcus 1998: 79–104; see also Merry 2006a: 29).

In the course of data collection, I have conducted 23 problem-centered expert interviews in Bangladesh (Witzel 2000; Bogner and Menz 2005a, 2005b; Meuser and Nagel 2005). An expert in the context of this field research was someone who had particular knowledge about the process of children's rights implementation through his or her function in at least one of the seven projects examined. The rationale behind the selection of interviewees was to gather as much information and detail as possible to draw a comprehensive picture of the implementation activities in the local sphere. Hence, the interview partners included representatives of all participating project stakeholders. These ranged from technical advisors from IOs like the ILO or UNICEF, project directors at the Ministry of Primary and Mass Education (MoPME) or national coordinators of the Ministry of Labour and Employment (MoLE), and directors or managers of larger nationally or internationally operating Bangladeshi NGOs (e.g. the Bangladesh Rural Advancement Committee (BRAC) or the Underprivileged Children's Educational Programs (UCEP)), to field workers engaged in the targeted communities representing local governmental or non-governmental institutions. Preference was given to respondents who were in direct contact with the rights-holders, the children and families, themselves. These were mostly field workers or project coordinators from implementing NGOs or, as in the case of the FFE programs, teachers from governmental schools. In projects that aimed at the realization of more than one of the three rights principles examined here, interviewees from each component were consulted, i.e. from the field team withdrawing children from the worst forms of child labor, from the colleagues providing education services in the communities, and from health care suppliers. Whereas a few interviews with local field workers had to be conducted in Bengali and were translated simultaneously, usually by another NGO colleague, most conversations could be held in English. Only one interview partner (who had been the national coordinator of a large governmental project) refused to have his interview taped due to his harsh critique of governmental corruption, which had made him quit his job and change his occupation.

What has been subsumed under field observation here was a combination of participant observation and visiting the individual project components in practice, particularly the existing infrastructure and respective institutions. Participant observation is a research method rooted in anthropology that allows the field worker to place individuals or communities in a certain context to gain a realistic picture of their behavioral dynamics (see Whyte 1984: 27). The main instrument of this method is taking field notes of formal and informal meetings, discussions, and any investigations made (Whyte 1984: 32). Entering the field often goes hand in hand with an exploration beyond the boundaries of personal knowledge and beyond facts that can be read in books and documents. Exploring requires a considerable amount of time to get acquainted with the new social terrain, gathering access to a locality and, in some cases, for gaining the acceptance of the resident communities. A local guide is valuable for learning insights, multiplying contacts, and managing difficult situations, while guides also attest to the researcher's sincerity (Whyte 1984: 63). Reverting to a few of these key informants can enrich the process of data collection; as soon as the researcher becomes accredited within a circle of relevant experts, the flow of accessible information increases considerably (compare Whyte 1984: 74–7). This relates to both, conducting field interviews and observations. Both can fruitfully complement each other; the synergy effect between them has been nicely summarized by Whyte:

> [...] Observation guides us to some of the important questions we want to ask the respondent, and interviewing helps us to interpret the significance of what we are observing. Whether through interviewing or other means of data gathering, we need to place the observed scene in context. (1984: 96)

This mutual complementarity was applied in the research endeavor on which this book is based. Whenever contacts to local implementing NGOs and field workers were established through an interview, they were asked whether a field visit to their project site was possible and if they could serve as a local guide.[2]

Visiting the field was extremely enlightening with respect to context-specificity. A learning center in Bangladesh's slums, as part of the established infrastructure to realize the right to education, is by no means comparable to what people from Western countries would understand as a school. Sometimes it is simply a provisional and fragile bamboo hut that is in some way fixed above the Buriganga River; entering and leaving it might already be a safety risk. As we will see later on, this impermanence and instability that marks the lives of the children and their families in these poor communities is one of the factors that explain why their own behavior frequently is not in accordance with children's rights (see also Schapper 2009).

Field observations included visits to learning and community centers in Dhaka's slums, pre-primary schools preparing children for integration into the governmental schooling system, rural and urban governmental schools, teachers' trainings, hazardous work places of children or work places from which hazards had been removed, women's groups of micro-credit components, a garment factory, and different non-governmental skills training facilities. Besides gathering observations and taking photographs, informal interviews and conversations with children, parents, teachers, trainers, community people, field workers and coordinators, monitoring and education officers, other field researchers, program directors, factory managers and representatives from NGOs, and development agencies were undertaken. Most of them were held in Bengali and either translated by the respective local guide or, if it was reduced to a simple dialogue, did not need any translation. The difference from Whyte's procedure was that the people observed, visited, and informally talked to were not necessarily the same as the consulted experts. Therefore, the methodological procedure was only partly complementary and can be described as rather supplementary. This means that expert interviews were supplemented with informal discussions held with local rights-holders and their social environment while taking field notes. Of particular relevance throughout conducting field research in Bangladesh was maintaining an overt research role that demanded sensitivity, understanding, cultural tolerance, patience, bearing frustration, a bit of courage, and most of all, being completely open to learning, to experiencing, and to what will happen next (see also Whyte 1984: 81).

Whereas research methods were borrowed from anthropology and sociology, evaluations methods, again, originated from Political Science and IR.

2 In some cases, project activities had already terminated. Nevertheless, most of the time either single components kept running beyond the project period or the same concept was accomplished in a different project. Then, visits to these respective sites were made to gain at least a basic understanding of the rationale behind it.

They have comprised process-tracing (Checkel 2005a, 2005b; George and Bennett 2005; van Evera 1997), a structured–focused comparison (George and Bennett 2005), a qualitative comparative analysis (Ragin 1987; Rihoux and Ragin 2009, read more about this in Chapter 4) and a content analysis of all the documents, i.e. the evaluation reports of the project, other project documents, interview transcripts and newspaper articles (Atkinson and Coffey 1997; Mayring 2000).

Altogether, this book project is a multi-disciplinary endeavor. It has applied anthropological and sociological field research methods and evaluation methods from Political Science and IR to answer a question that has meaning in a variety of disciplines, first and foremost in Human Rights Studies. The book focuses on human rights and their implementation, although many of its sections tackle questions relevant to development research. Here, however, the emphasis is on whether basic rights could be realized according to the measures set out in international conventions. The main concern is on protecting and providing for fundamental rights and freedoms – in a sustainable way – not so much on how education and health policy could be even further developed and improved. This book's accentuation of norm effectiveness, actors, responsibilities, regulative mechanisms and sustainability – as elaborated above – clearly situate it into Human Rights Studies within IR.

1.5 This book's outline

This book starts by highlighting inspirations from governance research that contributed to establishing an analytical framework on studying local rights implementation (Chapter 2). Of particular significance is the scope of governance concepts embracing "[...] all levels of human activity – from the family to the international organization [...]" (Rosenau 1995: 13). In this chapter, this is mainly relevant for a departure from the nation state and for considering vertical governance expansions towards the local level (Rosenau 1992: 2–3; Christiansen 1997: 51–2; Bache and Flinders 2004: 35; compare also Benz 2009: 16). Taking account of horizontal governance diversifications implies a shift away from state-centric government concepts and integrates regulatory activities of civil society and private business actors. In the second part of this chapter, these governance inspirations meet the more established study of human rights norms in IR scholarship, including socialization and compliance research as well as the Spiral Model of Human Rights Change. The analytical framework developed at the end of this chapter suggests to vertically and horizontally broaden our understanding of human rights realization to integrate regulatory activities at the local level and the involvement of non-state actors.

In the next part, the situation of children and their rights in Bangladesh – with reference to childhood, child labor, education, and health – will be introduced (Chapter 3). Moreover, global children's rights anchored in the

CRC and the C182 are specified. These are legally binding for Bangladesh and have been transferred into its national legislation and domestic policies. Nevertheless, these global norms so far have not trickled down to the local rights-holders. Problem-centered interviews conducted with field workers from IOs, the government, and NGOs reveal that the rights situation on the ground has not yet comprehensively changed. For making rights meaningful to the children at the grassroots, a local implementation process has to evolve.

The cases introduced in the following initiate such a local implementation process in one way or the other (Chapter 4). Subject to further investigation are seven projects and programs fostering rights implementation. Their basic components, features, strategies and participating actors will be briefly delineated. The second part of this chapter reveals which regulative mechanisms of these cases lead to a successful implementation outcome. Therefore, successful implementation has to become clearly defined and a logical configuration of mechanisms has to be established with the help of a crisp-set QCA. This results in a statement about necessary and sufficient conditions pertinent to regulative mechanisms that need to be at work to achieve an implementation outcome.

The second chapter on the local implementation process (Chapter 5) refers to the necessity of establishing a permanent local infrastructure and administrative institutions involving community members. Moreover, it describes and classifies multi-level actor partnerships that play a prominent role in compensating governmental implementation deficits. By systemizing the empirical evidence at hand, it singles out which partner takes over what role and functions in the process. Particularly local actors, whether governmental or non-governmental, are indispensable for directly reaching out to the rights-holders. Often, they are the only ones with access to local communities and they manage protective measures and rights-related services.

The area between outcomes and impacts is the subject of the next part of this book (Chapter 6). Despite strong empirical evidence of an observable outcome measurable through figures delivered from evaluation reports, only few policy activities seem to result in a sustainable impact. Most of the projects considered here operate within a limited time frame and are not supported by external donor funding beyond that. If the government has not taken over the infrastructure until then, protective measures and service delivery usually have to be stopped and the reduction of the problem, i.e. the impact, begins to stagnate. This chapter is divided according to indicators pointing to an impact beyond a respective program's outcome. It concludes with presenting the results of the entire case study on the implementation of children's rights obtained in the form of generated hypotheses.

This book's conclusion briefly reiterates main argumentative steps and elaborates on a new understanding of human rights implementation on the basis of all empirical and theoretical considerations made. In a further step, it refers to limitations and open research questions pertinent to the case study, it outlines political implications and suggests a route for further research departing from what has been elaborated and highlighted here.

Chapter 2

Governance inspirations meet the study of human rights norms

> In many countries the main tendency in recent years has been to shift the balance between government and society away from the public sector and more towards the private sector. [...] there are also efforts to shift the balance towards a sharing of tasks and responsibilities; towards doing things together instead of doing them alone.
>
> (Kooiman 1994: 1)

In International Relations (IR), we have observed a major shift from government to governance (e.g. Rosenau and Czempiel 1992). Just like Kooiman (1994) suggests above, there is a general tendency towards sharing functions and responsibilities that have been traditionally attributed to the government among different actors, public and private ones. This tendency can be observed in many policy fields. Hence, we speak of environmental governance, of security governance or even of (just) peace governance. We do not yet speak, however, of human rights governance. The policy field of human rights is traditionally considered to be a public and not a private domain. In the conventional understanding, it is the state government that ratifies a human rights treaty and that implements the rules and norms that are anchored in this treaty. Such an understanding of human rights government becomes particularly obvious if one contemplates human rights research that has been conducted by IR scholars.

In this chapter I argue that a governance perspective will broaden our understanding of how human rights evolve *after* they have been ratified and transferred into national law by the respective government. Governance research promises to provide valuable inspiration for studying human rights implementation, particularly in weak states in which deficits in several state functions, such as welfare, legitimacy and rule of law prevail (Schneckener 2007: 107–9). In these states, governmental and non-governmental actors operating at different regulatory levels can share human rights implementation responsibilities.

Concepts of governance are promising to fruitfully broaden the human rights research agenda: they embrace various forms of regulation and are suitable for analyzing political orders of social reality regardless of whether they have traditionally existed for a long time or are just recently evolving (compare Mayntz 2009a: 9). Governance terminology is attractive because it facilitates a perspective that grasps governing as an international system beyond the nation-state as well as domestic governance within a nation-state or the relation between both (see also Börzel 2005). This means that a governance perspective overcomes the traditional separation between international and domestic politics and between international anarchy and national hierarchy (Börzel 2005: 74–5).

2.1 Governance inspirations

Since the classical realist theory of international politics was concerned with the struggle for power and peace among nations (Morgenthau 1973), profound changes have taken place in what was once the discipline of "Inter-national Relations". Between the great debates and inter-paradigm exchanges, scholars have continuously broadened their research agenda in the face of growing interdependence, hoping to capture and explain emerging aspects of world politics. The interdependence literature of the 1970s still upholds the concept of the nation state as a separate unit within the international system but points to complex mutual dependence among countries and among actors in different countries (Keohane and Nye 1977: 8). It does not see the state system declining, however, and instead highlights an evolving international society (Bull 1977). In the late 1980s and throughout the 1990s, the significant boost of transactions across borders in numerous areas, such as finance, trade, and other capital flows but also in terms of information, communication, and cultural exchanges, as well as human mobility, has led to the use of the term globalization (Beisheim, Dreher, Walter, Zangl and Zürn 1999). After recognizing the increasing sensitivity and vulnerability between separate state units (Keohane and Nye 1977), the globalization literature of the 1990s brings the merging of these units into play (Zürn 2002: 235): "Globalization thus describes a process of transition towards one integrated global society and away from a cluster of merely internationalized societies" (Zürn 2002: 236).

Nevertheless, most of these transactions are not global but transcend national borders (Zürn 2002: 238). This goes hand in hand with a decoupling of territory and rule resulting in changes in the Westphalian order of the modern state system (Caparaso 2000) including the declining authority of states (Strange 1996) and traditional notions of state sovereignty. Whereas interdependence describes a condition, "globalization" refers to a process (Zürn 2002: 237). This process of political and social denationalization leads to a transformation of the state within the dimensions of welfare, rule of law, resources, and legitimacy (Beisheim, Dreher, Walter, Zangl and Zürn 1999; see also Zürn 2005). What has been emerging is a world order beyond national borders involving a variety of actors apart from governmental ones (e.g. Keck and Sikkink 1998); in other words: a post-national constellation (Habermas 1998; Leibfried and Zürn 2006).

In this world of complex interdependence, governance research has become increasingly prominent. With the aim of capturing the intricacy of world affairs, governance scholars continuously point to how interwoven regulatory arrangements are embedded in a multi-level system and how a variety of actors across these levels exert influence on a wide range of issues. Even though forms of regulation have largely shifted from government to governance (e.g. Rosenau and Czempiel 1992), world affairs are still controlled by intentional activities pursuing common objectives (e.g. Rosenau 1995).

Concepts of governance remain contested until today. A pioneering, open, and still broadly accepted definition has been offered by James Rosenau (1995) who suggests conceiving of governance as: "[...] systems of rule at all levels of human activity – from the family to the international organization – in which the pursuit of goals through the exercise of control has transnational repercussions" (Rosenau 1995: 13). According to Dingwerth and Pattberg (2006), Rosenau's definition embraces four constitutive elements. These are (1) systems of rule, (2) levels of human activity, (3) the pursuit of goals, and (4) transnational repercussions. (1) Systems of rule exist whenever regulatory mechanisms are in place that impact norms, expectations, and the behavior of actors in a particular issue area. These rule systems, i.e. the existence of norms and regulating standards that structure, enable, and constrain social activity, are an important recurrent element that can be found in almost every definition of governance (Dingwerth and Pattberg 2006: 189). (2) The inclusion of all levels of human activity, from the family to the IO, as a broadening constitutive element of this definition emphasizes an inseparably linked multilevel system, including activities at the global, regional, national, and local scale. (3) The pursuit of explicit goals is highlighted instead of solely considering intentional interactions that follow-up on a certain objective. (4) The fourth constitutive element of Rosenau's definition, transnational repercussions, relates to the impact rule systems can possibly have, even beyond national boundaries (Dingwerth and Pattberg 2006: 190).

Characteristic for governance is an ongoing relocation of authority outwards toward supranational and inwards toward sub-national entities (Rosenau 1992: 2–3). This leads to an even deeper interrelatedness between the macro and micro level. As macro-level changes are ongoing, the role of micro-level actors in the unfolding of governance without government has to be further explored (Rosenau 1992: 28). Recent definitions of governance do not only refer to purposive activities and the involvement of diverse actors but also include distributive power. In their volume on new modes of governance in the global system, Mathias Koenig-Archibugi and Michael Zürn emphasize that: "[...] governance can be understood as the creation and implementation of rule systems that facilitate the coordination and cooperation of social actors and determine the distribution of the costs and benefits of collective action" (Koenig-Archibugi 2006: 3).

In contrast, Mayntz (2009a) has suggested a narrower definition of governance embracing various forms of regulation. She refers to the concept of governance as subsuming miscellaneous approaches to intentionally regulating collective affairs (2009a: 8). This includes forms of institutionalized self-regulation in civil society, different means of cooperation between governmental and non-governmental or private business actors, as well as the classical sovereign exercise of control by state actors (Benz 2004: 21; compare Mayntz 2009a: 46). The cognitive interest of governance theory is in exploring possibilities for collectively regulating transnational issues and supplying common goods (Mayntz 2009b: 13). Concerted action for tackling and, in the most favorable cases, solving trans-sovereign problems has to be binding, as Rittberger (2009: 261) has added. It involves governance institutions that handle trans-boundary issues, which individual nation states cannot effectively address (Rittberger 2009: 262). Governance theory, therefore, constitutes an institutionalist theory emphasizing a regulatory structure (Mayntz 2009a: 47; compare also: Dingwerth and Pattberg 2006: 189).

Following these conceptualizations, governance in this book is understood as a term for intentional, binding activities that create order beyond national boundaries in a multilevel system involving both regulative and distributive interventions, which are exercised through a variety of governmental and non-governmental actors.

2.2 The vertical and the horizontal governance dimension

One important inspiration from governance research is its departure from the nation state. This departure takes two dominant dimensions into account, vertical expansions towards a system of multi-level governance, i.e. interactions between different regulatory levels, and horizontal expansions towards transnational governance, i.e. interactions between different types of actors. In this book, I argue that understanding vertical and horizontal expansions of regulation helps to comprehend human rights politics in weak states. The vertical dimension is useful to integrate processes between the global and the local sphere. In particular, local level processes – which tell us more about how human rights reach their target group – have been neglected in IR accounts of rights implementation so far. In addition to that, the horizontal dimension helps to reveal which actors beyond the nation state participate in such processes.

2.2.1 The vertical dimension

Scholars investigating the European Union (EU) and its political space between supranational and sub-national activities have pioneered research on the vertical governance dimension within the framework of *multi-level governance* concepts. A critical process in this was "the rise of regional Europe" (Christiansen 1997: 51) requiring intensified coordination in a governance system that encompasses a multitude of institutions at the supranational, national, and regional (in the sense of Europe's sub-national regions) level of decision-making (Hooghe and Marks 1997: 1). In other words, the European Community had to be governed although its characteristics did and still do not fit statehood criteria pertinent to territoriality, peoplehood, and sovereignty (Preuss 1996: 214).

European governance is characterized by three substantial criteria emphasized in the literature. First of all, the competence for making and implementing European regulations is not solely attributed to the EU but distributed among several governance levels including the supranational as well as the national, regional, and local spheres. Secondly, rule-making and realization is not limited to public but also private actors. Public and private actors are not in a hierarchical relationship but mutually depend on each other. Thirdly, the EU concentrates on regulative politics instead of redistributing resources. This de-politicization fosters the delegation of regulative competences to independent agencies (compare Börzel 2005: 80).

A plurality of actors from supranational institutions, member states, regions, as well as interest groups, the private sector, and other non-governmental organizations (NGOs) have all taken relevant roles and participate in the EU's policy process (Preuss 1996: 219; see also: Christiansen 1997: 66). This process, as stated by Preuss above, does not only lead to the integration of new actors into the governance system but also shapes the functions they have to take up. The principle of subsidiarity has thereby guided questions and debates about the distribution of powers and competences in community policy making and implementation (Weiler 1997: 123).

The multi-layered nature of European decision-making structures has been recognized as a unique system (Kohler-Koch and Rittberger 2009: 4) and led to the introduction of the concept of multi-level governance in the 1990s: "MLG [multi-level governance] posits that decision-making authority is not monopolized by the governments of the member states but is diffused to different levels of decision-making, the sub-national, national and supranational levels" (Kohler-Koch and Rittberger 2009: 8). According to Benz (2009), a multi-level governance system is characterized by four defining features. Constitutive of multi-level governance are (1) a political system in which competences and resources are shared across territorial levels and units and in which (2) actors belonging to institutions operating at various levels coordinate decisions. Furthermore, there is (3) a connection between structures and processes within a territorial level and between territorial levels and (4) actors interact within as well as between these levels (Benz 2009: 17–18).

Today, the research agenda of EU governance scholars largely concentrates on new modes of governance, participation of civil society organizations, and evolving governance arrangements including their problem-solving capacities (Kohler-Koch and Rittberger 2009: 4). Remaining challenges are to: "[...] tidy up the conceptual morass, to amend the inconclusive evidence, to oust the ghost of 'the state' as a major frame of reference, and to get beyond the tyranny of dichotomies" (Olsen 2009: 191). This means that despite the inspiration that European integration research has provided for investigating multi-layered systems, conceptual clarity is lacking in European multi-level governance approaches just as much as in others. Until today, for example, some researchers – in their use of the concept – exclusively stick to the vertical dimension of EU decision-making, i.e. integrating supranational and subnational governmental actors. This means that they rather refer to a concept of "multi-level government" (Bache 2012: 630). Other understandings of multi-level governance integrate both, vertical *and* horizontal dimensions of interdependence within the EU system (Bache 2012: 630; Bache and Flinders 2004: 35; compare also Benz 2009: 16). Hence, according to their understanding, the intertwining of state and non-state actors leads to even more complexity. This tendency towards intricacy and the consequent need to share competencies among a multitude of heterogeneous actors results in increasing coordination difficulties across levels (Benz 2009: 16) in which forms of multi-level governance have to prove their functioning under respective conditions (Benz 2009: 233).

Such interwoven multi-layered systems can neither be governed in a centralized way nor can public entities be treated or coordinated separately from each other (Benz 2009: 15). This means that there is not one single mode of EU governance (Börzel 2012). A systematic analysis of policy-making in the EU suggests that a combination of decision-making procedures guided by three main principles is in place. (1) Hierarchy is the principle for supranational centralization and supranational decision-making, (2) negotiation systems encompass inter- and transgovernmental cooperation and competition can be subsumed under (3) the market principle. Different forms of political coordination in the EU can be typologized according to these principles as institutionalized rule structures and the respective actors involved. Therefore, the complexity of European decision-making procedures has been recognized as a "governance mix" (Börzel 2012: 614–24).

Recently, Michael Zürn (2012) has claimed that the EU is not the only system of multi-level governance. He has introduced the concept of global multi-level governance as a form of global governance under two particular conditions. On the one hand – and this is a clear demarcation to intergovernmental coordination – he claims that global institutions need to hold authority. And on the other hand, he argues, that the different governance levels do not operate independent of each other. In contrast, they are mutually dependent and each level performs particular functions which points to at least "[...] some extent [of] functional differentiation" (Zürn 2012: 731). Thus, the nation state does not carry out all of its traditional functions anymore (Zürn and Leibfried 2005), it rather shares these with different non-state actors and takes the role of an "authority manager" (Genschel and Zangl 2008) that orchestrates a system of transnational governance (Abbott and Snidal 2009: 501).

2.2.2 The horizontal dimension

Whereas the vertical governance dimension is usually reflected in multi-level governance concepts, another important research strand on *transnational governance* has evolved around the horizontal governance dimension. Transnational governance comprises the development, enforcement, and implementation of norms and rules with significant participation of private actors with a scope beyond national borders (Dobusch and Quack 2009: 236). Crucial in transnational governance concepts is the increasingly important role of non-state actors, among them multinational corporations, employers' associations, NGOs, and social movements. These non-state actors can be categorized into firms and industrial groups on the one hand and NGOs and civil society organizations on the other hand. Various constellations and arrangements of actors from both of these two categories increasingly appear on the world stage and take over governance functions (compare Abbott and Snidal 2009: 506).

Comparing rather traditional and more recently evolving modes of governing, Abbott and Snidal (2009) contrast two ideal governance types. Whereas old governance comprises mandatory laws and regulations, is state-centric, and organized around a centralized authority and bureaucratic expertise, new transnational governance encompasses soft law, state orchestration promoting stakeholder engagement and broad participation, and is characterized by decentralized authority and dispersed expertise (Abbott and Snidal 2009: 520). In contrast to the central role of the state in more traditional governance concepts, the new governance ideal type implies that the state:

> [...] modifies its regulatory responsibilities to emphasize orchestration of public and private actors and institutions rather than direct promulgation and enforcement of rules [...] Orchestration includes a wide range of directive and facilitative measures designed to convene, empower, support, and steer public and private actors engaged in regulatory activities. (Abbott and Snidal 2009: 509–10)

Orchestration and shared regulatory responsibilities imply a progressive shift from single-actor to multi-actor schemes (Abbott and Snidal 2009: 519). The emerging collaboration of diverse actors enables pursuing common goals while combining complementary competencies (Abbott and Snidal 2009: 526) along with sharing expertise, capacities, resources, and commitment. Besides collaboration, the multiplicity of actors and a corresponding bundling of their respective strengths facilitates the fine-tuning of regulation according to local circumstances and conditions (Abbott and Snidal 2009: 527).

Although states remain the central actors in the international system, even today (Hasenclever and Mayer 2007: 12), the new governance ideal type embracing state orchestration and public–private cooperation can increasingly be found in the world. Modes of transnational governance may result in fluid and fragile social orders and many of its organizational forms and processes have not yet been extensively explored (Dobusch and Quack 2009: 236–7). The cooperative actor constellations investigated in the IR literature so far are global policy networks (Reinicke and Deng 1999), public–private partnerships (Börzel and Risse 2005; Beisheim, Liese and Ulbert 2007; Huckel, Rieth and Zimmer 2007; Schäferhoff 2009), and inclusive multipartite institutions (Rittberger 2009). All of them have one thing in common: the increasing involvement of non-state actors in transnational actor constellations.

Non-state actors and even NGOs themselves constitute an extraordinarily heterogeneous group with only limited within-group differentiation in the relevant literature (Seifer 2009: 15). Both terms describe diffuse categories comprising economic actors such as transnational companies – disposing of a range of material capabilities – but also trade unions, powerful international NGOs based in Northern countries, small NGOs of the South – endowed with only scarce resources – and others (Seifer 2009: 13). They actively participate in governance at various levels including the local, national, regional, supranational, and international levels (Seifer 2009: 16). For the purpose of this analysis, some basic characteristics of those NGOs engaging in collaborative networks with governmental actors to undertake governance functions are outlined here.

NGOs are political actors distinguished by high flexibility and the corresponding ability to adjust to the complex demands of multi-level arenas. In contrast to democratically elected governments that are intimately involved in legitimization procedures, NGOs easily and flexibly handle themes and adapt positions. In their activities, modern communication technologies count as important tools for processing information, framing issues, and adding them to the public agenda. NGOs usually engage in the governance of certain policy fields, among them human rights, democratization, environmental protection, and development (Seifer 2009: 28). Particularly in areas of limited statehood, people who are affected by inequality, social grievances, discrimination or exploitation often do not see themselves represented by their government but rather by particular IOs or NGOs (Seifer 2009: 29).

Within transnational actor constellations, NGOs commonly cooperate with IOs. The United Nations have made "arrangements for consultations with non-governmental organizations" in the Economic and Social

Council's (ECOSOC) resolution 1296 from 1968, providing the basis for their definition of the term 'non-governmental organization' (UN 1968: 21). According to that resolution, NGOs are organizations that have not been established by an intergovernmental agreement (UN 1968: 21, Article 7). Further defining features designate NGOs to be a representative body that is democratically organized; that works on a non-profit basis and that aims at supporting the spirit and objectives of the United Nations. NGOs do not belong to a political party, they need to be non-violent, and they have to respect the principles of non-interference and state sovereignty (UN 1968: 21; compare Seifer 2009: 31–2). The non-state and non-profit character of NGOs has also been highlighted in the Union of International Associations' (UIA) definition. According to their understanding, an NGO is a: "[...] legally constituted organization created by private persons or organizations with no participation or representation of any government. It is usually non-profit. [...] NGOs can be organized on a local, national or international level [...]" (UIA 2010).

A narrower definition was formulated by Anthony Judge (1995), who claims that NGOs mediate between the state and its citizens, taking over essential functions pertinent to sustaining democratic culture. These include (1) expressing a society's needs, (2) motivating citizens to actively participate in society, (3) promoting pluralism and diversity, (4) providing alternative possibilities to state agencies for the delivery of services with enhanced flexibility and independence, and (5) creating mechanisms of accountability pertinent to governments and the market (Judge 1995). The compatibility of some of these aspects has been questioned by Deacon (2007). Pointing to an extensive increase in NGOs and social movements from the global South, he refers to the paradox that international and domestic NGOs act as policy advocates and service providers at the same time. There might be a conflict of interest in NGOs' commitment for justice and social change and their ambition to secure a lucrative aid contract when providing services on a sub-contracted basis (Deacon 2007: 94–5).

Yet, these definitions still leave us with a bulk of empirical heterogeneity, which is also reflected in the variety of scientific usages of the term 'non-governmental organization' (compare Seifer 2009: 37). For the purpose of a clear understanding of NGOs in this book, and guided by the definitions outlined above, at least some broadly accepted characterizing features will be determined here. It apparently is easier to begin with a negative definition and to determine what NGOs are not rather than what they actually are. Hence, NGOs are:

- non-governmental,
- non-profit,
- non-violent, and
- non-partisan.

A positive definition is much more difficult to formulate. Due to the complexity of tasks, responsibilities, and activities NGOs undertake and the heterogeneity of existing organizations, the characteristics of their engagement are blurry and hard to grasp. In this book, NGOs are understood to:

- express, represent (not necessarily democratically), and advocate the views and needs of society or particular groups or minorities within society to the state (see also Judge 1995),
- pursue objectives that are usually coupled with the *Charter of the United Nations*, human rights treaties and declarations, and that reflect the necessity of reducing democratic, social, and economic inequalities in the world and of promoting environmental sustainability, peace, and security (e.g. UN 1968; Seifer 2009),
- engage in the flexible delivery of social services (e.g. Judge 1995; Deacon 2007),
- be organized at the local, national, and international levels and interact across these levels (UIA 2010),
- function as oppositional pressure groups or engage in coalitions and networks with other NGOs, private actors (businesses and business associations), and state organizations (including IOs) where they can become part of decision-making structures and governance processes (Seifer 2009: 38),
- center their work on values and ideas; creatively handle and use information, develop sophisticated political strategies and campaigns (compare Keck and Sikkink 1998).

These characterizing features still embrace a number of divergent organizations but also help to delimit some. The non-profit orientation, for example, is important for a demarcation from business and the private sector (see also: Seifer 2009: 35) and NGOs' role in not representing their own views and interests but rather those of social groups and minorities distinguishes them from interest groups.

NGOs increasingly carry out governance functions through less formalized and more flexible arrangements, partnerships, networks, and projects (compare Deacon 2007: 158). They usually become involved in providing public goods in a demand-tailored and efficient way whenever governmental institutions cannot meet the challenges of complexity in modern societies (Seifer 2009: 30). Thus, a state-centered understanding of politics has shifted towards a society-oriented perspective in which non-state actors become meaningful protagonists in shaping political processes (Seifer 2009: 87). In IR scholarship, this society-oriented perspective becomes visible in research on cooperative modes of governance in which state actors share traditionally governmental responsibilities with private business actors or actors from civil society. Research on public–private partnerships (PPPs) has most prominently entered the IR agenda in the past decade and is of further importance for the research results presented in this book.

Global or transnational PPPs are institutionalized forms of cooperation between public and private actors beyond the nation state for the delivery of regulatory or governance services pertinent to setting and implementing norms (Börzel and Risse 2005: 198). One decisive conceptual differentiation of PPPs from other institutions is that PPPs allow for non-state actors not only to participate but to be, to the greatest possible extent, equal partners in the policy process from agenda-setting to implementing decisions (Huckel, Rieth and Zimmer 2007: 116). This contrasts with "exclusive" executive multilateralism that allows informal access for non-state actors (like the United Nations Security Council) and a form of more progressive and "open" executive multilateralism granting consultative status to NGOs (such as the United Nations Economic and Social Council) (Rittberger 2009: 264).

Scholars emphasize that PPPs between state actors, i.e. governments and international organizations, and non-state actors, i.e. commercial enterprises and associations, foundations and NGOs, are trans-boundary and institutionalized on a permanent basis (Beisheim, Liese and Ulbert 2007: 247). Degrees of institutionalization vary; in highly institutionalized PPPs, clear decision-making structures are installed that include bodies, councils, precise rules, and defined procedures (Huckel, Rieth and Zimmer 2007: 140). In addition to these clear governance structures, a high degree of institutionalization goes hand in hand with a precise formulation of tasks to be completed, explicit delegation of responsibilities to partners, transparent criteria and conditions for tendering partners, and the monitoring and evaluation of projects (Beisheim, Liese and Ulbert 2007: 258). Monitoring and evaluating PPPs' outcomes tends to be even more important if their projects concentrate on the provision of services or material goods (Beisheim, Liese and Ulbert 2007: 255).

PPPs increasingly emerge in developing and transformation countries that lack the capabilities, resources, and administrative capacities to implement and enforce political decisions (Beisheim, Liese and Ulbert 2007: 248). To achieve common objectives, PPPs exchange and mutually provide material resources, among them money, goods, and infrastructure, as well as ideational ones including knowledge, information, and experience (Brühl and Liese 2004: 166; Huckel, Rieth and Zimmer 2007: 118; Beisheim, Liese and Ulbert 2007: 253). Thus, they address and complement each other's deficits and pursue common goals with combined strengths (Reinicke and Deng 1999: VII, 98). In areas of limited statehood, besides internal PPP management and external capacity building mechanisms (including material and immaterial transfers), the institutionalization of learning and persuasion processes and strengthening of local ownership through the involvement and participation of affected actors count as success factors for PPP projects (Beisheim, Liese and

Ulbert 2007: 259–62). PPPs are emerging in an increasing number of policy fields, particularly those focused on environmental, health, and social issues and standards. Consequently, these constitute the domains in which most focused research on transnational actor constellations has been conducted (see for example Beisheim, Liese and Ulbert 2007; Schäferhoff 2009).

In sum, despite its fuzziness, its lack of conceptual clarity, and the prevalence of research gaps yet to be filled, governance scholarship provides some fresh insights and inspiration to the traditionally rather state-centered theorizing in IR. These inspirations comprise a vertical governance dimension and a horizontal governance dimension. Applied to the study of human rights norms, they help to understand how norms travel from the international to the local sphere (vertical governance dimension) and which institutions and actors make these norms travel (horizontal governance dimension). Before governance inspirations "meet" the study of human rights norms, however, the latter – in its rather state-centric version – will be briefly introduced below.

2.3 Norms, socialization and compliance in IR scholarship

Generally speaking, norms do not only define suitable behavior but – compared to ideas that are mostly individualistic – have been ascribed an explicit inter-subjective quality: "Because norms involve standards of 'appropriate' or 'proper' behavior, both the intersubjective and the evaluative dimensions are inescapable when discussing norms" (Finnemore and Sikkink 1998: 891). An often-cited definition of social norms that goes beyond that and attributes appropriate behavior to a certain identity has been suggested by Jepperson, Wendt and Katzenstein (1996). According to them: "Norms are collective expectations about proper behaviour for a given identity" (1996: 54). In contrast to this sociological understanding, Chayes and Chayes' (1998) conception is more legally influenced. They refer to norms as treaties that are legally binding on the states, which ratify them. In most cases, state and society actors are ready to accept that they are obliged to obey the law, and thus, the most fundamental norm of international law is *pacta sunt servanda* – treaties are to be obeyed (Chayes and Chayes 1998: 8).

This book largely follows an understanding of social norms that constitute a certain identity as suggested by Jepperson et al. The empirical study of children's rights implementation later reveals that norms pertinent to education, health, and the abolition of child labor are most effectively socialized if the entire affected community is being addressed. Whenever children's rights are protected, their role and most probably their identity within the community is changing from an income-earning towards a school-attending child.

Whether one behaves in accordance with a norm is reflected by the way the social environment or the society as a whole reacts. Norm-violating behavior might lead to critique while conformance to norms is praised, or in cases of a deeply internalized norm, norm-violation does not lead to any reaction at all since compliance is taken for granted. Representing shared moral values, norms initiate communication between respective actors. Norm creation is frequently guided by so-called entrepreneurs, such as agents or organizations, with particular ideas about proper behavior in a community. These norm entrepreneurs are crucial for the emergence of norms; they raise public attention to specific themes and problems using a dramatizing and interpretive language. Social movement theories use the term "framing" for these reinterpretation processes. The construction of cognitive frames is one of the most important political strategies of norm entrepreneurs. The creation of new frames is successful whenever there is public resonance and new discussions emerge (Finnemore and Sikkink 1998: 896; Joachim 2001: 232).

After ideas have become norms, questions about whether and how these norms influence the behavior of state actors arise. These can be further explored by considering the theoretical distinction between norms operating as rule defining, and thereby constituting identities according to social constructivism, and norms regulating the behavior for already constituted identities like rational choice theories would suggest (Jepperson, Wendt and Katzenstein 1996: 54). Hence, differentiating between regulative and constitutive effects of international norms is rooted in controversies between social constructivist and rational choice paradigms in IR theory. These are, among others, embedded in the framework of institutionalism. Institutionalism in IR departs from the assumption that structures of international politics are characterized by complex interdependence and explains that institutions matter and not only explain peace and cooperation, but also constitute a condition for both (Axelrod and Keohane 1985).

IR research on norms, particularly on norm socialization and norm compliance, has contributed to bridging the divide between rational and constructivist reasoning regarding norm effects, therefore, pleading for more integrative approaches. This bridge-building leaves room for explaining norm effects by focusing on hypothetical mechanisms according to a logic of consequences *and* a logic of appropriateness, under the heading of "conventional constructivism" (Checkel 2007).[1] Integrative approaches have been criticized for neglecting the positivist-interpretative epistemological divide, not only between rational choice and constructivist scholars, but also between social constructivism's conventional and interpretative (or critical) strands, as well as for meta-theoretical inconsistency. To address this critique, a call for meta-theoretical and methodological pluralism emerged, in particular from researchers studying European integration through a socialization lens (Checkel 2007; see also Checkel and Zürn 2005). Seeking these

1 In a chapter on "Constructivism and EU Politics", Checkel suggests three major distinctions in approaches to social constructivism, namely conventional, interpretative, and critical or radical constructivism (Checkel 2007).

complementarities between rationalist and constructivist, as well as within constructivist accounts, has been advocated by socialization and compliance researchers. Both, however, require openness to methodological pluralism (Checkel 2007).

Scholars of both research strands make use of mechanisms to explain how norm socialization and compliance can be fostered. In this regard, mechanisms can be understood as a set of hypotheses explaining a specific social phenomenon with regard to interactions among individuals and interactions between individuals and some sort of social aggregate. They enable fine-grained explanations operating at an analytic level below that of a comprehensive theory (Checkel 2005b: 4). This means that mechanisms are not only useful for relating cause and effect but for producing middle-range socialization approaches (Checkel and Zürn 2005: 1048). Therefore:

> [...] the term causal mechanism refers to the intermediate processes along which international institutions may lead actors towards accepting norms, rules and modes of behaviour of a given community. Mechanisms connect things; they link specified initial conditions and a specific outcome. (Checkel and Zürn 2005: 1049)

Hence, mechanisms explain how processes towards *norm adoption*, i.e. socialization, and how processes towards *norm adherence*, i.e. compliance, come about (Schimmelfennig 2002: 405–7). In both of these research strands, however, mechanisms are addressed at state actors and there is very little knowledge about what leads to norm conformity among society. Earlier research on socialization suggested *normative persuasion* in conjunction with *material incentives* (Ikenberry and Kupchan 1990: 314) and *external inducement*, i.e. economic and military incentives and sanctions (Ikenberry and Kupchan 1990: 290–1), to be relevant socialization mechanisms. *Internal reconstruction* occurs in cases in which a hegemon reconstructs the domestic political institutions of a state that it intervened in. Hence, reconstruction leads to an imposed policy change to provoke norm change, as a gradual result of accepting the re-established institutions as the state's own (Ikenberry and Kupchan 1990: 291–2).

Within the framework of European Integration research, Checkel identifies causal socialization mechanisms with the help of which institutions socialize state agents to internalize community roles and norms (2005a: 802). *Strategic calculation* (Checkel 2005a: 808), *bargaining*, *social influence* (Checkel and Zürn 2005: 1052), *role playing* (implying a shift from a logic of consequences to a logic of appropriateness, see Checkel 2005a: 810–12) and *arguing* (Checkel and Zürn 2005: 1052) are relevant mechanisms fostering socialization.

Compliance research stresses mechanisms such as *monitoring* and *sanctioning* (Zürn and Neyer 2005: 191), *cost-benefit calculations*, *enforcement* mechanisms (e.g. van Aaken 2005), *juridification*, and *legal* as well as *civil internalization* (Zürn and Neyer 2005: 195). In addition to that, a number of authors point to the meaning of *compliance management* (Chayes and Chayes 1998; Chayes, Chayes and Mitchell 1998; Jacobsen and Brown Weiss 2000; Tallberg 2002; Mitchell 2005; Zürn and Joerges 2005; Mitchell 2007). They usually stress *capacity-building* including the provision of administrative, technological, and financial resources to be most relevant (Zürn and Joerges 2005: 30). Chayes, Chayes and Mitchell add informational and regulatory capacities as significant factors in fostering compliance with an international treaty (1998: 40).

If one considers legitimacy aspects, however, mechanisms like participation opportunities in rule-making and the social acceptance of regulations – both addressed at society – become more important (Zürn and Joerges 2005: 26). Earlier research, e.g. on compliance with environmental agreements, has also touched upon such ideas by emphasizing the considerable impact of public attitudes on overall compliance (Vogel and Kessler 2000: 32).

Table 2.1 maps the entire range of mechanisms elaborated in socialization and compliance research. Here, it becomes obvious that only participation and social acceptance have been identified as relevant mechanisms addressed at society for achieving adherence to international norms.

Table 2.1 Socialization and compliance mechanisms

Mechanisms **Addressees**	**Socialization**	**Compliance**
State *Logic of Consequences*	external inducement, internal reconstruction, material incentives, strategic calculation, bargaining, social influence	monitoring, sanctioning, juridification, legal internalization, civil internalization (access to courts)
State *Logic of Appropriateness*	role playing, normative persuasion, arguing	capacity building, participation
Society *Logic of Consequences*		civil internalization (access to courts)
Society *Logic of Appropriateness*		participation, social acceptance

Source: author's compilation

2.4 Human rights change and its state centeredness in IR

Human rights are special among norms since they involve particular collective expectations of appropriate behavior (compare norm definitions by Finnemore and Sikkink 1998: 891; Jepperson, Wendt and Katzenstein 1996: 54) that are addressed not only at state governments but also targeted at every single one of their citizens, every human being:

> Human rights are principled ideas about the treatment to which every individual is entitled by virtue of being human. These ideas have gained widespread acceptance as international norms and law defining primarily the relationship between the state and its citizens, but are also increasingly invoked as rules governing the behavior of corporate and other nonstate entities. (Schmitz and Sikkink 2013: 827)

These obligations and behavioral principles are usually codified in international treaties and agreements. The Universal Declaration of Human Rights (UDHR), adopted by the United Nations General Assembly in 1948, was the first (albeit non-binding) agreement about shared principles that were hoped to become universal and to evolve into global and not only domestic validity. Attempts to create a binding world charter of human rights as a response to the Second World War and the resulting awareness that the nation state had failed in its traditional role of guaranteeing civil rights, flagged during that time (Riedel 2004: 11–12). Instead, it took another two decades and the formulation of separate treaties to make human rights norms binding (compare Liese 2006: 59).

Derived from the UDHR, three main dimensions of human rights can be identified (Krennerich 2010: 7). The first dimension, civil and political rights, refers to Articles 3 to 21 of the UDHR and is anchored in the legally binding International Covenant on Civil and Political Rights (ICCPR) from 1966, which entered into force in 1976 (UN 2005: 31–53). Civil and political rights, among others, encompass freedom from torture, degrading treatment, and arbitrary detention, as well as freedom of speech, association, and religion. They are often conceptualized as "negative" rights obliging states to refrain from action that violates the human beings' dignity (Uvin 2004: 14).

Economic, social, and cultural rights are known as the second dimension of human rights set forth in Articles 22 to 27 of the UDHR and enshrined in the 1966 International Covenant on Economic, Social and Cultural Rights (ICESCR), another legally binding human rights treaty (UN 2004: 229). These rights consist of the right to education, the right to an adequate standard of living, the right to the highest attainable standard of health (Uvin 2004: 14), the right to just and favorable conditions of work (UN 2006a: 13), and others. They are considered as the dimension of "positive" rights in the sense that often costly action has to be undertaken by ratifying governments to implement them (Uvin 2004: 39) and "to achieve progressively the full realization of the rights" (UN 2006a: 9; compare also Uvin 2004: 39).[2] Economic, social, and cultural rights have been traditionally marginalized by Western countries, especially during the Cold War, and emphasized by all

2 Some authors do not subscribe to the clear distinction between civil and political rights as *negative* rights and economic, social, and cultural rights as *positive* rights (e.g. Hamm and Kocks 2006).

communist and most developing countries. Many international human rights organizations (e.g. Amnesty International or Human Rights Watch) and more developed nations have focused on promoting civil and political rights. The third dimension of human rights introduces a shift in human rights thinking. Whereas previously, individual rights were exclusively emphasized, collective or solidarity rights have more recently been introduced to the human rights edifice. These embrace rights pertaining to development, environment, sustainability, etc. (Uvin 2004: 14–16). Third dimension rights have often been treated as mere aspirations and legally binding treaties could hardly become established around them.

Despite this distinction between the three dimensions, all human rights are considered universal, indivisible, interdependent, and interrelated under the umbrella of the United Nations. The 1948 UDHR has already determined the equality between all kinds of human rights in terms of their validity and importance (OHCHR 2006b: 2). In 1950, the General Assembly declared that "the enjoyment of civic and political freedoms and of economic, social and cultural rights is interconnected and interdependent" (resolution 421 (V), sect. E, in: UN 2006b: 5). Particularly with respect to the first two dimensions, the Office of the High Commissioner for Human Rights (OHCHR) states that:

> Economic, social and cultural rights must be respected, protected and realized on an equal footing with civil and political rights. The principle of their *interdependence* recognizes the difficulty (and, in many cases, the impossibility) of realizing any one human right in isolation. (OHCHR 2006b: 2)

In short, no hierarchy among human rights exists. Kaufmann (2004) goes even further in stating that there is a causal link between human rights of the first dimension and improvements in socio-economic outcomes. So does Alston who precisely summarizes the interdependency issue by stating:

> [...] the diverse human rights – civil, political, economic, social and cultural – are causally linked and this can be mutually reinforcing. They can create synergies that contribute to poor people securing their rights, enhancing their human capabilities and escaping poverty. Because of these complementarities, the struggle to achieve economic and social rights should not be separated from the struggle to achieve civil and political rights. And the two need to be pursued simultaneously. (Alston 2005: 789)

One more recent argument pertinent to complementarities brought forwards by the United Nations is that there are three interlinked duties pertinent to the implementation of all kinds of human rights, whether they are civil and political or economic, social and cultural rights. These are the duty to respect, the duty to protect and the duty to fulfill (Krennerich 2010: 7). Obligations to protect and promote are usually considered to be a state responsibility. It might require international cooperation within the framework of the United Nations System (intergovernmental governance), the establishment of an international court, such as the European Court of Human Rights (supranational governance), or the external pressure of civil society actors on governmental policies or procedures (transnational governance) (cf. Rittberger and Zangl 2006: 193–5). Beyond that, human rights norms define the identity of nations in the international community: Since 1994, there has not been a single state government that did not accept and ratify at least one of the central conventions pertinent to the human rights regime[3] of the United Nations. This means that human rights norms have internationally become a binding behavioral demand (Liese 2006: 60). Human rights violations therefore contradict the liberal identity of most states and citizens in the international system and can lead to pressure, critique, and even "shaming" (Risse, Ropp and Sikkink 1999: 23) from an international public (compare also Risse, Jetschke and Schmitz 2002: 38). Hence, states are usually eager to either comply with human rights or to keep violations invisible from the eye of the international community to facilitate cooperation and avoid any sanctions.

2.4.1 A global consensus on children's rights

Children's rights constitute a special type of human rights norms. Respective entitlements gained a prominent role during the First World War and were formulated as a matter of human rights in the *Geneva Declaration of the Rights of the Child* under the League of Nations in 1924 and the 1959 *United Nations Declaration of the Rights of the Child*. Binding children's rights norms, however, were not adopted by the international community until the 1989 UN *Convention on the Rights of the Child* (CRC) (UN 2006c: 3).[4]

Today, three conventions mark the global reference point for children's rights: the 1973 *ILO Minimum Age Convention*, the 1989 CRC, and the 1999 *ILO Worst Forms of Child Labour Convention* (C182) (compare Myers 2001: 44). Especially the latter two, the CRC and the C182 accommodate diversity and leave room for situational particularity in the countries of the South.

3 Human rights regimes are special in the sense that states have to cooperate to create and promote international human rights norms, but they do not necessarily work together to implement or enforce them since this is still largely considered the responsibility of the sovereign state (compare Zwingel 2005: 26–8; Krasner 1993). How this is changing towards more cooperative implementation cooperation is part of the argument developed in this book.

4 A notable exception are the various sector-specific ILO conventions stipulating a minimum age for admission to employment that were adopted from 1919 on and eventually were subsumed under the umbrella of the 1973 *ILO Minimum Age Convention*.

Both refrain from formulating details and talk in rather broader principles with flexibility for context-specific implementation (Myers 2001: 48). Representatives who drafted the (C182) decided to refrain from condemning child labor and instead, embrace a global consensus on the issue by focusing on abolishing all forms of children's work that "is likely to harm the health, safety or morals of children" (ILO 1999a). It became the first ILO convention adopted by unanimous vote and achieved the fastest ratification rate in ILO history (Myers 2001: 51–2; see also ILO 2010). Similarly, the CRC has been nearly universally ratified with the United States of America (USA) and Somalia being the only exceptions (Myers 2001: 51). Although these regulations are inter-governmentally initiated, bindingly anchored in international conventions and neither represent any private nor any public-private scheme, they do reflect the flexibility and guideline character of "soft law" raised by Abbott and Snidal as typical of transnational governance (2009: 530).

All of these binding agreements belong to the so-called "targeted treaties" integrating civil and political as well as economic, social, and cultural rights into one legal document. Hence, these conventions demonstrate the indivisibility and interrelatedness of human rights, as stated in the 1948 UDHR and recalled at the 1993 Vienna World Conference on Human Rights (Alston 2005: 789). The three children's rights investigated in this book do so as well; whereas (1) protection from hazardous forms of child labor belongs to the first dimension of human rights, (2) the right to education and (3) the right to health pertain to the second human rights dimension often involving costly action in a progressive realization process (UN 2006a: 9). All of these principles are closely intertwined; hazardous work by children, for example, has a strong effect on children's education and health situation.

The concept of the child as an autonomous and individual rights-holder contradicts the intuitive understanding of children who are vulnerable and in need of adult protection (Burr 2002: 52; compare also Reynolds, Nieuwenhuys and Hanson 2006: 292). Nevertheless – although children are considered to be rights-holders in the language of these conventions and the United Nations – the fulfillment of children's rights is largely dependent on the socio-economic conditions under which their parents live. This is particularly true with respect to parents' (and family members') situation pertaining to food, shelter, health, decent work, and remuneration, but also to all entitlements regarding their personal integrity (compare Arat 2002: 190). Individual rights have initially been a Western construct, whereas a communal sense of rights is much more relevant in societies of the South. In the latter contexts, the wellbeing of the family and the community is given more prominence, whereas the individual plays a rather subordinated role. Children and their rights cannot be abstracted from this social context. Guaranteeing social and economic justice for them also includes justice for their families and vice versa (see also White 2002: 1103). This might be inconsistent with certain children's rights principles highlighting individuality and universality, such as the "best interest of the child," a leading principle of the CRC, and "the views of the child" calling for endowing children's free opinion with more weight in all matters affecting them (compare Burr 2002: 51; Reynolds, Nieuwenhuys and Hanson 2006; UN 2006c: 5):

> The notion of the global child as the subject of rights has provoked a critique of the CRC's claim to universalism against what many observers suggest is a hardly obscured Western-centric view of "normal" child-adult and child-society relations that condemns other styles of upbringing as "outside" childhood. (Jones 2005: 338)

Taking this into account, this book applies an understanding of children's rights in accordance with Reynolds, Nieuwenhuys and Hanson (2006: 298) suggesting that rights build a global consensus but need "local emphasis, refurbishing and interpretation" (Reynolds, Nieuwenhuys and Hanson 2006: 298). Hence, one has to be aware of distinguishing between global ideas on children's rights and those that represent Euro-American ethnocentrism: "[…] practical experience suggests that valid global standards also should reflect widely shared values and avoid ethnocentric impositions by the rich and powerful" (Myers 2001: 43). "The 'right rights' seem not to be those imposed by the rich and powerful but those that are more broadly defined and more democratically adopted" (Myers 2001: 53).

The "right rights" in this book refers to certain principles agreed upon in conventions that highlight benchmarks and are more flexible in taking the situation of various, developed and developing contexts, into account. A basic global consensus will be stressed here. Global minimum standards are those that societies and states from the North, the South, and in between can agree upon, namely (1) protection from the worst forms of child labor that are detrimental to children's physical and mental development, (2) the provision of basic education, and (3) the provision of primary health services. These are the three basic rights further considered here.

2.4.2 *The spiral model of human rights change*

In IR, the Spiral Model of Human Rights Change has for a long time been the reference model to explain human rights implementation. In this book, I argue that this model comes along with major limitations that are of crucial importance for understanding how global rights reach their local rights-holders. These limitations pertinent to the model's neglect of the local level, its state-centeredness and its lack of specificity on how to proceed from a phase, in which human rights have been ratified, towards state (and societal) behavior that is consistent with these rights will be elaborated here. First of all, however, the model itself will be briefly introduced.

Inspired by Keck and Sikkink's (1998) assumptions on transnational human rights networks in the 1990s and the three phases model of a norm life cycle resulting in norm internalization and change (Finnemore and Sikkink 1998), the Spiral Model of Human Rights Change seeks to explain the influence of transnational actors on a domestic human rights situation (Risse, Ropp and Sikkink 1999). The Spiral Model comprises five phases and refers to repressive regimes adopting personal integrity rights (Risse, Ropp and Sikkink 1999) through processes of norm socialization with sustained compliance as the desired outcome (compare Jetschke and Liese 2009: 13). It introduces the main stages – conceptualized as five phases – of a transition from authoritarian practices to democratic ones, i.e. to protecting human rights and fundamental freedoms. These major assumptions have been validated by several additional case studies later on (see Risse, Jetschke and Schmitz 2002). Risse, Jetschke and Schmitz further assume the Spiral Model to be valid in connection with economic, social, and cultural norms – a postulation not yet backed by sufficient empirical evidence (2002: 182). Beyond that, the authors claim: "[. . .] that the model is generalizable across cases irrespective of cultural, political, or economic differences among countries" (Risse and Sikkink 1999: 6) which means that it could be applied to Northern as well as Southern countries, to developing as well as to transition states but also to Western democracies. The starting point of this complex model is the existence of international human rights regimes. After the end of the Cold War, these were strengthened through explicit human rights policies and the establishment of respective institutions. All too often, the emergence of human rights regimes can be seen as a response to severe human rights violations (Risse, Jetschke and Schmitz 2002: 35–7).

With the help of the Spiral Model, it was shown that the improvement of a human rights situation is a process composed of five phases. Phase 1 (repression) describes a situation in which a repressive government systematically commits human rights violations and critical domestic (non-governmental) opposition groups are unable to initiate change. This phase can last for a long time since information about a human rights situation within a country can possibly remain inaccessible to the world public for a longer period. Whenever oppositional groups manage to establish links to transnational human rights networks and provide information about the norm-violating behavior of the repressive government, this situation starts to change (Risse and Sikkink 1999: 22; Risse, Jetschke and Schmitz 2002: 37–8; Risse 2007: 28). The transnational networks addressed involve international NGOs, churches, trade unions, foundations, etc. (Risse, Jetschke and Schmitz 2002: 202).

After these links have been established, phase 2 (denial) comes into play. This phase comprises to provide information about the human rights situation in the respective country and to mobilize IOs and Western states (via transnational human rights networks) to highlight how repression and violations are in contradiction with their own liberal identity. Shaming is part of a moral persuasion strategy and indicates that the norm-violating state does not belong to the "in-group" of the international community anymore. Denying these facts usually is the first reaction of the respective government and is already part of the socialization process. By doing so, the repressive government frequently points to the principle of non-interference and sovereignty rather than questioning the prevalence of human rights norms as such (Risse and Sikkink 1999: 22–4; Risse, Jetschke and Schmitz 2002: 38–9; Risse 2007: 29–30).

One result of a so-called "boomerang throw"[5] can be observed in phase 3 (tactical concessions) in which growing pressure "from above", through Western states and IOs, and "from below", through national opposition groups, has an effect on the repressive government. To counter the critique raised, the state admits slight changes in its behavior – it makes tactical concessions. These could result in permitting demonstrations or releasing prisoners. Making concessions can lead to important consequences such as strengthening domestic human rights activists and local civil society. The acceptance of human rights discourses increases under the protection and attention of international networks and the world public. An emerging dialogue between the government, the opposition, and transnational human rights networks eventually leads to an exchange about how to implement the respective norm (Risse and Sikkink 1999: 25–8; Risse, Jetschke and Schmitz 2002: 39–42; Risse 2007: 30–2).

In phase 4 (prescriptive status), an institutionalization of the human rights norm is initiated. With the transfer of international norms to national law, its practical application becomes more likely. A ratified human rights convention, however, is not a sufficient criterion to decide whether the prescriptive status has actually been reached. The state government could be acting out of strategic-instrumental calculations without really accepting the legitimacy of the norm (Risse, Jetschke and Schmitz 2002: 42). Nevertheless, some indicators help in identifying whether the stage of prescriptive status has indeed been reached. Among others, these comprise the institutionalization of ratified norms within the national constitution and/or within national legislation, the establishment of complaint mechanisms that enable citizens to report human rights violations, and an integration of human rights language into the discursive practices of the government. In this phase, state actors do not denounce critique as interference and engage in a dialogue with anyone

5 The boomerang pattern emerges in a situation in which channels between the state and its domestic actors, national non-governmental opposition groups, are blocked and cooperation becomes impossible. In cases like that, domestic NGOs may bypass the state level and directly search for international allies with the aim of exerting outside pressure on the respective state government (Keck and Sikkink 1998). These international allies could be transnational human rights networks, Western democracies, and international human rights organizations. So what has been initiated by critical groups and organizations *within* a state comes back like a boomerang and has the effect of *outside* pressure addressed at the repressive government of the same state.

addressing criticism towards them (Risse and Sikkink 1999: 29). Additional criteria introduced by Risse, Jetschke and Schmitz (2002: 43) comprise argumentative consistency within the government's communication, an improving human rights situation after external and internal pressure decreases (or even after a potential regime change), and visible governmental effort to convert human rights norms into practice.

Nevertheless, the prescriptive status has to be distinguished from phase 5 (rule-consistent behavior). Transition to this phase is only possible if domestic and international mobilization remains existent. Pressure from national and transnational networks is indispensable for achieving the continuous improvement of a human rights situation. In this last phase of the socialization process, international human rights norms are entirely institutionalized and compliance becomes a habitual practice of actors demanded by the rule of law. Furthermore, it is assumed that respective state actors have internalized the human rights norms ratified (Risse and Sikkink 1999: 31–5; Risse, Jetschke and Schmitz 2002: 43–4; Risse 2007: 33).

In sum, transnational networks, in connection with international human rights regimes, organizations, and Western states, are of particular relevance in early phases of the socialization process. Later on, argumentative processes play an important role. After the prescriptive status has been reached, institutionalization and habitualization processes become dominant (Risse and Sikkink 1999: 33–5). Social constructivists go even further than referring to institutionalization and habitualization. Risse explicitly argues that norm socialization will not be achieved without the internalization of norms by relevant state actors (2003: 119).

Risse et al.'s model helps explain how transnational networks challenge the repression of individual governments and help change their domestic human rights situation. Human rights change, however, is put on one level with a legislative and domestic policy change initiated by local forces in cooperation with transnational advocacy coalitions, instead of being viewed as a change for the people whose human rights are being violated. In addition, there is not much scope for explaining a stagnating human rights situation in cases in which governments have willingly ratified norms but their implementation still does not come about. This means that the Spiral Model is limited in its applicability, namely to repressive state governments that deny personal integrity rights in their domestic policies.

2.4.3 Criticizing the neglect of the local level, state centeredness and under-specificity

This book applies a governance lens to comprehensively explain a human rights implementation process. From a governance perspective, Risse et al.'s model, first of all, neglects the local level. It stresses that in phase five, state actors have internalized human rights standards and they need to act in consistence with them. Hence, there is hardly any reference to local institutionalization processes. Considering interaction between the international, national, regional and local level within multilevel systems, however, has been central to all governance concepts. Particularly emphasized is the need to analyze how decentralized systems function (Christiansen 1997), the relocation of authority towards sub-national entities (Rosenau 1992), the role of micro-level actors and predominantly, the participation and role-taking of local non-governmental actors in the policy process (Christiansen 1997). This emphasis on local governance systems and actors in the issue area of human rights has been emphasized by the United Nations which demand that human rights need to gain meaning beyond their ratification. Policy researchers and human rights practitioners highlight that despite increasing ratification rates and norm adoption (i.e. norm socialization) key gaps in implementation prevail, first and foremost at the local level (OHCHR 2006a). They go even further by noting that "[…] if [human] rights don't have meaning locally they will have little meaning elsewhere" (Robinson 2002) and that "Human rights are best protected when they are rooted in the local culture" (UN 2004: 239).

The Spiral Model of Human Rights Change does, similar to studies on socialization and compliance, not depart from IR's focus on national activities and actors. Human rights change is viewed as a modification of the national constitution, legislation, institutionalized complaint mechanisms, and discursive practices (Risse and Sikkink 1999: 29) all of which are embedded in the overall assumption of governmental responsibility. This could be due to the model's concentration on personal integrity rights anchored in the ICCPR of 1966 obliging states to abstain from human rights violations (Uvin 2004: 14). Though, case studies within the discipline have verified that even with respect to civil and political rights, active support at the local societal level is particularly relevant for achieving human rights change (e.g. Liese 2006: 281). In the framework of the model, transnational and domestic oppositional pressure are taken into account, but only to change the behavior of state actors, and not to contribute to the implementation process itself. Transnational and local actors therefore remain external to the process of norm realization, while norm socialization and compliance are viewed to solely concern governmental actors. This concept of implementation continues to be limited to the national and the governmental domain, and does not touch upon the sub-national and societal sphere at all.

Neglecting vertical and horizontal governance dimensions, secondly, points to a state-centeredness of IRs' scholarship pertinent to norm socialization, compliance, and human rights change. This is astonishing considering the deep roots socialization research – also applied in IR studies – has in symbolic interactionism according to Mead, who emphasized self-society relations (Stryker and Burke 2000: 285). Hence, IR have borrowed from psychological and sociological theories' explanations about how an individual becomes a member of society to provide explanations for how individual states become members of the international community. This has been largely done without taking society and state–society relations within the respective state into account (a pioneering work in this direction was undertaken by Flockhart 2006). Norm internalization by state actors constitutes the outcome of a socialization process. Internalization, however, is a psychological concept that can hardly be measured with the methodical toolkit of a political scientist and can therefore, in most studies, merely be assumed.

Studies of international socialization and mostly also of compliance research neglect the targets of international treaties who, in the case of human rights, are a state's citizens. Such a departure from the focus on actors of the political-administrative system and the integration of societal actors into politics implementation and compliance (compare also Mayntz 2009a: 43) is a new direction in the study of norms that still has to be elaborated in greater detail. Risse et al.'s Spiral Model of Human Rights Change, for instance, implies a limited understanding of horizontal expansions. It does ascribe a prominent role to non-state and transnational actors, but this remains external to the actual human rights implementation process and is reduced to exerting and keeping up pressure on the state government. Transnational actor networks, involving international NGOs, churches, trade unions, foundations, etc. (Risse, Jetschke and Schmitz 2002: 202) are necessary to pressure the government prior to, during, and following human rights ratification, but the norm implementation process itself is regarded as a purely governmental responsibility. Implementation is restricted to transferring norms to the national constitution, legislation and policies, and installing complaint procedures (Risse and Sikkink 1999: 29). Although the model has been exclusively tested to be valid for civil and political rights, i.e. rights implying that the state has to refrain from certain actions, it claims to correspond to social rights in certain cases as well (Risse, Jetschke and Schmitz 2002: 182). Human rights, however, are mutually reinforcing. Guaranteeing civil and political rights goes hand in hand with providing for economic, social, and cultural rights as well. Disregarding societal actors in the implementation process not only neglects the horizontal governance dimension, it also contradicts the fact that it is society, i.e. a nation state's people, for whom human rights are made. These citizens need to participate in the implementation process or they at least have to accept the behavioral standards at stake.

Third, the Spiral Model underspecifies how norm compliance (i.e. rule-consistent behavior) can be reached after national institutionalization processes (i.e. prescriptive status). The five phases model of human rights change differentiates between a stage of (4) prescriptive status in which international norms have been ratified and transferred to domestic legislation and policies and (5) the phase of rule-consistent behavior. The latter, according to the model, can only be achieved if transnational and domestic oppositional pressure can be upheld, i.e. if an active civil society is present. Since this remains the only perquisite outlined in the model, demarcations between these two phases remain blurry and "underspecified" (see Schapper 2010: 9, compare also Jetschke and Liese 2013: 26-42).

But also other critical questions need to be raised in the face of recent political developments, such as: Is it only state actors that commit human rights violations? And, is it solely state actors who can protect human rights and their targets? Terrorism, for instance, is a crucial counterexample that completely turns the tide (see Jetschke and Liese 2013: 42). It teaches us that human rights can be violated by other forces than the government and that the state – despite its willingness and efforts – cannot always protect its citizens. In particular for weak states with limited welfare functions, other scenarios can be opened up as well. What if state governments simply commit themselves on paper without taking further action – a strategic move towards avoiding criticism, securing their reputation as an accepted member of the international community, and avoiding costly public spending? And, considering the human rights situation of local communities, children, and their parents in such countries, are domestic legislative reforms and policy modifications really enough for things to change? Doesn't it require further resources, the establishment of structures, regulative measures, and the involvement of additional actors to make these rights meaningful for their targets? Is it simply the pressure transnational and non-governmental actors provide or do they indeed, as suggested by governance research, take up a more crucial role in the process towards rule conformity?

To sum up, all of the critical issues raised here are closely intertwined. Vertical and horizontal stretches in governing human rights have not been comprehensively considered in IR scholarship yet. Hence, consulting the analytical lens of a governance researcher, a basic underlying assumption of this study is that the state has to cooperate with society (compare Mayntz 2009a: 43) after ratifying international treaties. These cooperation processes that aim at transporting global rights to their local targets will be further explored in this book. Other less state-centered research from different disciplines provides valuable insights in this respect. Some useful aspects and results from anthropological, sociological and developmental studies will be introduced in the following.

2.5 Anthropological, sociological and developmental perspectives on children's rights

In childhood studies, an important bulk of empirical research has been conducted at the disciplinary intersection of anthropology, sociology and development scholarship. Various analyses investigating the situation of children in developing countries (e.g. Myers 2001; Khair 2001; Burr 2002; Reynolds, Nieuwenhuys and Hanson 2006) suggest that a comprehensive understanding of the local context is an essential prerequisite for implementing global rights therein. Scholars emphasize that global norms need "local emphasis, refurbishing and interpretation" (Reynolds, Nieuwenhuys and Hanson 2006: 298) to become meaningful in a particular context.

The meanings of childhood, development and wellbeing are socially and contextually constructed (e.g. Ungar 2004; Boyden and Mann 2005: 12) and differing cultural discourses pertaining to rights and responsibilities of children exist (Woodhead 2006). As a consequence, outside interventions by international governmental and civil society organizations towards fostering children's rights and development within a particular context are not necessarily appropriate (Boyden and Mann 2005: 4). Or to put it in other words: there is no "[...] one-size-fits-all model that is often used by those endeavoring to put in place childcare programs in different societies" (James 2008: 266; see also Woodhead 1996). Hence, there is a need for an understanding of child development that is culturally appropriate (Woodhead 1996) and programmatic interventions should at best reflect children's own reality (Boyden and Mann 2005: 4).

Woodhead (1996) refers to such interventions and programs as "Contextually Appropriate Practice". Pertinent policies are designed to take account of children's situation from a comprehensive perspective including not only material, but also social and cultural resources that children themselves but also their parents and the entire community have at their disposal (Woodhead 2006: 17–18; see also Woodhead 1996). A similar argument is made by Sarah C. White (2002) who suggests that economic as well as cultural (and identity) factors need to be recognized and combined in order to design effective policy mechanisms: "Development agencies and political activists thus need to address the material, social and political factors that make and keep children poor, [...]" (White 2002: 734–5). Abstracting children from their own social environment and treating them as one (of many) independent client groups in development policies, she claims, leads to a situation in which the intricacy of the relationship between children, their families and the entire community within certain contexts is being neglected (White 2002: 734).

Jo Boyden and colleagues (1998) have even moved one step further by arguing that what is needed to design appropriate policies is not only a contextual knowledge of children's reality but that this knowledge shall be provided by the children themselves. Only then, they emphasize, can the complexity of problems, which for instance working children face, become addressed most effectively (Boyden, Ling and Myers 1998). In line with this argument, children are viewed as social agents that participate in and shape their own environment (Woodhead 2006: 29–31; Boyden and Mann 2005: 19). Children, anthropological and sociological scholars claim, shall be participating subjects (even with an active role in research processes relating to them) that need to be personalized and individualized (James 2008: 270). Such an understanding of children and childhood has also been fostered by the CRC and its underlying principles, like the "best interest of the child" and the "views of the child" calling for endowing children's free opinion with more weight in all matters affecting them (compare Burr 2002: 51; Reynolds, Nieuwenhuys and Hanson 2006; UN 2006c: 5).

Although not concerned with the implementation of children's rights but with the protection of women, the work of Sally Engle Merry has been path-breaking in explaining how global rights become meaningful in local contexts (Merry 2006a, 2006b). One important step the anthropologist makes in her writings is that she does not conceptualize culture as an obstruction to human rights implementation. Quite the contrary, she rather "[...] encourages attention to local cultural practices as resource for change" (Merry 2006a: 9). Merry introduces the concept of vernacularization as the adaptation of global norms to local communities, their institutions and their meanings (Merry 2006b: 39). One key dimension of a vernacularization process, she claims, are the agents that connect behavioral standards codified in international law with local realities and practices. The anthropologist refers to these "translators" or "intermediaries" as people who engage at various levels, including the local, regional, national and global sphere (ibid.). Human rights intermediaries can be activists of a social movement, lawyers, NGO leaders, academics or others that: "[...] have one foot in the transnational community and one at home" (Merry 2006b: 42). This means that they need to apply the language of IOs and external donors but, at the same time, they need to reach out to the local norm targets and present issues in a way that is appropriate for them. Translating NGOs continuously depend on external funding and, therefore, shape their strategies in a way that attracts donor governments and organizations. Nevertheless, they have to create a suitable frame that resonates within the particular cultural context (Snow 2004: 401). Intermediaries "indigenize" meanings; they make them comprehensible within prevalent cultural terminology, ideas, traditions, and practices (Merry 2006b: 39–41): "Human rights intermediaries put global human rights ideas into familiar symbolic terms and use stories of local indignities and violations to give life and power to global movements" (Merry 2006b: 42). They need to be aware of two sides simultaneously by combining globally constructed human rights concepts with local problems and the ways people think about these. As a consequence, translators are endowed with the power to direct those rights-holders, often vulnerable populations, who are less informed and educated. And on the other hand, translating intermediaries are vulnerable themselves due to their dependencies on their principals and assignments (Merry 2006b: 40). Often, NGOs take the positions of intermediaries: they have legal expertise, they know the human rights system and how to apply the language of pertinent conventions (Merry, Levitt, Rosen and Yoon 2010: 102; Merry 2006a; see also Jenichen 2012) and they have access to the local target populations. The effort of civil society organizations becomes even more important in the absence of state commitment or lacking state functions. Interventions of NGOs as intermediaries of human rights translation, however, can lead to informal protection processes and institutional support (Boyden and Mann 2005: 8).

Human rights have the potential to create new alliance, coalitions and partnerships. They can reshape institutions, e.g. by hybridization, to mobilize the participation of grassroots actors (Merry, Levitt, Rosen and Yoon 2010: 125). Translators can build cooperative networks or "layers" consisting of a complex set of activists to transport global rights norms to their local targets (Merry and Stern 2005: 387). These layers build "[...] critical bridges between a human rights discourse connected to modernity and universalism and more particular and individualized ways of thinking about injuries" (Merry and Stern 2005: 388). Layer networks integrate actors that are characterized by crucial differences with respect to their rights awareness, their education level, their international outreach and their language skills (Merry and Stern 2005: 396). Only few of these intermediaries serve as a connecting belt between the various layers and help to establish a movement that works towards making people conscious of human rights, towards integrating pertinent meanings into everyday practices and towards creating political change (Merry and Stern 2005: 399; Merry 2006a: 3).

Besides the actor perspective, Merry identifies two prevailing forms of vernacularization. One is replication defined as a more superficial way of translating global human rights into local contexts. Here, international norms or behavioral standards are imported and hardly adapted to the particular circumstances. The other is hybridization which constitutes a more interactive mode of appropriation. This means that a merging of structures, knowledge and practices takes place and leads to the establishment of new hybrid institutions (Merry 2006b: 45–8). If intermediaries are more committed to local norm targets, Merry suggests, they tend to produce hybrid norm translations. And in cases in which they are closer to their principals, mediating agents choose replicating models of appropriating rights (Merry 2006b: 48).

From Merry's perspective, translating global norms to local places remains a top-down process from more powerful international arenas to less powerful contexts. She identifies several paradoxes that occur in the process of human rights vernacularization. First, standards that are considered to be universal might be difficult to adapt to the particularities of a local context. Within the framework of a human rights system highlighting individualism, personal integrity, autonomy and equality, it might be problematic to attain resonance among local target communities (Merry 2006a: 4; Merry 2006b: 48–9). Second, ideas of human rights are accepted with less hesitance "[...] if they are packaged in familiar terms [...]" (Merry 2006a: 5). They have a greater impact, however, if they question existing power relationships. Third, utilizing local language and symbols leads to an increased acceptance of human rights ideas among the rights-holders. Moreover, to secure funding and to enhance legitimacy, these ideas have to be framed in the language of IOs and the transnational human rights regime. Fourth, to increase the awareness of rights among society, institutions need to comprehensively implement these. At the same time, lacking awareness leads to a situation in which little advocacy for rights implementation is being mobilized within civil society. Fifth, there is an ambivalent relationship between the human rights system and the state. On the one hand, the concept of human rights has emerged from a situation of distrust into the willingness and capability of the state to protect its citizens. On the other hand, rights advocacy and demands for rights-related provisions are usually targeted at the state (Merry 2006a: 5).

2.6 Governance, children's rights and the local sphere: an analytical framework

In this book, I will try to provide some answers to the paradoxes between the global and the local Merry has formulated. Although this study is situated in IR, I will use insights and field research methods from anthropology and sociology to explore how global children's rights reach their local norm targets in Bangladesh. Utilizing anthropological methods seems fruitful due to the discipline's focus on the local level and on small-scale social units (Merry 2006a: 28–9). During my field research in Bangladesh, I have identified sites, in which global, national and local processes are reflected in the social reality of children, their families and entire communities (compare Merry 2006a: 29). Hence, with my comparison of norm implementation in seven local cases, I will engage in what anthropologists call multi-sited ethnography (Marcus 1998: 79–104; see also Merry 2006a: 29).

For integrating the global, the national and the local sphere as well as governmental and societal actors, I suggest applying a governance framework to the study of human rights realization. This means that this book builds on multidisciplinary field research, in which methods originating in Anthropology, Sociology and Political Science are combined. The research questions raised, however – in contrast to Merry's work (e.g. Merry 2006a, 2006b) – pertain to the installation of regulative mechanisms, the institutionalization of collaboration, the sharing of responsibilities and sustainability issues and can therefore be situated within IR and Political Science.

Table 2.2 provides an overview of the research questions considered in this book. The analysis focuses on a global consensus on children's rights that is anchored in international conventions adopted by most governments in the world. Bangladesh is one of the nation states that have swiftly committed themselves to two of these international conventions. This study departs from a situation in which these global children's rights have been ratified by Bangladesh's government and first of all, traces the national implementation process, i.e. the process of norm translation into the constitution, into national legislation and domestic policies. Second, it asks whether national implementation leads to a change for the local target group and it clarifies

Table 2.2 Analytical framework

The Vertical	⟵ **Governance Norms** ⟶	**The Horizontal**
Global	Conventions	Intergovernmental
National	**(1) *National Implementation:*** (Constitution, Legislation, Policies) **(2) *From National to Local Implementation:*** *Do national implementation processes lead to a human rights change for the local target group? How are national implementation processes linked to local implementation?*	Governmental
Local	**(3) *Local Implementation:*** *How does a local human rights implementation process evolve? What structural, institutional changes does it imply and which regulative mechanisms have to be installed?*	**(4) *Local Actors and Actor Arrangements:*** *Which actors and actor constellations engage in local implementation processes?*

relations between national and local implementation processes. In a third step, inductive empirical research reveals how a local human rights implementation process evolves and which structural, regulative and institutional changes it implies. Finally, actor constellations, including governmental and societal ones, between different levels are being examined. Here, the book focuses on their temporal institutionalization, their sharing of responsibilities and on aspects of sustainability. The overall objective of this book is to generate hypotheses on how global human rights norms reach their local targets in a weak state context.

Chapter 3

Children's rights in Bangladesh: national versus local implementation

আমার সোনার বাংলা, আমি তোমায় ভালবাসি...
Amar shonar Bangla, ami tomae bhalobashi... –
My Bengal of gold, I love you...

(National Anthem of Bangladesh)

> [...], two official stances are prominently observed in Bangladesh. First, those who matter in Bangladesh repeatedly take the public posture that children are the greatest treasure of the country, and that all efforts would be taken to ensure their protection, participation, welfare and development. Second, since Bangladesh is one of the earliest signatories of the CRC, it demonstrates her commitment to the cause of children. The utter hollowness of such promises and claims becomes obvious when one is confronted with the grim reality at the ground level.
>
> (Siddiqui 2003: xi)

With its rich cultural heritage and fertile land, Bangladesh[1] was once known as "Shonar Bangla" or the Golden Bengal[2] (BBS 2009: 2) although its history and presence is marked by struggle for independence and survival (Feldman and Larson 2004: 13). The People's Republic of Bangladesh, formerly known as East Pakistan, was born in 1971 gaining independence from West Pakistan after almost two decades of – a partly violent – commitment to achieve autonomy. East and West Pakistan had, mainly due to religious reasons, separated from India after British decolonization in 1947. Since then, they were not only spatially disconnected from each other but also divided along languages, cultures, social and economic development, and political endeavors. Even before Pakistan fell apart, an inequality between the Eastern and the Western part had emerged. Among other reasons, this was because of the

1 বাংলাদেশ: bangla=Bengali, desh=country, Bangladesh means Bengali-speaking country.

2 Bangladesh forms the larger and more populated part of the former Bengal, the remainder of it being the Indian State of West Bengal (see among others: Shrestha 2002: 202–4).

preferential channeling of funds from the United States of America (USA) and several European donors towards West Pakistan enabling its military, industrial, and infrastructural development (van Schendel 2009: 144–51). Even though the roots of aid dependence had been gradually established even before Bangladesh existed, the bloody Liberation War of 1971 and a post-independence period coined by political turbulences, military coups, and a severe famine in 1973 and the year after, marked the birth of Bangladesh as a birth into poverty (Thanki and Dhingra 2006: 10).

Until today, Bangladesh belongs to the least developed nations in the world, ranking 146th out of 187 countries with available data, according to the Human Development Index (HDI) (UNDP 2011). About 49.6 percent of its population lives below the poverty line of 1.25 US Dollars a day, compared to 22.6 percent in Pakistan and 55.1 percent in Nepal (UNDP 2011). Bangladesh disposes of a predominantly agrarian economy accommodating a rural labor force. Apart from agriculture, dominant industries are readymade garments and textiles, chemical fertilizers, tea processing, paper, newsprint and cement production, light engineering, sugar making or the production and processing of leather goods. All of these industries operate according to free market principles (BBS 2009: 8). Particularly well-known in Western countries are products from the readymade garments and knitwear industry, which together constitute Bangladesh's biggest export sector (BBS 2009: 8).

With a population of about 149.7 million people in 2011 (BBS 2011), of which about 90 percent are Muslims, Bangladesh belongs to the most densely populated countries in the world, accommodating 1,015 inhabitants per square kilometer (BBS 2011). In 2008, about 13 million people lived in the national capital Dhaka alone. This, however, is a figure that can only be estimated given the explosive growth of the city (BBS 2009: 7). Landlessness, famines, and widespread poverty in the rural areas lead to a major land exodus with families migrating to the bigger cities in search of more and better opportunities. More than often, they end up living in shanties and urban slums in even worse situations (BSAF 2008: 15).

Bangladesh's indigence and reliance on foreign aid is perpetuated and worsened by natural disasters, such as cyclones, recurring (monsoon) floods, and riverbank erosion (BSAF 2008: 15). Natural calamities and their consequences affect the poorest of the poor even more than others:

> Such dramatic changes in weather are especially devastating for the rural poor and landless, who are among the least able to fight against the high prevalence of waterborne diseases, water pollution, groundwater contamination by naturally occurring arsenic, soil degradation and erosion, and deforestation. (Feldman and Larson 2004: 14)

Neither these environmental consequences, which have a devastating effect on the poor's health and living situation, nor other poverty issues can adequately be addressed in Bangladesh's political system with its rampant turmoil and instability. The 1975 assassination of Sheikh Mujibur Rahman, the first President of Bangladesh and commonly known as the father of the Bengali nation, was followed by two decades of military rule. Even after military leadership was overcome, political restlessness and the recurrence of corrupt leaders have remained characteristic for Bangladesh. During recent years, the country has either been governed by Khaleda Zia of the Bangladesh National Party (BNP) (Kumar 2007), Sheikh Hasina of the Awami League (AL) or a caretaker government that has frequently been accused of acting as a tool of the military. Both leading ladies have continuously been involved in corrupt affairs, detained, and again and again, forced to leave the country. The last elections on 29 December 2008 swept AL leader Sheikh Hasina, the eldest daughter of Sheikh Mujibur Rahman, back to power as Prime Minister (The Daily Star 2008a).[3] Only about a year before, in July 2007, she had been arrested and sent to jail for extortion (The Daily Star 2008b).[4] As a consequence of such corrupt, unsteady, and volatile political leadership, the People's Republic of Bangladesh frequently scores high on Transparency International's Corruption Perception Index (CPI). Although a *de jure* parliamentary democracy is in place, it ranks 144 out of 176 countries and remains one of the most corrupt countries in the world (Transparency International 2012). Despite democratically functioning institutions such as a parliament, an active opposition, free print media, a judiciary, open elections, and an official commitment to human rights, only very limited accountability and hardly any public input can be observed in the country (Feldman and Larson 2004: 14).

In a context of such severe poverty like Bangladesh's, children are particularly disadvantaged and vulnerable. The "Save the Children" Child Development Index (CDI),[5] an assessment tool of child wellbeing, ranks Bangladesh 107th out of 141 countries with available data (Save the Children UK 2012: 24). Taking recent years' developments into account, child wellbeing in Bangladesh has improved. According to the CDI, it belongs to the countries that achieved notable progress between the last measurement period in the 1990s (1994–1999) and the first one in the 2000s (2000–2006) with an improvement of 43 percentage points (Save the Children UK 2008: 13). How this progress, in particular with respect to health, education, and

3 "Landslide mandate" in *The Daily Star* (internet edition), 30 December 2008, Dhaka, Bangladesh: http://www.thedailystar.net/newDesign/news-details.php?nid=69338 [retrieved 26 August 2009].

4 "Freed Hasina asks for quick election" in *The Daily Star* (internet edition), 6 December 2008, Dhaka, Bangladesh: http://www.thedailystar.net/story.php?nid=40807 [retrieved 26 August 2009].

5 The CDI is comparable to the HDI. Its main difference is that it takes child-focused indicators into account. Child well-being according to the CDI considers (1) health measured by the under-five mortality rate, (2) nutrition assessed by the percentage of children under five years old who are underweight, and (3) education quantified by the percentage of primary school children not enrolled (Save the Children UK 2008: 5).

the reduction of hazardous child labor, has come about is further investigated in this chapter.

3.1 Children in Bangladesh: a situation analysis

The concept of childhood in South Asia and Bangladesh differs from Western perceptions. In local communities, children's developmental stages are not understood in a standardized way according to age limits, and the age of a child is not necessarily linked to skills he or she should have attained and to what he or she should be able to perform (Blanchet 1996: 62–4). Direct translations of the Bengali shishukal (শিশুকাল) to childhood and correspondingly, shishu odhikar (শিশু অধিকার) to children's rights misinterpret local conceptions in this respect. A shishu (শিশু) rather grasps a small child from infancy to pre-school childhood. School-age children whose rights are at stake to be protected the most – since they are particularly at risk of being drawn into child labor – can, in the local understanding, already take care of themselves and are not considered to be a shishu anymore (see also Blanchet 1996: 37–40). Thus, there is no single Bengali word or phrase for childhood (Bissell 2003: 58) and the term in use among children's rights advocates might be misleading or at least does not correspond to local realities.

Bangladesh's children themselves associate childhood with an absence of authority in decision-making, with performing fewer responsibilities, and with contributing less to the family income. Marriage is viewed as a rite of passage connected to leaving the life stage of childhood (Bissell 2003: 60–4). Developmental phases of childhood and adolescence in Bangladesh are determined by the role a child is taking, such as commencing school and being able to comprehend, working or taking other responsibilities, and acquiring gender roles, rather than by any age standards (Blanchet 1996: 45). This indeed means that according to local realities, children enter adulthood, which includes income-earning, marriage, responsibilities, and decision-making much earlier than seemingly appropriate by Western standards. Additionally, due to a widespread absence of birth certificates throughout the country, the age of children is often unknown or can only be estimated if the birth of a child can be related to a certain event, like a natural disaster. This, of course, makes law enforcement with respect to children's rights even more problematic (Khair 2005: 40; Blanchet 1996: 43).

According to Muslim beliefs, childbearing is viewed as a compulsory duty: "[...] if one has more than one child he will earn God's approval more as Allah's name is raised in voices" (Maloney, Aziz and Sarker 1981: 99). Giving birth to a number of children is religiously seen as an enhancement of the entire family's honor (Maloney, Aziz and Sarker 1981: 101). Children are also considered to be an integral part of their relatives' social and economic network; they provide income security for the elders, particularly after their retirement from work (Maloney, Aziz and Sarker 1981: 105). From an economic perspective, male children are preferred as future income earners, while females usually remain without a salary as most of their duties are limited to the private sphere. In addition to girls' lacking income contribution, families have to spend considerable amounts of money for arranging their marriages and for paying their dowries (Maloney, Aziz and Sarker 1981: 107). After marriage, daughters are considered to belong to their husband's family (McNicoll and Cain 1990: 108), which often leads to parents' hesitance to invest in their education from childhood on. Sons, in turn, are viewed as an important source of income for their widowed mothers and the remaining family after the father or the head of the family has passed away (McNicoll and Cain 1990: 41). Investing in their education, therefore, can be considered an investment in the entire family's future wellbeing.

Only a thorough understanding of these childhood particularities in Bangladesh can fruitfully inform a children's rights implementation process (compare Bissell 2003: 69). To pursue this research objective and learn more about that process, this descriptive situation analysis concentrates on aspects that are the most relevant with respect to the three rights under investigation. As such, the upcoming sections delve deeper into the children's situation in terms of child labor, education, and health.

3.1.1 Child labor

To understand the multidimensional and complex phenomenon of child labor in Bangladesh and in any part of the world, it is indispensable to take a closer look at what exactly determines and causes it. Standards defining child labor are set by the International Labour Organization (ILO), which refers to its complexity as a conceptual dilemma (ILO 2002a: 16). Significant factors for a definition are children's age, the nature of work they undertake, and their working hours summarized in different categories of working children. According to the *ILO Minimum Age Convention* (C138) of 1973, which comprises the most comprehensive international definition for admission to employment (ILO 2006: 6), the age at which a child is allowed to take up an occupation should generally not be below 15 years and the completion age of compulsory schooling. Regulations in countries with insufficiently developed economic and educational facilities slightly differ. Here, the minimum age for admission to employment should not be below 14 years. Light work that does not impede a child's development, health or education, and does not exceed 14 hours a week, may be carried out from the age of 13 on, and in less developed countries can be taken up at the age of 12. Hazardous work, on the contrary, can only be commenced at the age of 18 in all countries regardless of their developmental stage. Exceptions can be made for children who are at least 16 years old and are adequately trained and protected (ILO 1973a).

The definition of a minimum age for admission to work elaborated above takes account of children's age, nature of employment, and working hours and constitutes the basis for regulations put forward in the 1999 *ILO Worst Forms of Child Labour Convention* (C182). From these defining features, categories of working children can be derived. According to internationally recognized categories established by the ILO, economically active children are all children between five and 17 engaged in any form of productive work whether it is paid or not. These could be legally acceptable forms of employment, such as an apprenticeship, as well as unacceptable types of child labor. Whether economically active children are regarded as child laborers depends on the nature of work and the quantity of hours they are engaged in it. This means children below 13 years of age (12 years in developing countries) engaged in any occupation are child laborers. As devised above, children between 13 and 15 years of age (12 and 14 years in developing countries) are child laborers, except if they are undertaking light work of less than 14 hours a week. Children above 15 years are child laborers if they work for more than 43 hours a week. Children of all ages are considered as undertaking hazardous work if they work more than 43 hours weekly or if they are employed under certain hazardous conditions defined by the C182 and its accompanying recommendation. All children engaged in the unconditional worst forms of child labor are exposed to a work situation which is, according to the C182, the most abusive and damaging to their physical and mental health and their development. Examples for the worst forms of child labor are forced or bonded labor, children engaged in (drug) trafficking, pornography, prostitution, and child soldiers (ILO 1973a, 1999a, 1999b; Bannerman and Berghuys 2008: 12).

The most recent National Child Labour Survey published by the Bangladesh Bureau of Statistics (BBS) reveals that in the country, according to the child labor categories outlined above, almost 7.5 million children are economically active. Of these, 3.2 million are child laborers and almost 1.3 million children engage in hazardous work. Figure 3.1 provides an overview of the categories of working children in Bangladesh according to gender.

Data from the BBS shows that, of these almost 3.2 million child laborers in the country, 77 percent are boys and only 23 percent are girls (Khundker 2005: 8). In absolute numbers, this would mean that 2.5 million boys are engaged in child labor compared to only 0.7 million girls. Gendered data on child labor, however, do not necessarily provide a realistic picture of how labor among boys and girls is indeed being shared. Girls are frequently engaged in the private sphere, in domestic child labor or home-based work often hidden from the public eye and official statistics. Hossain (2007: 145) stresses this reality for women and female children in Bangladesh: "While a large number of women and children are employed as domestic workers, there are no statistics available on their actual numbers. Because of the nature of their work they are isolated within the home and given their lack of any bargaining power they cannot negotiate their wage" (Hossain 2007: 145).

	Total	Boys	Girls
□ Children in Hazardous Work (CHW)	1.291.000	1.172.000	120.000
▨ Child Laborers (CL)	3.179.000	2.461.000	718.000
■ Economically Active Children (EAC)	7.423.000	5.471.000	1.952.000

Figure 3.1 Economically active children, child laborers and children in hazardous work
Source: Data from National Child Labour Survey 2002–2003; BBS 2003: 63 (variations in presentation: A.S.)

Shoishab Bangladesh, a local non-governmental organization (NGO), brought to light that indeed more than 300,000 child domestic workers are employed in Dhaka City alone. A comparatively recent study involving 5,092 domestic child laborers, of whom 78 percent were female, revealed that these children have little or no access to education, start working approximately at the age of ten and on average, work 6.99 days a week and 15.5 hours per day. These children are engaged in various household tasks while they are dependent on the goodwill of their employers who usually agree to provide food, clothes, and shelter to them. Domestic workers are not necessarily paid and if they are, an average monthly salary was found to be about 223.60 Bangladeshi Taka (BDT).[6] The majority of children, namely 81 percent, had to hand over this sum to their parents (Khair 2004: xv–xx).

6 One euro corresponds to 102 BDT, one dollar corresponds to 79 BDT [18 March 2013].

Most children in Bangladesh work in the informal sector in enterprises that neither recognize nor protect their workers under national legal and regulatory frameworks (ILO 2002b: 3).[7] The BBS reveals that 93.3 percent of all working children in the country are engaged in the informal economy (BBS 2003: 70). Informal businesses operate beyond the reach of the national tax system and employees usually do not sign formal labor contracts, they earn lower wages, they have no formal representation, and are not protected by the labor law (Bannerman and Berghuys 2008: 7–8). Occupations of children in the informal sector include working as mechanics, messengers, packers, shoe-shiners, cleaners, junk collectors, vendors, flower or foodstuff sellers, porters, transport helpers, rickshaw pullers and, as already mentioned above, domestic workers. Construction work or earth digging and filling are other types of informal work children can possibly undertake. Especially in the rural areas, children are active in agriculture, weaving, and fishing. In the course of their work, they can be exposed to dangerous processes and substances (Khair 2005: 12; Khan 2001: 81; Khondker 1993: 92).

In Bangladesh's formal economy, which operates within the national tax system with labor contracts and protections under national employment regulations, children are occupied in the shrimp and garment industries or in small-scale factories producing bidis,[8] cigarettes, glassware or leather goods in tanneries. Further light-ware industries employing children comprise food processing and canning enterprises, bakeries, spinning and weaving businesses, pottery shops, toy shops, embroidery and metal works, cottage industries, handicrafts, and other small workshops (Khair 2005: 8). Formal transport and communication sectors also employ children (National Child Labor Policy Draft 2007: 5), and frequently, they also crush bricks on construction sites. Boundaries between the informal and the formal sector, however, are blurry and cannot always be accurately delineated. While sub-sectors and sub-contractors of the formal economy can exist in informal arrangements, the semi-organized sector is a category that still needs to be further investigated (see for example Khan 2001: 102). Beyond that, children and other workers can be engaged in both a formal and an informal employment arrangement at the same time.

The salary children receive varies considerably and depends upon their age, experience, skills, and the working activities they perform. A comparably recent study undertaken by the Foundation for International Research on Working Children (IREWOC) revealed that child laborers in Bangladesh usually start working as apprentices and only get paid after acquiring more

7 This does not refer to legal protection under international conventions. The C182, for example, clearly defines the forms of labor that it applies to (ILO 1999, Article 3). Most of these forms, such as slavery, prostitution, illicit or hazardous work, are activities in the informal working sector (see also the accompanying recommendation: ILO 1999b).

8 Bidis are small hand-rolled cigarettes usually containing tobacco or herbs that are very common in South Asian countries.

skills and experience. Working conditions and income are rarely regulated and vary according to the goodwill of the employer. In 2008, the salary of children in Dhaka's leather sector varied between 1,000 and 2,500 BDT in the tanneries, between 1,500 and 3,000 BDT in small scale factories and between 1,000 and 2,200 BDT per month among child shop assistants selling leather products (Ensing 2009). The ILO, in a less recent study, published data according to which children earn between zero and 36 BDT per day with a daily average of 14 BDT. Parents, however, receive an income of 100 to 125 BDT per day. This means that the average household income with three or more earners is about 4,000 BDT monthly (ILO/IPEC 2006: 14).

The supply of child labor, first and foremost, can be explained by a poor economic household situation. An employer's decision to hire children, instead of adult workers, points to dysfunctions in a labor market where child labor serves as a cheaper and more competitive substitute for unskilled adult labor (ILO 2001: 19). Increasing women's participation in the labor market, for instance, could lead to a decrease of children's labor force participation.[9] One important example is Bangladesh's garment industry, which now employs even more women since it has become virtually child labor-free (compare Bissell 2003: 49). From the employers' perspective, it is usually the temptation to gain a competitive advantage, which leads to hiring cheap laborers who are easier to exploit, mostly unaware of their rights, unorganized, less likely to contradict and not difficult to control, eager to acquire skills, and to contribute to their family's income (Khair 2005: 10). Some employers, however, are trapped in a poverty cycle, similar to the children they hire, and struggling for the survival of their businesses.

In Bangladesh, socialization according to particular socio-cultural values contributes largely to children participating continuously in the national labor force. Broadly speaking, child labor has been and still is an accepted practice in Bangladesh (Feldman and Larson 2004: 17). In a predominantly agrarian economy, parents attribute economic value to their children, and thus, raise large families. The family in Bangladesh is not only perceived as a close circle of trust and social company but also as needing to secure welfare for all of its members. Frequently, elder siblings are exempted from attending school to watch their younger brothers and sisters at home while both parents are engaged in full-time employment.[10] Traditional authoritarian attitudes of parental power, control and regulation, and filial duty are being transmitted inter-generationally, and it is taken for granted that children contribute

9 I would like to thank Prof. Alaka Basu for this useful comment, which again highlights the cultural dimension of the child labor problem in Bangladesh. The work that is undertaken by children could be performed by women if they were able to emancipate themselves from traditional gender roles and participate in public life.

10 See, for example, the interview with Md. Monwer Hossain Khandker, Bangladesh Rural Advancement Committee (BRAC), Programme Manager, Field Operations, BRAC Education Programme, 8 June 2008.

to the family income (Khair 2001: 79–80). In some cases, employers are simply not aware of the fact that child labor is prohibited by international and national law and that they are exploiting the children that they employ.[11] Social attitudes and behavior are particularly discriminating towards certain groups of children like child domestic workers and street children; they face neglect as well as psychological and physical abuse although they are, at the same time, the most vulnerable and disadvantaged (Shishu Adhikar Sangjog 2001: 15; Ghuznavi and Ghuznavi 2001: 31).

Moreover, socio-cultural perceptions and attitudes towards child labor are closely linked to education. Parents, especially in poor rural areas, are skeptical about sending their children to school for a variety of reasons. To begin with, they are not educated themselves and do not necessarily attach any value or meaning to literacy and schooling (Khair 2005: 11).[12] Uneducated parents cannot relate to the contents being taught at school and view it as too elitist or academic. They would prefer a more practical education that transmits employable skills to their descendants (Khair 2005: 31–2). Parents, indeed, are afraid that their children will not find employment after schooling since it, according to their opinion, does not provide them with marketable skills.[13] Awareness among parents and their children about the way education could change their economic situation in the long run by breaking the intergenerational cycle of poverty is very often simply lacking.[14] It could even turn out to be a delicate issue for poor parents to get their children admitted to formal schools due to prevailing societal class differences and stigmatization.[15]

In addition to that, even though primary education in Bangladesh is free and compulsory, and secondary education is free for girls, there are hidden costs attached to children attending school. These include school materials, especially paper and pencils, but also uniforms and school transportation (ILO 2004b: 2). Of further relevance are the opportunity costs involved whenever children attend school, and thus, earn less or do not earn at all (Dorman 2008: 3). These are differently assessed for boys than they are for girls. If a decision is made to invest in a child's education, boys are more likely to be sent to school. They are the ones who can become engaged in a job later on and receive a salary that pays off the schooling investment (Khair 2005: 6; Dorman 2008: 1–2).

11 See, for example, the interview with Profulla Chandra Barman, BRAC, former Project Coordinator, 17 July 2008.

12 See also the interview with M. Mohiuzzaman, Underprivileged Children's Educational Programs (UCEP), Manager Technical Education, 2 June 2008.

13 Interview Shafiqur Rahman Bhuian, Ministry of Labour and Employment (MoLE), former Deputy Chief Planning and Project Director Eradication of Hazardous Child Labour in Bangladesh, 18 June 2008.

14 Interview Profulla Chandra Barman, BRAC, former Project Coordinator 17 July 2008 and Interview Musbah Alim, CATALYST, Executive Director, 19 June 2008.

15 Interview Musbah Alim, CATALYST, Executive Director, 19 June 2008.

This nexus between child labor and education is of particular significance and demands a closer analysis of the education situation in Bangladesh which will be undertaken in the following.

3.1.2 Education

The *World Conference on Education for All* held in 1990 in Jomtien, Thailand was a milestone in the development of Bangladesh's education system.[16] Since then, astonishing progress with respect to basic education has been achieved. After signing the *World Declaration on Education for All* in 1990, a *Compulsory Primary Education Act* was adopted and enacted in the same year, making primary education compulsory for all children between six and ten years of age (Blanchet 1996: 184). This legal commitment to major reforms and advancements in the education sector initiated institutional developments and substantial growth in public expenditure on primary education (Ehsan 2001: 148). Consequently, in 1992, a Primary and Mass Education Division was installed in Bangladesh's ministerial structure, which turned into the Ministry of Primary and Mass Education (MoPME) in 2003. Whereas the MoPME is responsible for basic education, including formal free and compulsory and non-formal education (NFE),[17] the Ministry of Education takes care of secondary and higher education as well as religious educational streams (MoPME 2009).[18]

As a result, primary school enrollment in Bangladesh increased remarkably during the last two decades, particularly for girls among whom the net enrollment ratio[19] in the period from 2007 to 2010 was at 93 percent, compared to 86 percent for boys (UNICEF 2012: 104). This means that in Bangladesh, universal primary education, i.e. the second Millennium Development Goal (MDG), is most likely to be achieved by 2015 even though serious concerns about completion rates[20] and the quality of education remain (BSAF 2008: 11). Another concern is the high number of drop-outs; from the children enrolling in primary school, only 76 percent successfully graduate, taking an average of 6.6 years (Khan 2008: 36).

Local development NGOs, who are usually externally funded, play a decisive role in providing primary education in Bangladesh. They frequently offer NFE to children that, for different reasons, are hampered from attending

16 See, for example, the interview with Tapan Kumar Chakravorty, Deputy Director, Primary Education and Stipend Program (PESP), Ministry of Primary and Mass Education (MoPME), 17 July 2008.

17 NFE is a widespread phenomenon in Bangladesh and refers to schooling outside of the formal governmental education system. This is particularly attractive for working children.

18 MoPME, official website: http:/www.mopme.gov.bd/ [retrieved 30 April 2009].

19 The net enrollment ratio refers to the number of students enrolled at a certain education level belonging to the respective age group.

20 An overview is provided by the United Nations Development Programme: MDGs and Bangladesh, http://www.undp.org.bd/mdgs.php [retrieved 30 April 2009].

mainstream governmental schools or drop out before completing the primary education cycle. NFE is usually offered in provisionally set-up and unpretentiously arranged learning centers in poor rural areas and urban slums, often in locations where governmental schools are missing. These NFE centers provide basic education in reading and writing Bengali and sometimes even English. Here, children are taught how to calculate and write; but the curriculum also includes training on health care or other issues relating to children's rights (Hossain 2008). NFE programs are characterized by unconventional teaching methods, teachers who refrain from corporal punishment and authoritative pressure, and flexible teaching hours that are highly appreciated among children. Most NFE participants are unable to attend a mainstream governmental school program due to their working times, an earlier drop-out or financial constraints.

To coordinate governmental and non-governmental efforts in NFE program implementation, a Bureau of Non-Formal Education (BNFE) under the MoPME was established. Assessment studies in Bangladesh reveal that the NGOs' NFE centers, in general, do not only perform better than governmental primary schools with regard to academic achievement and supervision, they also offer more instruction time, are better equipped with teaching material and resources, and profit from better functioning school management committees and community participation. This performance success is believed to be due to the constant training and motivational work undertaken by NGOs (Ehsan 2001: 151–6).

NFE provided by NGOs, however, largely depends on external funding and predominantly caters to the needs of certain groups of students like the ones engaged in child labor. Even today, there is no governmental institutionalization for NFE.[21] This means that even though many of Bangladesh's children depend on more flexible forms of schooling to receive any kind of education at all, the government completely relies upon NGOs and donor money to reach out to these students. Whereas NFE largely contributes to an overall improvement of the educational situation in the country, its integration into a functioning governmental education system is not yet given.

For the year 2005, the Bangladesh Bureau of Educational Information and Statistics (BANBEIS) reported the existence of 37,672 governmental primary schools compared to 22,049 registered and non-registered non-governmental primary schools and 23,497 other primary level institutions (BANBEIS 2008), among them the so-called "ebtedayee madrassash" or Islamic-oriented

21 The BNFE coordinates non-governmental efforts with respect to primary education; nevertheless, it does not create or institutionalize governmental initiatives in the area of NFE. This means that the government does not offer any flexible forms of education, considering the number of children who have to work and contribute to the family income. Therefore, at the moment, child laborers depend on the educational supply of NGOs (see also: Interview Mohammad Golam Kibria, UNICEF, Education Section, Education Officer, 4 June 2008).

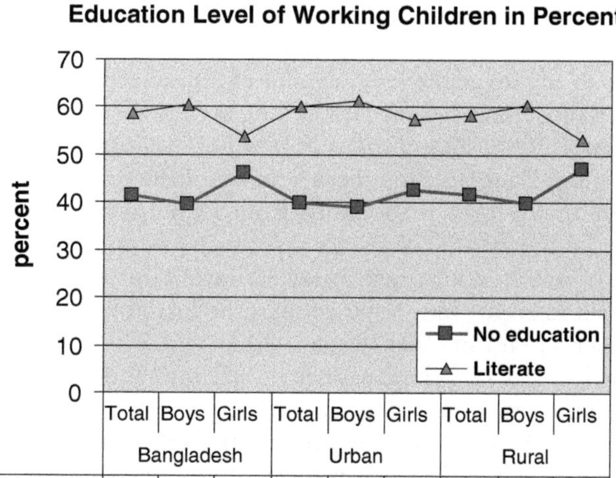

	Bangladesh Total	Bangladesh Boys	Bangladesh Girls	Urban Total	Urban Boys	Urban Girls	Rural Total	Rural Boys	Rural Girls
No education	41,3	39,5	46,1	39,8	38,8	42,6	41,6	39,7	46,9
Literate	58,7	60,5	53,9	60,2	61,2	57,4	58,4	60,3	53,1

Figure 3.2 Working children by level of education and gender in percent
Source: Data from National Child Labour Survey 2002–2003; BBS 2003: 66 (variations in presentation: A.S.)

and religion-based schools (Ehsan 2001: 153). For the children of middle class families, there are also private kindergartens, English medium schools or even army and cadet educational facilities (Blanchet 1996: 181).

Among working children, rural girls are particularly disadvantaged when it comes to educational attainments. In concrete figures, this means that 46.9 percent of working girls in rural areas have no educational opportunities at all, compared to 39.7 percent of rural boys. The situation proves to be only slightly better among working children in urban domains. Figure 3.2 highlights working children's education level according to gender.

Gender parity in primary education, one target of the third MDG, has already been reached in Bangladesh. Drop-out rates among girls, however, remain particularly high and parents facing serious economic hardships try to marry off their daughters at a very young age, in many cases when they are not older than 15 or 16 years (BSAF 2008: 14). The rate of child marriage, referring to boys and girls under 18 years of age, is at 64 percent, in general, and with 69 percent, even higher in rural areas (UNICEF 2008: 150). Early marriages of girls, which are mostly due to poverty, happen at the expense of secondary school education. In addition to that, child marriage increases the risk of maternal death due to early pregnancy and child birth.

Nevertheless, attitudes in Bangladesh have shifted from a situation in which educating daughters is considered to be watering a neighbor's tree[22] and in which any investment in a female child is viewed as a waste of resources since she will be married off and belong to a different family in her adulthood (Raynor 2005: 83). Various regulative mechanisms introduced by the Government of Bangladesh and other stakeholders increased secondary school enrollment among girls remarkably, from 18 percent in the year 1970 to 50 percent and more in 2000. Significant for such a development was not only the initiation of free compulsory primary education but also free tuition for girls in classes six to eight from 1990 on, and the introduction of a female secondary stipend program in 1994 (Raynor 2005: 88). The increasing involvement of women in local school management schemes and in parent-teacher associations might contribute to girls enrolling and remaining in the education system (Shishu Adhikar Sangjog 2001: 18). Girls' school education, however, does not necessarily reflect a transformation of gender roles. Ultimately, the purpose of education could again be driven by marriage (Blanchet 1996: 49) in order to find a husband who prefers to wed an educated wife.[23]

Most schools in Bangladesh, whether governmental or non-governmental, primary or secondary, have unique characteristics of school coordination. These include school management committees, composed of local leaders and elites, teachers, the headmaster, parent representatives,[24] and parent-teacher associations (Ehsan 2001: 151). The rationale behind these institutions is to improve community involvement for certain school-related aspects. These school management committees involving a range of community members can play a crucial role in implementing the right to education and other children's rights at the grassroots level as will be shown later on. Before delving into concrete implementation practices, the link between educational concerns, in particular the literacy levels of parents, and the health situation of their children, will be elaborated below.

3.1.3 Health

When analyzing children's health and nutritional status, it is indispensable to realize that the situation of the child can hardly be separated from his or her mother's health situation. This is particularly true during a mother's reproductive years, including the time a child is being breastfed and beyond that, when it comes to passing on health and nutritional knowledge (Shishu Adhikar Sangjog 2001: 5). Female adolescents and women in Bangladesh frequently suffer from malnutrition, which can lead to stillbirth, premature delivery, low birth weight, and neonatal death.

22 This indeed is an old Bengali saying (compare Raynor 2005).

23 Interview Tapan Kumar Chakravorty, Deputy Director, PESP, MoPME, 17 July 2008.

24 Ibid..

South Asia remains as the only region in the world with clear evidence of gender discrimination in food distribution among female children under five years of age and adolescent women (UNICEF 2008: 28): "In Bangladesh, deep-rooted gender discrimination often manifests itself in unequal distribution of food at the household level, whereby boys are given more and better quality food than girls" (Sultana and Ahmed 2001: 34). Discrimination in food distribution hampers the development of girls and results in the delivery of underweight infants. The risk of giving birth to a low-weight infant increases with early pregnancies carried out by mothers under 18 years of age (Sultana and Ahmed 2001: 43).

Between 2006 and 2010, a high number of Bangladeshi children, i.e. 41 percent, between zero and five years of age were underweight, a rate which is among the worst rate in the entire world (UNICEF 2012: 92). However, not only infants and small children are affected; clear evidence demonstrates how an improved health and nutrition status has an impact on the achievements of school children and adolescents. It fosters school enrollment, attendance and performance, economic productivity, and the health of future generations (del Rosso and Marek 1996: v). Hence, an improved health and nutritional situation would significantly contribute to human and economic development (Sultana and Ahmed 2001: 35).

The sharp increase in global food prices and domestic crop losses caused by natural calamities lead to both a rise in domestic food prices and, consequently, to food insecurity (ADB 2009: 193). Malnutrition is not only a severe health problem in itself but also increases additional health hazards and the prevalence of diseases that have proved to be difficult to control. Health issues malnourished children are confronted with include acute respiratory infections, diarrhea, and diseases requiring preventative vaccinations. Fever is a major manifestation of malaria and of other infections that children are exposed to. Both, malaria and fever, in turn, contribute to malnutrition and high mortality rates. The treatment of children suffering from fever increases considerably in urban areas, with a respective income, and in cases where mothers have completed primary or higher education (National Institute of Population Research and Training, Mitra and Associates and Macro International 2009: 143–4).

The prevention of infectious diseases through vaccinations has improved significantly in Bangladesh. In 2010, between 93 and 99 percent of all one-year-old children were fully vaccinated against tuberculosis, diphtheria, measles, tetanus, polio, and hepatitis. Vaccination coverage, of course, is higher in urban areas and for the children of educated mothers (UNICEF 2012: 96).

Diarrhea and other water-related illnesses are most commonly triggered by limited access to clean water and sanitation facilities (Sultana and Ahmed 2001: 41) to which only 32 percent of the rural and 48 percent of the urban population have access to in Bangladesh (UNICEF 2008: 126). Other frequently occurring diseases are, for instance, measles, traditionally regarded as the visit from a sacred goddess and therefore not always treated, and neonatal tetanus, in many cases caused by the South Asian custom of applying cow dung to the newborn infant's umbilical cord. Using unsterilized household instruments to cut the cord also leads to tetanus infections (Sultana and Ahmed 2001: 40). The presence of trained birth attendants would not only prevent the spread of these diseases but would also contribute immensely to saving the lives and improving the health situation of newborns and their mothers (UNICEF 2008: 35).

Whereas it is clear that hazardous labor is harmful to children's health, a raw correlation between working children and reported health problems has not yet been systematically established (Dorman 2008: 39). Whether and how child labor affects health is determined by the work context (i.e. the nature of work undertaken, work hours, and conditions, risks and hazards), the involvement of hazardous chemicals, machinery or equipment, and the individual situation, such as the age of the child, his or her health and nutritional status and a child's previous experience with the specific work being undertaken. In her study on child labor in Bangladesh, Sumaiya Khair (2005: 12–13) differentiates among health hazards as detrimental to physical health and safety, on the one hand, and to the mental and psychological wellbeing of children, on the other hand. Occupational health and safety risks encountered by children are injuries, mutilation, burns, and infections, but also anemia, tuberculosis, kidney disorders, and respiratory diseases. In the informal sector, child laborers may be exposed to dangerous processes and substances like dust, fumes, chemicals, and other lethal substances that could result in respiratory problems, skin infections or even cancer. Moreover, awkward work positions can lead to deformities in a child's body height and structure, as well as his or her spinal column and pelvis. Khair (2005: 13) emphasizes that certain occupations, even though they are regarded as safe under family supervision, might bear particular health risks, such as agricultural work. Sexual harassment and abuse are other dangers working children are confronted with; girls being even more susceptible to any forms of sexual exploitation. These and other incidences at work can have an impact on the psycho-social development of children. Emotional stress and feelings of insecurity and frustration are examples of mental and psychological health consequences child laborers might encounter (Khair 2005: 13).

In sum, this rather basic delineation of the context in which children in Bangladesh are situated does not aim at completeness but rather on highlighting how aspects pertaining to child labor, education, and health are closely interwoven. The analysis shows recent progress that has been attained relating to these aspects. Examples include a considerable advancement in primary school enrollment and the achievement of gender parity in basic education. Furthermore, there have been relevant improvements in vaccination coverage and significant progress in the wellbeing of children, according to Save the Children's CDI, which measures health, nutrition, and education. Before searching for the roots of this change, however, the concrete rights that are relevant and binding for Bangladesh are considered more closely. What exactly are the agreements the Government of Bangladesh has committed itself to guarantee? The following section analyzes the international legal framework in which the situation of Bangladesh's children is embedded. Here, the focus is on international children's rights conventions and their translation into Bangladesh's legislative framework.

3.2 Legally binding children's rights principles

It is beyond dispute that the UN *Convention on the Rights of the Child* (CRC) (UN 1989) can be regarded as a milestone in the establishment of an international legal framework for children. With 193 ratifications, it has almost been universally ratified (ILO 2006: 16) and constitutes the most widely accepted human rights treaty in the world (UN Treaty Collection [c]: Website) (see also UN 2006c: 3; Lansky 1997: 237). Particularly after two early declarations on children's rights, the *Geneva Declaration of the Rights of the Child* and the *Declaration of the Rights of the Child*, were adopted by the League of Nations (1924) and the United Nations (1959) respectively, UN member states felt that legally binding regulations were indispensable to protect and promote the wellbeing of children (UN 2006c: 3). Alongside conventions concerned with racial discrimination or discrimination against women, the CRC belongs to the so-called targeted treaties incorporating civil and political as well as economic, social, and cultural rights (Alston 2005: 789). The CRC embodies so-called universal and forward-looking principles, namely non-discrimination (Article 2), primary consideration of the best interests of the child (Article 3), the right to life, survival, and development (Article 6), and the idea that children's opinions have to be heard and taken seriously, which is summarized as the views of the child (Article 12) (UN 2006c: 4–5).

Considering the situation analysis pertaining to child labor, health, and education in Bangladesh as elaborated above, the following provisions of the CRC are of relevance. Whereas Article 31 calls for providing children with rest and leisure, with time to play and undertake recreational activities, Article 32 refers more explicitly to the elimination of hazardous child labor or work that has detrimental effects on a child's education and health:

> States Parties recognize the right of the child to be protected from economic exploitation and from performing any work that is likely to be hazardous or to interfere with the child's education, or to be harmful to the child's health or physical, mental, spiritual, moral or social development (UN 1989: Article 32.1; UN 2006c: 30).

Concrete measures to be undertaken by states parties for ensuring the full implementation of this article are:

- the provision of a minimum age for admission to employment (Article 32.2.a),
- providing for regulations with respect to work hours and conditions (Article 32.2.b), and
- providing for penalties and sanctions to enforce this provision (Article 32.2.c) (UN 1989: Article 32; UN 2006c: 30).

In addition to that, regulations pertaining to realizing the right to *education* are reflected in Article 28 of the CRC, which recognizes the:

> Right of the child to education, and with a view to achieving this right progressively and on the basis of equal opportunity, they shall, in particular (UN 1989: Article 28.1)

- provide free and primary education (Article 28.1.a),
- develop forms of secondary education, including general and vocational education, and make them accessible to all children (Article 28.1.b),
- make educational and vocational information accessible (Article 28.1.d),
- create measures to foster regular school attendance and reduce drop-outs (Article 28.1.e),
- promote and encourage international cooperation to foster education (Article 28.3). (UN 1989: Article 28; UN 2006c: 28).

Finally, the following provisions for the progressive realization of the right to health are accounted for in Article 24 of the CRC, which comprehensively describes the:

> Right of the child to the enjoyment of the highest attainable standard of health and to facilities for the treatment of illness and rehabilitation of health (Article 24.1). (UN 1989: Article 24; UN 2006c: 26).

To implement this right to the fullest extent, the following measures have to be taken:

- the reduction of infant and child mortality (Article 24.2.a),
- the provision of necessary medical assistance and health care (Article 24.2.b),
- combating disease and malnutrition through the provision of nutritious food and clean drinking water (Article 24.2.c),
- ensuring prenatal and postnatal health care for mothers (Article 24.2.d),

- ensuring access to basic knowledge regarding child health and nutrition (Article 24.2.e),
- developing preventive health care and family planning services (Article 24.2.f), and
- encouraging international cooperation to progressively ensure the full realization of this right (Article 24.4). (UN 1989: Article 24; UN 2006c: 26).

Bangladesh committed itself to the CRC with only a single reservation regarding Article 21 on child adoption.[25] The government ratified it even before it officially entered into force about a month later (Khair 2005: 20). Thereby, Bangladesh agreed to progressively provide for the measures laid out in the legal instrument, beginning with harmonization of national legislative provisions.

Another children's rights convention that Bangladesh acceded to is the C182 (ILO 1999a), which in its long form is called the *Convention Concerning the Prohibition and Immediate Action for the Elimination of the Worst Forms of Child Labour* (ILOLEX [a]). This treaty and its accompanying Recommendation (R190) (ILO 1999b) are part of a new strategy that the ILO has been promoting since the 1990s to advance the gradual elimination of child labor with a primary emphasis on its worst forms (ILO 2006: IX; Liese 2005: 2). Although the convention requires immediate action towards eradicating the worst forms of child labor by its ratifying states parties, it achieved the fastest, and until today unsurpassed, ratification pace in the history of the ILO and even encouraged governments to commit to other child labor-related standards (ILO 2000; ILO 2006: 15).

Just like the CRC, the C182 defines children as all persons under the age of 18 years (ILO 1999a: Article 2). Whereas Article 3 determines the worst forms of child labor as all forms of slavery, sale, and trafficking of children, forced and compulsory child labor, and the engagement of children in armed conflict, prostitution, pornography, illicit activities like drug trafficking, and any work that is harmful to the health, safety, and morals of children, Article 1 demands that:

> Each Member which ratifies this Convention shall take immediate and effective measures to secure the prohibition and elimination of the worst forms of child labour as a matter of urgency (ILO 1999a: Article 1).

Major implementation measures to be taken by state governments as a consequence of ratifying the C182 include the establishment of:

25 The Government of Bangladesh claims that Article 21 on child adoption is not in accordance with Muslim law.

- national laws and regulations that shall determine the worst forms of child labor for the respective national context (Article 4.1),
- a competent authority that shall determine where these types of work exist (Article 4.2),
- monitoring mechanisms pertaining to these types of work (Article 5),
- action programs to eliminate the worst forms of child labor (Article 6), and
- penal or other sanctions to ensure enforcement of the convention (Article 7.1) (ILO 1999a).

The importance of education as one significant and viable alternative that supports the elimination of child labor is recognized in Article 7.2, which states that:

> Each Member shall, taking into account the importance of education in eliminating child labour, take effective and time-bound measures to (ILO 1999a: Article 7.2)

- prevent children from becoming engaged in the worst forms of child labor (Article 7.2.a),
- provide assistance for the removal of children from the worst forms of child labor as well as for their rehabilitation and social reintegration (Article 7.2.b),
- ensure free basic education and vocational training for children formerly engaged in the worst forms of child labor (Article 7.2.c),
- consider the special situation of the female child (Article 7.2.e), and
- to designate a competent authority to take account of the implementation of these measures (Article 7.3) (ibid.).

Regarding the right to health, no particular provisions are laid out in the convention except for the definition of the worst forms of child labor as harmful to children's safety, morals, and health (ILO 1999a: Article 3.d).

Recommendation R190 (ILO 1999b) defines in greater detail what the initiated action programs, as part of the implementation mechanisms, should focus on and what should be considered when defining forms of hazardous work that are harmful to the health, safety, and morals of children as stated in Article 3.d. It furthermore elaborates on implementation details emphasizing data collection, as well as information processing and reporting to the ILO, domestic monitoring to be undertaken by competent authorities, and ensuring that certain worst forms of child labor become criminal offences prosecuted by law. Alongside other measures mentioned are the need to supervise enterprises, to offer information and training concerning the elimination of the worst forms of child labor, to establish complaint procedures, to enhance the educational infrastructure, and to strengthen international cooperation and assistance (ILO 1999b). The Government of Bangladesh has ratified C182 in due course on 12 March 2001 (ILOLEX [b]) and actively cooperates with the ILO's technical assistance program, the International Programme on the Elimination of Child Labour (IPEC), to put its implementation measures into force.

Beyond these two conventions, there are two legal documents that play a decisive role in the context of Bangladesh. One is the C138 (ILO 1973a) which has not been ratified by the Government of Bangladesh as yet, although this has led to major international critique. Surprisingly, however, Bangladesh's labor legislation has been reformed according to the standards of the convention stipulating a minimum age for admission to employment of 14 years. This legislative reform is used by the government to excuse its refusal to legally commit to the international standards brought forward by the C138 (Khair 2005: 18).

The other legal instrument relevant for Bangladesh's children's rights situation is the *Child Labor Deterrence Act*. This act, also known as the Harkin Bill, was brought before the US Senate in 1992 (Khair 2005: 19–20). It was proposed by Senator Tom Harkin and Republican George Brown. Referring to the *Declaration of the Rights of the Child* from 1959, it aimed to place trade sanctions on all goods produced with child labor (Bissell 2003: 55). If the bill had come into force, it would have banned or imposed sanctions on the import of any products to the USA that were completely or partly manufactured or mined by children under the age of 14 (USDoL). The Bill's introduction in 1992 was too late for passage that year and a reintroduction in 1993 did not lead to its enactment in the USA. However, it resulted in a massive dismissal of child laborers from Bangladesh's garment factories since pertinent employers' associations were afraid that they would lose one of their most important sales markets. The dismissed children, mainly girls, lost their income from one day to another and ended up as street children, taking up jobs in the informal sector or even worse, became victims of traffickers or engaged in prostitution (ILO/UNICEF 2004: 5–6; see also Feldman and Larson 2004: 20). Only about two years later, responsive policy programs were initiated providing these children with viable alternatives, such as education and skills training. Even though the Harkin Bill has never been enacted, it had considerable repercussions on the child labor situation in Bangladesh. At first it led to a worsening of the rights situation. And at a later stage, it resulted in the introduction of a comprehensive policy response strengthening children's rights (read more about this in Chapter 4 on local policy programs).

3.3 Children's rights principles reflected in national laws and domestic policies

In the course of implementing international legal instruments ratified by the state government, the first measure to be taken is to harmonize national legislation and domestic policies accordingly. The following section takes a closer look at how Bangladesh's laws and policies reflect the three children's rights principles considered here. Furthermore, it will be outlined which principles were already anchored prior to ratification and which legislative or policy reforms were initiated following the ratification process of respective conventions.

3.3.1 Relevant legislation

Constitutional law in Bangladesh directly refers to the right to education and the right to health and nutrition as fundamental principles of state policy. Part two of the *Constitution of the People's Republic of Bangladesh* codifies these as basic necessities including, among others, food, education, and medical care (Article 15.1). As an integral part of rural development and the agricultural revolution, the state commits itself to the improvement of education and public health (Article 16). Furthermore, free and compulsory education is stipulated (Article 17). Raising the level of nutrition and improving public health is considered the state's primary duty (Article 18), and there are special provisions for the benefit of children (Article 28.4) (The Constitution of the People's Republic of Bangladesh, as modified up to 17 May 2004).

With the 1990 *Primary Education Act*, the Government of Bangladesh reserved the right to declare primary education obligatory in all areas of the country (Article 3) and for all children between six and ten years of age. In relation to that, it announced the creation of education committees responsible for monitoring school enrollment and attendance (Article 4) (The Primary Education (Compulsory) Act, 1990; see also Siddiqui 2001: 19). Whereas Bangladesh's constitution already embraced education and health provisions at the time of the country's inception, the ratification of the CRC and the adoption of the *Primary Education Act* came hand in hand and were introduced in the same year. This reflected an increased awareness among the government and Bangladesh's civil society regarding the need for educational and literacy improvements from 1990 onwards (ILO 2009).

Pertinent to the protection from the worst forms of child labor, only indirect provisions were enshrined in Bangladesh's constitution. Part two refers to fundamental principles of state policy; it stipulates the right of workers to be free from exploitation (Article 14) and anchors the right to recreation, rest, and leisure (Article 15.3). Part three, determining fundamental rights guaranteed to the citizens of Bangladesh, prohibits all forms of forced and compulsory labor (Article 34) (The Constitution of the People's Republic of Bangladesh, as modified up to 17 May 2004; see also Sengupta and Hossain 2007: 184). Hence, there is no particular article codifying the prohibition of child labor in general or putting forward a minimum age for admission to employment within the framework of the constitution. Nevertheless, forced and compulsory labor, as well as economic exploitation, is prohibited by law.

Within Bangladesh's national legislation, there are several sector-specific acts with their own definitions of who is considered a child and at what age it is permitted to enter the respective occupational sector. These partly originate from the period when Bangladesh was still East Pakistan or even from British colonial rule. Today, most of the regulations are antiquated and inconsistent with one another, particularly regarding the minimum age for admission to employment (ILO 2004a: 2). Examples for these earlier laws are the *Mines Act* (1923), the *Children (Pledging of Labor) Act* (1933), the *Employment of Children Act* (1938, and amended in 1974), the *Tea Plantations Labour Ordinance* (1962), the *Shops and Establishment Act* (1965), the *Factories Act* (1965) and the *Factory Rules* (1979). The rationale behind the *Children Act* adopted in 1974 was to consolidate legal provisions pertaining to custody protection and the treatment of children, as well as to the trial and punishment of adolescent offenders (Khair 2005: 37–9). It bears provisions taking account of working children and the exploitation of children for which the Act imposes penalties.

The 2006 *Labour Code*, prepared by a National Labor Commission taking up work in 1992, has finally harmonized and consolidated the bulk of national labor laws in force in Bangladesh. Most of the laws replaced by this code originated in the British Colonial regime or the Pakistan period. These laws were outdated, often overlapping, and partly inconsistent with each other (Halim and Rahman 2007). The *Labour Code* is also known as the *Bangladesh Labour Act*, and it replaced 22 Acts and Ordinances pertinent to labor issues (ILO NATLEX). Other sources mention the repeal of 25 previous labor-related laws (Halim and Rahman 2007), among them the *Children (Pledging of Labour) Act* (1933), the *Employment of Children Act* (1938), and the *Factories Act* (1965) (Sengupta and Hossain 2007: 185). According to the *Labour Code*'s definition, persons who have not reached the age of 14 are considered children (Halim and Rahman 2007: 36), and those over 14 but below 18 years of age are regarded adolescents (Halim and Rahman 2007: 25). It clearly prohibits child labor; children below the age of 14 are not permitted to take up employment, with exceptions made for children aged twelve years or older, who are allowed to undertake light work that does not interfere with their education and school attendance or is not detrimental to their health and development (The Bangladesh Code 2006, Article 44). If there is doubt about the age of a child or an adolescent, proof issued by a registered medical practitioner is necessary to take up any forms of occupation legally (Khair 2005: 39; The Bangladesh Code 2006, Article 36). Additionally, the *Labour Code* includes provisions protecting adolescents from hazardous work; it prohibits them from engaging in cleaning, lubricating or processing any dangerous machinery (unless they have received training and particular precautions have been taken), and from employment underground or under water (Sengupta and Hossain 2007: 185; The Bangladesh Code 2006, Article 39, 40, 42). Working hours of adolescents, in general, are not allowed to exceed five hours per day and 30 hours per week in any factory or mine, and seven hours per day or 42 hours per week in any other establishment. Night work is completely prohibited for adolescents (The Bangladesh Code 2006, Article 41).

The regulations of the *Labour Code* reflect the standards put forward in both ILO treaties, the C182 but also the C138, even though no legal commitment regarding the latter exists:

> An analysis of the abovementioned laws reveals that provisions in the domestic laws relating to working children are in many ways on par with ILO Conventions in the area. Just as relevant ILO Conventions set different age standards for admission to work on the basis of the nature of the occupation, the laws of Bangladesh demonstrate a similar trend. (Khair 2005: 39)

Despite these legislative improvements and harmonization, the government has for a long time refrained from defining the worst forms of child labor for Bangladesh's national context, as required in the convention.[26] Another considerable point of criticism is that these legal provisions are only valid for child labor undertaken in formal working sectors (ILO 2004b: 2), even though more than 90 percent of children are engaged in informal activities (BBS 2003: 70). This means that most of Bangladesh's child laborers cannot be reached through the national labor legislation put forward. These children, however, can be supported by national policies installed to realize children's rights. The following section introduces Bangladesh's most significant domestic policies, which promote the right to education and health and protect children from hazardous forms of labor.

3.3.2 Domestic policies

Children's rights principles are reflected in quite a number of domestic policies and development plans in the People's Republic of Bangladesh. While it seems difficult to identify a coherent policy strategy, a link between abolishing child labor and guaranteeing education and health services is usually established. The *Fifth Five Year Plan* (1997–2002), a major development program, emphasized a multi-sectoral approach to child development, which integrated key development areas such as health, education, social services, and the progressive elimination of child labor. The plan formulates a rights-based approach to child development, and calls for universal access to primary education, decreasing child labor, and protecting children from exploitation and violence. One major strategy put forward embraces the promotion of income-generating facilities for parents and the provision of education in rural areas to eventually eradicate child labor. Even though formulating

26 Informal interview with Sumaiya Khair, Professor, Department of Law, University of Dhaka, 23 June 2008.

broad-based objectives, these plans have been criticized for lacking concrete strategies to effectively deal with the child labor problem (Khair 2005: 23–4). After the introduction of the *Fifth Five Year Plan*, no further five-year development plan has been compiled. Instead, emphasis has been placed on the preparation of a *Poverty Reduction Strategy Paper* (PRSP) (Kabir 2009). The current PRSP for the period between 2009 and 2011 comprises a special section on protecting children. It proposes to take concerted action in advancing children's health, food and nutrition, their education, improved access to water and sanitation as well as child empowerment through awareness-raising programs and community mobilization (IMF 2012: 65–8).

The 1994 *National Children Policy* outlines intervention areas to ensure the protection of children's rights and children's healthy development in all respects. It provides for the formation of the National Council for Children, which works under the auspices of the Ministry of Women and Children Affairs (MWCA). The council observes the implementation of laws relating to children and initiates legal reforms with the overall aim of realizing the CRC. Major intervention areas identified include birth and survival, education and psychological development, family environment, assistance to children in difficult circumstances and providing for their protection by legal rights. The *National Children Policy* directly refers to the need to protect children from hazardous child labor and to provide them with free and compulsory education. However, it has also been criticized for concentrating on very general policy objectives and for failing to formulate precise policy outputs (Khair 2005: 25–6). A new draft of the *National Children Policy* was passed by the Government of Bangladesh in 2011 (Ahmed 2011); its content, however, has not been published yet.

Another policy instrument, the *National Plan of Action for Children* (1997–2002), a follow-up requirement for state governments that have ratified the CRC, frames two major strategies for achieving the gradual elimination of child labor. These encompass the establishment of a safety net for marginalized children to prevent their engagement in full-time work through the provision of educational opportunities and the initiation of urban and rural interventions that reduce vulnerabilities. This policy document has been critically assessed for its focus on satisfying the demands of donor agencies. In addition to that, its guidelines are considered as too vague and not concrete enough to achieve successful outcomes (Khair 2005: 28). A new *National Plan of Action* designed to implement the *National Child Labour Elimination Policy* of 2010 is currently being developed (USDoL 2011: 46).

After several drafts were controversially discussed for a considerable number of years, the Government of Bangladesh finally passed a *National Child Labour Elimination Policy* in 2010. This policy is a follow-up requirement of admission to the C138. The main objectives of the policy are, among others, to withdraw children from the worst forms of child labor, to engage their parents in income-generating activities, to offer stipends for (re-)integrating children in schools and to raise awareness among society to eliminate several forms of child labor by 2015 (MoLE 2010: 4–5). In contrast to what is demanded by the C182, however, the policy lists very general – instead of country-specific – working conditions under which children's occupational activities would be considered hazardous (MoLE 2010: 7). In the text of the policy, "pragmatic strategies" and responsible coordinating and implementing institutional units are identified (MoLE 2010: 10–19). For ensuring effective coordination of all governmental and non-governmental initiatives aiming at eliminating the worst forms of child labor, a Child Labour Unit has been installed within the Ministry of Labour and Employment (MoLE) (MoLE 2010: 19). In 2011, this Child Labour Unit initiated a Child Labour Monitoring Information System (CLMIS) that handles data pertinent to child labor collected by the various ministries (USDoL 2011: 46). In addition, a National Child Labour Welfare Council comprised of several stakeholders was called into life as part of the national policy to monitor the child labor situation in the country. Until 2012, however, the council had never met (USDoL 2011: 46). What remains to be done despite of all advancements initiated with this policy, is to clearly state which forms of hazardous work are prohibited in Bangladesh, to place occupations undertaken in the informal sector, such as agricultural and home-based work, under legal protection, to raise the age of compulsory schooling to the minimum age for admission to employment, which is at 14 years, to channel adequate funds into the implementation of the *National Child Labour Policy* and to ensure that the National Child Labour Welfare Council takes up its work (USDoL 2009: 48; USDoL 2011: 47).

Certainly, numerous policies aiming to realize the right to education have been formulated in Bangladesh as well. The most recent ones are in line with the demands of the *World Conference on Education for All*. A first *National Plan of Action* (NPA) for the period between 1992 and 2000 concentrated on fostering free and compulsory primary education through the establishment of a General Education Project (1990–1996), a Primary Education Development Program (PEDP) and the Food For Education (FFE) Program and Female Secondary Stipend Program (FSSP), which aim to increase school attendance and decrease dropout rates (MoPME (without publication date): 25). As a follow-up to the first NPA, the *National Plan of Action II* (2003–2015) restates the Education For All (EFA) vision of providing access to education not only for all students, but also for pre-school children and for adults at continuing education institutions. Its major components include (i) Early Childhood and Care Education, (ii) Universal Primary Education, and (iii) Non-Formal Education (MoPME (without publication date): 34–50).

Several *National Education Policies* were formulated in recent years. The latest one, adopted in 2010, highlights the importance of pre-primary education, beginning at the age of five years, and it makes enrollment into primary schools compulsory from the age of six years on. In addition to that, it states that Bangladesh's national education system shall remain in the hands of the government, instead of being delegated to NGOs and other private actors. Nevertheless, the 2010 *National Education Policy* makes reference to the fact that NGOs will continuously provide NFE, e.g. for child laborers who do not meet the demands of the formal governmental education system (MoE 2010).

Reporting on past and future action to improve the situation of children's rights is a requirement for governments that have ratified the CRC. Bangladesh accomplishes reporting obligations with its *National Plan of Action for Children*. The latest national plan (2004–2009), prepared by the Ministry on Women and Children Affairs, highlights the empowerment of girls in education. It stresses the need to enhance capacities for girls in school as well as in technical and vocational education. Moreover, it aims to increase opportunities for out-of-school children to make education more meaningful for female children (MWCA 2005: 33).

Last but not least, the right to health and nutrition is similarly promoted by a multitude of policy strategies in Bangladesh. The *Fifth Five Year Plan* (1997–2002) formulated the objective of ensuring universal access to quality health care services for all citizens of Bangladesh. Here, the need to reduce infant and maternal mortality and to improve their nutritional status was emphasized (Sultana and Ahmed 2001: 37). Another five-year program, launched in 1998 as the *Health and Population Sector Programme* (HPSP), acknowledges adolescents as one priority target group. The HPSP made provisions for the delivery of an Essential Services Package (ESP) that comprises basic reproductive and child health services, including family planning, maternal care, and immunization, but also information on communicable diseases and behavioral change towards health protection (Sultana and Ahmed 2001: 37).

The 1994 *National Children's Policy* comprises provisions for guaranteeing the right to survival after birth through fostering nutritional and physical security, and improvements in the entire family's health. Health services pertaining to reproductive health, safe motherhood, family planning, menstrual regulation, care of post-abortion complications, the management of reproductive tract infections, and sexually-transmitted diseases are provided for in the 1997 *National Reproductive Health Strategy*. An accompanying essential service package addresses the particular issues of female children (Sultana and Ahmed 2001: 39).

The *Bangladesh Decade Action Plan for the Girl Child* (1991–2000) primarily sought to reduce gender disparities with respect to health, education, access to social services, and protection. Implementation strategies encompassed inter-ministerial cooperation, community participation, increased participation of women's groups, capacity building among local government institutions, mobilization of NGOs, partnership-building between governmental, and non-governmental groups, as well as awareness raising, training, and monitoring on issues regarding girls (Khair 2005: 25).

Approved by the Cabinet in 2000, the *National Health Policy* (NHP) formulates the overall goal of providing basic medical utilities to all citizens of Bangladesh. These health services should be of an optimal quality (National Health Policy 2000: 2nd and 3rd objective). One objective of the health policy is to reduce child and maternal mortality within the next five years (ibid.: 5th and 6th objective). These rights-relevant services are to be carried out in collaborative efforts between governmental and nongovernmental organizations (National Health Policy 2000: Principle 5).

The *Bangladesh Integrated Nutrition Programme* (BINP) launched under the Ministry of Health and Family Welfare in 1995 stipulates the need for comprehensive national nutrition and the reduction of malnutrition, first and foremost among women and children. These aims shall be reached by ensuring household food security, behavioral changes related to food intake, infant feeding, growth monitoring, and caring practices (Sultana and Ahmed 2001: 38). The most recently adopted 2006 *National Food Policy* puts forward adequate nutrition for all individuals, particularly for women and children, as one of its three major objectives. Under the framework of a Public Food Distribution System, food is directly disseminated to poor households that participate in training and development activities (MFDM 2006: 10). The *National Food Policy* does not only highlight the need for macro- and micronutrient food consumption, but also emphasizes nutrition education and preventing diseases through water, sanitation, and other health service developments (MFDM 2006: 12). Sufficiently nutritious food shall especially be supplied to vulnerable groups, such as disabled people, adolescent girls, and pregnant or nursing mothers. To achieve these objectives, cooperation with NGOs and development partners is being advocated (MFDM 2006: 12). Local NGOs are supposed to play a crucial role in the delivery of pertinent services (MFDM 2006: 14).

A simple congruence procedure undertaken with the help of reviewing Bangladesh's constitution, its social and labor legislation, as well as its policy initiatives reveals that children's rights principles derived from major international conventions are reflected therein. Whereas only few legislative changes had to be made following the ratification of international conventions, numerous policies and development programs – in some cases, under the influence of international organizations (IOs) – were formulated and implemented. Table 3.1 summarizes which legislative acts and domestic policies are in congruence with at least one of the three children's rights principles examined here.

Table 3.1 shows that there is no child-related legislation addressing protection from the worst forms of child labor, the right to education and the right to health care at once in Bangladesh. Not even the constitution makes reference to all of these – very basic – rights. Instead, it neglects protection from the worst forms of child labor and determining a minimum age for admission to employment. In contrast to that, domestic policies usually encompass a broader range of issues at the same time, such as the *National*

Table 3.1 Bangladesh's legislative acts and policies in congruence with children's rights

<table>
<tr><th rowspan="2"></th><th colspan="3">Children's Rights Principles</th></tr>
<tr><th>Protection from the Worst Forms of Child Labor</th><th>Right to Education</th><th>Right to Health Care</th></tr>
<tr><td>Legislative Acts</td><td>The Labour Code</td><td colspan="2">Constitution of the People's Republic of Bangladesh</td></tr>
<tr><td></td><td></td><td>Primary Education Act</td><td></td></tr>
<tr><td>Domestic Policies</td><td colspan="3">Fifth Five Year Plan (1997–2002)</td></tr>
<tr><td></td><td colspan="3">Poverty Reduction Strategy Paper</td></tr>
<tr><td></td><td colspan="3">National Children Policy</td></tr>
<tr><td></td><td colspan="3">National Plan of Action for Children (1997–2002), (2004–2009)</td></tr>
<tr><td></td><td>National Child Labour Elimination Policy</td><td>National Education Policy</td><td>National Health Policy</td></tr>
<tr><td></td><td></td><td>National Plan of Action I+II</td><td>Health and Population Sector Programme</td></tr>
<tr><td></td><td></td><td colspan="2">Bangladesh Decade Action Plan for the Girl Child (1991–2000)</td></tr>
<tr><td></td><td></td><td></td><td>National Food Policy</td></tr>
</table>

Source: Author's compilation

Children Policy, the PRSP, the *Fifth Five Year Plan* and the *National Plan of Action for Children*. All of the rights investigated here, however, are anchored in national laws and policies indicating that – at large – a national implementation process has come about. In the following section, I will examine whether national implementation, the harmonization of Bangladesh's legislation and policies, has really made a difference in the lives of the children at the grassroots level. Did legislative reforms and policy installations indeed lead to an improvement of the children's rights situation?

3.4 National versus local implementation

Although global children's rights have accessed Bangladesh's national system and implementation processes seem to be on a good way forward, conducting field level research leaves you with a completely different picture. Interviewing representatives from IOs, national ministries, and field staff from local NGOs, and visiting the areas in which the most disadvantaged children live, suggests that comprehensive implementation has only very selectively taken place. Empirical evidence indicates that Bangladesh's children could not always be reached by national legislative and policy measures. This proves to be particularly true for the indigent ones living in the urban slums and poor rural areas of Bangladesh. A large number of those children live in disastrous conditions far away from any entitlements regarding education, health, and the protection from hazardous labor. The following pages provide a brief overview of how norm targets in Bangladesh, i.e. the children themselves but also their families and their entire community, perceive children's rights. Do they know about their own entitlements as rights-holders or do they at least have basic knowledge of the most important rights they should be enjoying? If yes, what is their attitude towards these rights? And, are they in any position to claim these rights at all?

The target areas under consideration are usually poor local communities with a high prevalence of child labor and with few schooling or health care opportunities. These have been the focal point for certain project interventions, which are introduced later on (in Chapter 4). This section's main purpose is to show how little of the national implementation process had trickled down to these communities before any local interventions were in place, and before targeted implementation strategies were applied.

In Tongi, District Gazipur, and in Mirpur and Keranigonj, District Dhaka, three poor urban industrial areas, local people who later on participated in the non-governmental *Bangladesh Institute of Labour Studies' Child Labour Elimination Project* report that they – even prior to local project implementation – were aware of the importance of education. Nevertheless, due to poverty, they did not always send their children to school since they could not afford the school fees required for enrollment. In addition to that, problems with respect to educational infrastructure persist. Particularly in rural areas, schools can be far away from a child's home and reaching a school either means to bear additional transportation costs or to expose school children to certain safety risks. Governmental schools are often overcrowded with up to 100 children in one class with only a single teacher available. In some cases, communities prefer alternative forms of teaching, such as passing on traditional knowledge from generation to generation. This can lead to a child's engagement in labor arrangements[27] at a very young age for learning marketable skills.

27 Interview Sajjad Hossain, BILS, Child Labour Elimination Project Coordinator, 21 May 2008.

A government official from the MoPME reports that in economically disadvantaged rural areas, even among very poor families, the consciousness about the importance of education is growing as well. This also holds true with respect to education for girls. According to the Deputy Director of the governmental *Primary Education Stipend Project* (PESP), the interest in sending children to school has been generally increasing even before local project interventions were in place that offered material benefits and incentives. Local people consider it their duty to facilitate their children's school attendance: "I must send my kid to school. If I don't have a meal in a day but I want to send my child in the school. I don't want to keep him or her illiterate. I don't want to do that. [...] It is the common expectation that has already been settled in the mind".[28] This generally growing awareness among the public – even in remote rural areas – is the result of several wide-ranging awareness-raising activities, such as the UNESCO's global *Education For All* initiative and its follow-up arrangements that the government of Bangladesh has committed itself to.[29]

In Chittagong, the second largest city of Bangladesh, poor families are not very well educated. They realize the importance of schooling but at the same time, the perception that education is meant for wealthy people prevails. Before any regulative mechanisms of the governmental *Eradication of Hazardous Child Labour Project* were at work here, local people did not know much about human rights, in general, or children's rights, in particular. However, people feel that sending their children to work, instead of to school, is due to poverty as reported by a colleague of the local NGO Padakhep: "Families are sending their children to work, they know this is painful but they actually don't know the rights [...] because they are not very educated; [...] they don't know the rights and other things, human rights, children's rights [...]".[30] From this statement, one can conclude that daily challenges linked to poverty are too pressing to even care about children's education. At the same time, there is some realization about the importance of education even though no definite understanding about the abstract term of "rights" exists. Primary education is not perceived as a universal entitlement, but rather as a benefit for wealthy families and their children.

Another NGO employee working with Jano Seba Kendra (JSK) explains what children's rights mean to an impoverished slum community of Hazaribagh, a Dhaka metropolitan area with a high prevalence of formal and informal leather tanneries. Before local project interventions in this overpopulated shanty town came into effect, the residents were not aware of any rights related to their children. There was no access to the governmental education system, the water and sanitation situation was disastrous and children's

28 Interview Tapan Kumar Chakravorty, PESP, MoPME, Deputy Director, 17 July 2008.

29 Ibid.

30 Interview Sanwar Moni, Padakhep, Coordinator Executive Director's Secretariat, 1 July 2008.

nutrition was insufficient: "[...] the children, the boys and girls, [...], they are staying in very unhygienic conditions, they are suffering from malnutrition [...]".[31] Poverty is strongly connected to a general lack of education of these poor people, which results in a prevailing ignorance regarding child labor, education, and health issues.

A UNICEF Education Officer responsible for the *Basic Education for Hard to Reach Urban Working Children* (BEHTRUWC) Project explains how disadvantaged communities in the urban slums all over Bangladesh experience basic children's rights before any local interventions were installed. Almost all of the people in the targeted metropolitan areas have no awareness about children's rights at all: "Our general perception is that, I mean, in 90 percent of the cases the children are not aware of their rights and even the parents and the communities they are not well aware about the children's rights issues and the other related issues, related to child labor [...]".[32] Parents in these disadvantaged territories are usually illiterate or semi-literate and they send their children to work when they are not older than seven or eight years in order to cover the family's basic needs. In the resulting intergenerational cycle of illiteracy and poverty, these children's children will continue to neglect the value of education. One of their major concerns is that an investment in children's education would not pay off due to lacking employment opportunities:

> [...] since there are very few employment opportunities in the country [...], they feel that instead of sending children to school, if I involve him at the early stage in the job [...], whether he is paid or unpaid but he is involved after three, four years of experience, he'll be getting good jobs and more options because there is competition.[33]

Poor people rather accredit vocational or skills training, which they consider as purposive. They appreciate passing on traditionally acquired skills that the family has performed and engaged in for several generations already. However, as Mr. Kibria points out, some of the local factory owners have enjoyed some marginal extent of education, sufficient for them to know that the legal age for admission to employment is set at 14 years in Bangladesh. Nevertheless, this knowledge does not prevent them from hiring children below this minimum age, due to lacking financial means for recruiting adult labor in their informal businesses, which all too often operate at the edge of survival.

Before the urban ILO/IPEC project *Preventing and Eliminating the Worst Forms of Child Labour in Selected Formal and Informal Sectors in Bangladesh*

31 Interview A.N.M. Shamsuddin Dewan, Jano Seba Kendra, Director, 26 June 2008.
32 Interview Mohammad Golam Kibria, UNICEF, Education Section, Education Officer, 4 June 2008.
33 Ibid.

became operative, the Executive Director of the local NGO Lighthouse described how hazardous child labor in the bidi[34] factories and tobacco industries of Haragas in Rangpur, Bangladesh belonged to everyday life: "[...] it is something like that is part of their life, they can work. But it is illegal and it is the worst forms of child labor, they didn't consider it at all".[35] Local community members do agree that education may be necessary, but there is much more relevance attached to earning money as a first priority. In Rangpur, even local government officials disregard children's rights[36] and not many non-hazardous employment opportunities apart from the bidi factories exist. Hence, lacking economic alternatives lead to a large number of children ending up in the worst forms of child labor.[37] Knowledge regarding sanitary and hygienic issues is completely lacking and child laborers occupied in hazardous work did not even greet with the obligatory Muslim "Salaam Walekum" (সালাআম ওয়ালেকুম) before any local interventions promoting their rights but also their social status were in effect.

Most urban slum children in Dhaka City do not have any notion of what their rights are, describes Mr. M. Ehsanur Rahman, the Deputy Executive Director of the Bangladeshi non-state organization, Dhaka Ahsania Mission (DAM), an implementer of the ILO/IPEC project *Prevention and Elimination of Selected Worst Forms of Child Labour in the Informal Economy in Dhaka City*. Some of them, however, might have access to media broadcasting, including the favorite Meena cartoon,[38] to public shows or street dramas. The latter two are popular advocacy tools among organizations working with local communities. Consuming media can lead to the development of a certain basic understanding of rights-related issues:

> So it's not, it's not saying about what law is, it's more understanding what is the inner meaning of the law and what the law is for. So we more just on those aspects, on understanding elements, on the understanding

34 Bidis are small hand-rolled cigarettes usually containing tobacco or herbs and frequently to be found in South Asian countries. They are either produced in factories which all too often involve child labor or in home-based work by either children or women.

35 Interview Md. Harun-or Rashid, Lighthouse, Executive Director, 20 May 2008.

36 Interview Md. Hamidul Islam, Bangladesh Development Service Center, Assistant Director, 24 May 2008.

37 Interview Profulla Chandra Barman, Bangladesh Rural Advancement Committee, former Project Coordinator, 17 July 2008.

38 Meena is a South Asian comic character developed by UNICEF. In books and on TV, she experiences stories related to the life of a South Asian girl. The Meena cartoons are very popular among children in South Asian countries and translated to several regional languages. They are made to promote children's rights, in general, and the rights of girls, in particular. Examples of themes tackled in Meena comic books are immunization, child labor, and attending school, but also sexual exploitation, trafficking, and dowry payment. For further information, visit the website of UNICEF South Asia: Meena Communication Initiative http://www.unicef.org/rosa/ media_2479.htm, [retrieved 17 November 2009].

> part of the law rather than communicating the law itself [...] they can pick up the message from there [...].

Hence, rights remain an abstract concept for these children but a certain broad understanding can be developed by interacting and communicating with NGOs or by utilizing sensitizing media or certain cultural events.

The amount of pressure created for children in situations in which the general public does not have any idea about child protection was expressed by the Executive Director of the Underprivileged Children's Educational Programs (UCEP), a domestic Bangladeshi NGO. Situations like these create an environment that shapes children's main role as income earners: "[...] these working children, the basic role that they have is, in fact they don't have any rights. They feel they are told to go and earn something and it's [...] a pressure [...] by the guardians and the parents that you have to go and work. They have got no rights,[39] [...]".[40] This implies that it is impossible for children to participate in decisions regarding their own lives. Even very fundamental entitlements like protection from hazardous occupations are being denied. Usually, not the children themselves but their parents decide whether they have to take up a certain labor arrangement or not.

A representative of an NGO called Gonoshahajjo Sangstha (GSS) that was responsible for supplying educational services within the framework of the *Bangladesh Garment Sector Projects* highlights how difficult it is to approach child laborers from the garment factories. From his experience with these child laborers, he suggests that children need to learn how to claim their own rights concerning safer work conditions and appropriate wages, but also regarding fundamental health, education and reproductive rights and rights related to marriage. Before the Garment Sector Projects became operative for the children engaged in the factories, these basic rights were completely unknown to them: "[...] before starting their learning in the centers, they are not very conscious about their rights, even they are not, they didn't know completing the primary education is compulsory [...]".[41] This situation had to be addressed through NGOs' continuous interaction with garment workers and their families embedded in the framework of local level policy initiatives.

In sum – despite the variety of information and detailed assessments provided by the diverse interview partners – there are some common patterns indicating why the implementation process has not yet trickled down to the local norm targets. First and foremost, it is poverty that forces children to

39 This rather harsh statement "[...] in fact they don't have rights. [...] They have got no rights, [...]" has an irritating effect, especially since it has been vocalized by an NGO representative engaging in the fight against child labor. Judging from the interview situation, he meant to point to the fact that these children are not in a situation to enjoy their rights.

40 Interview Aftab Uddin Ahmad, UCEP, Executive Director, 25 June 2008.

41 Interview Ali Hossain Sarder, Regional Coordinator Monitoring and Evaluation, Education Programme, Gonoshahajjo Sangstha, 22 June 2008.

engage in hazardous occupations and to neglect school education and health protection. In other words, poor children do not have the opportunity to concentrate on schooling while their family is starving. Second, people are lacking a general awareness of their rights. The whole concept of rights is too abstract and far away from their daily fight for survival. In addition to that, it requires some level of education to comprehend the meaning of these fundamental rights every human being is entitled to. The interview results, however, made clear that the hierarchical structure of Bangladesh's society leads to the widespread perception that education is reserved for children from well-off families. Accepting this hierarchy leads to a continuous reproduction of it. Poorer people – whose families have been trapped in a cycle of poverty and illiteracy for generations – favor early vocational training that leads to faster integration into the labor market and to income earning. This corresponds to the perception that school education is dysfunctional and will not lead to a better job placement. In too many instances, particularly in poor rural areas and urban slums, no schooling infrastructure exists. Therefore, local people keep thinking that education is not meant for them.

From these first empirical results, two preliminary conclusions can be drawn. First of all, regardless of the ratification of international children's rights conventions by the government of Bangladesh and pertinent legislative and policy reforms, the rights situation of the children at the grassroots has not necessarily changed. Correspondingly, a second implication must be that for the rights investigated, a national implementation process is necessary but not sufficient to guarantee these rights. The interview results put forward that even after national implementation, economic and social opportunities, an appropriate infrastructure, and rights awareness among the local norm targets are lacking. This means that national and local implementation are different processes; the one does not necessarily imply the other. Whereas it is obvious what measures have to be taken to accomplish national implementation, how to realize these rights at the local – and societal – level is not entirely clear. The case of local children's rights implementation in Bangladesh through local policy initiatives will inductively be investigated in greater detail in the following chapters.

Chapter 4

The local implementation process

> Without the Forum, we would have no knowledge about rights at all. It would be like having a Jackfruit without knowing how to eat it.
>
> (quote from a child participating in CLEP, Børnearbejde 2003: 31)

In this book, local implementation is investigated by comparatively analyzing seven project initiatives that contribute to realizing at least one of the rights examined here for Bangladesh's children. Included in the analysis are major policy programs launched in Bangladesh following its ratification of international children's rights conventions. From the 1990s on, a variety of different programs became installed in the country, either initiated by international organizations (IOs), by the government or by non-governmental organizations (NGOs). In this book, I investigate a broad range of these projects, including the:

(1) ***Child Labour Elimination Project*** (CLEP) initiated by an NGO,
(2) ***Food for Education Programs*** (FFE) including the successive ***Primary Education Stipend Program*** (PESP) launched by the government,
(3) ***Eradication of Hazardous Child Labour*** (EHCL) initiated by the government,
(4) ***Basic Education for Hard to Reach Urban Working Children*** (BEHTRUWC) started by UNICEF,
(5) ***Preventing and Eliminating the Worst Forms of Child Labour in Selected Formal and Informal Sectors in Bangladesh*** (ILO/IPEC USDoL) called into life by the International Labour Organization (ILO),
(6) ***Prevention and Elimination of Selected Worst Forms of Child Labour in the Informal Economy in Dhaka City*** (ILO/IPEC Net) initiated by the ILO, and
(7) ***Garment Sector Projects*** that were conducted by the ILO and UNICEF in cooperation with the Bangladesh Garment Manufacturers and Exporters Association (BGMEA/ILO/UNICEF).

4.1 Introducing the cases

The following sections briefly introduce all of these governmental, non-governmental and intergovernmental policy programs. Particularly emphasized is the context into which each project was installed and the particular features that characterize the respective initiative.

4.1.1 CLEP

The CLEP was founded by the Bangladesh Institute of Labour Studies (BILS), an NGO established in 1995 by Bangladesh's trade union movement with a view to strengthening basic workers' and human rights.[1] BILS' close ties to trade unions and its engagement in promoting national labor laws led to the initiation of several local level activities, among them the CLEP. CLEP was launched in March 2002 with the financial assistance of BILS' development partner, the Danish Trade Union Council (LO/FTF) Denmark, a trade union council for international development cooperation. The project's pilot activities started in 2002 in Tongi, District Gazipur, an industrial area close to Dhaka City. In 2003, a project expansion towards Mirpur and Keranigonj, both situated in District Dhaka, took place. Within these three project areas, the target group for interventions comprises child laborers between 12 and 14 years of age who are engaged in both hazardous and non-hazardous occupations. CLEP is a rather small-scale initiative; during the first project period, from March 2002 and until October 2006, 2,054 children, 1,042 girls and 1,012 boys, completed one of its skills development courses offered. By 2008, 3,144 children accomplished basic skills training and a total of 1,386 children graduated from CLEP's non-formal education (NFE) classes.[2]

The project is implemented with the help of several major intervention strategies. Through a two-step targeting mechanism, the three project areas, Tongi, Mirpur and Keranigonj, and the target group, child laborers between 12 and 14 years of age, were selected. For the first step – targeting of the intervention areas – predominant selection criteria were the on-site prevalence of child labor in big industries and the number of children involved in small-scale industries, i.e. in shops, in the transport sector, as station loaders or as garbage collectors. Besides the significant child labor problem in these areas, strong ties and access to trade unions in the communities played a major role in the selection process. In a second step, the targeting of the child laborers was carried out through a baseline survey. Information about the situation of the local working children, including their living conditions, level

1 Interview Sajjad Hossain, BILS, CLEP Project Coordinator, 21 May 2008.

2 Data from personal correspondence with Sajjad Hossain (former Project Coordinator of the BILS/CLEP Project), 7 November 2009.

of education, and nature of occupation was collected. In addition to that, the survey was used to analyze the local market situation to design an appropriate vocational training program that would provide respective trainees with employable skills (Hossain 2008: 12).

In the course of the project's implementation, local centers were established in the intervention areas. Through these local structures, several rights-related services could be offered; the provision of NFE constituting one of them. As a particular opportunity outside the formal governmental education system, NFE benefits those children of the target group who cannot read, write or calculate. They receive a 12-month basic education course in the community centers that includes reading and writing Bengali, acquiring basic mathematical skills, and obtaining a fundamental knowledge of English. The children attending NFE classes usually keep working for their employers. This flexible education approach, taking place in daily, two to three hour sessions, helps them maintain their income while learning at the same time. Additionally, students receive a 250 BDT stipend per month to cover eventual income losses and maintain or even improve their living standard (Børnearbejde 2003: 7). One important element of BILS' NFE program is teaching about the UN *Convention on the Rights of the Child* (CRC), as well as providing basic leadership and communication training. A particularly context-specific component of CLEP's NFE strategy is a recreational part, ensuring that participating children learn about Bangladesh's art, music, stories, and games (Hossain 2008: 13).

Next to NFE, basic skills trainings are offered to the students in the local community centers. BILS offers four trade courses for those children who have completed NFE or have completed a governmental school program. These comprise tailoring and embroidery or block-batik for girls, and electrical house wiring and motor mechanics, particularly for auto rickshaws and motorcycles, for boys. The project participants keep obtaining their monthly stipend during their skills training course. Other modules continue as well, such as the rights and communication training, primary health services and the recreation element. In addition, an instruction in job searching strategies accompanying vocational training is offered. This is meant to help these children find better and decent employment opportunities guaranteeing their workers' rights after completion of the course. If the adolescents do not find acceptable occupational alternatives after they have completed skills training, certain strategies are applied that aim to help them become self-employed using the practical knowledge they have gained.[3]

Next to basic education, primary health care issues are taught and materials on health care are disseminated to the participants of the program (Hossain 2008: 13). Apart from informing them about health-related issues, an appointed physician and a medical assistant come to the community center

3 ibid.

three days a week for two hours in order to treat the beneficiary children and provide them with medicine, free of charge.[4]

Another of CLEP's strategies focuses on awareness raising and advocacy, in- and outside the NFE classroom and the skills development course. This is carried out by printing and disseminating brochures, leaflets, and posters, as well as organizing and conducting rallies, workshops, roundtable discussions, and press conferences on child rights issues. Involved in this advocacy component are various actors of the community, but also employers' organizations and the Ministry of Labour and Employment (MoLE) (Hossain 2008: 13). To coordinate these awareness-raising activities, a development committee was established in the respective local project areas. Members of these committees are community leaders, local government and trade union representatives, social activists, teachers, children's guardians,[5] parents, and employers. Their main function is to monitor and evaluate the project's proceeding and outcome, to make suggestions, solve problems, and to follow-up with graduates after completion of their skills development course (Hossain 2008: 13–14).[6]

The establishment of a Children's Rights Forum constitutes another major strategy of CLEP. Each of these forums is composed of six children taking part in the NFE component of CLEP; these children usually live in the same area and have the opportunity to interact with each other. The six members of a group elect one leader who obtains a special training on children's rights, as well as on communication and leadership skills. These leaders act as multipliers within their forum, motivating their peers and spreading the word on children's rights within their community.

With the help of CLEP's income generation component, consisting of a savings scheme, 50 BDT per month are put aside for each student during project participation. This means that students are provided with a financial basis for acquiring working equipment in case they plan some form of self-employment after finishing their skills development training (Børnearbejde 2003: 6–7; Hossain 2008: 14). In addition, some tool boxes and machines necessary for establishing their own small-scale businesses are distributed upon successful completion of the vocational training course. Furthermore, graduates receive a certificate of completion with which they can apply for a permanent position (Hossain 2008: 13).

CLEP is a solely non-governmental initiative that operates on a small scale, in only three target areas of Dhaka City, and reaches out to only a few thousand children and their families. In contrast to that, the FFE and its

4 Interview Sajjad Hossain, BILS, CLEP Project Coordinator, 21 May 2008.

5 In many of these areas, children grow up as orphans for different reasons. Many of these orphans live with so-called guardians, though. Guardians are adults that agree to provide these children with shelter and food often in return for domestic work, watching younger children or other material and immaterial contributions.

6 Interview Sajjad Hossain, BILS, CLEP Project Coordinator, 21 May 2008.

successor, the PESP, are purely governmental and have such an immense outreach all over Bangladesh's rural areas that they became well-known even beyond Bangladesh's borders.

4.1.2 FFE and PESP

Following the 1990 *World Conference on Education for All* (EFA) in Jomtien, Thailand and the adoption and signing of the *Declaration on Education for All*, many nations – among them Bangladesh – committed themselves to provide children with unrestricted access to primary education and to reduce illiteracy comprehensively. As a response to this commitment – besides initiating the 1990 *Primary Education (Compulsory) Act* – Bangladesh's government called the FFE programs into life in 1993. The FFE's main objectives were to increase primary school enrollment and attendance rates and to reduce children's drop-out rates.[7] Another area of concern was to improve the quality of education in participating schools (Ahmed and del Ninno 2002: 36). Its large-scale programs cover rural areas exclusively and not only include governmental primary schools, but also registered non-governmental primary schools, community (low-cost) schools, satellite primary schools, and *ebtedayee madrassash* (religion-based and Islamic-oriented) schools (Meng and Ryan 2003: 2–3).[8] The FFE initiative remains one of the very few exclusively governmental undertakings in this context, with local government officials and school management committees at the Upazila or Thana level[9] as implementing agents and in monitoring functions. Whereas the Ministry of Primary and Mass Education (MoPME) has administered the FFE, it is implemented by the Ministry's own Project Implementation Unit (PIU) and executed locally by the Thana Nirbahi (Executive) Officer and the Thana Education Officer (Ahmed and del Ninno 2002: 8). Information on who has provided the food supply and the funding, however, diverges; some sources claim that food aid donors, such as the United States of America, contributed a significant proportion of the grain for the program (Meng and Ryan 2003: 2), national government officials affirm that all the expenses, including food stuff and stipend, were met by the government of Bangladesh.[10]

7 Interview Tapan Kumar Chakravorty, MoPME, PESP, Deputy Director, 17 July 2008.

8 Ibid.

9 Bangladesh is administratively divided into six regional divisions, namely Dhaka, Chittagong, Rajshahi, Khulna, Barisal and Sylhet. These divisions are split into 64 districts which again are divided into 489 political sub-units called *thanas* or *upazilas*. Political entities at the community level are 4,451 Unions and the smallest subdivision is into villages (Phillips and Gritzner 2007: 68; Ahmed and del Ninno 2002: 6; see also: Auswärtiges Amt 2009: Bangladesh Innenpolitik: Staatsaufbau http://www.auswaertiges-amt.de/diplo/de/Laenderinformationen/Bangladesch/Innenpolitik.html [retrieved 16 October 2009]).

10 Interview Tapan Kumar Chakravorty, Deputy Director, 17 July 2008.

One salient program mechanism of the FFE is the sophisticated two-step targeting procedure. The first targeting step is an area-based one that selects two to three economically disadvantaged Unions with low literacy rates from the rural Thanas, and includes all governmental, registered non-governmental, community, satellite, and one of the religion-based schools into the program. In a second step, within each targeted Union, a household-based selection takes place. Provided that children of primary school age belong to the household, it becomes eligible if at least one out of these four criteria is in place:

(1) A household owns less than half an acre of land,[11]
(2) The main income earner is day laborer,
(3) The household is female-headed,
(4) The household is dependent on low-income occupations, such as fishing, pottery, smithery, weaving or cobbling (Meng and Ryan 2003: 3; see also Ahmed and del Ninno 2002: 8).

However, even if these conditions are met, primary school students can only benefit as long as they are enrolled in one of the FFE schools targeted in the first step. Altogether, not more than 40 percent of the students in the respective FFE school are eligible to receive benefits (Meng and Ryan 2003: 4). These 40 percent of primary school children are selected and listed jointly by the school management committee, which comprises the headmaster and teachers of that school and the Compulsory Primary Education Ward Committee.

As suggested by the title of the programs, eligible beneficiaries, the students, receive a particular amount of food grain on a monthly basis delivered as 15 kilograms of wheat or 12 kilograms of rice. If a family has more than one child and sends all children of primary school age to one of the FFE schools, they become eligible to receive up to 20 kilograms of wheat or 16 kilograms of rice (Meng and Ryan 2003: 3).[12] The food ration obtained can either be consumed by the family or it can be sold to cover other needs and expenses (Ahmed and del Ninno 2002: 2). Grain distribution had initially been arranged by the school management committees who – together with local government officials – provided for its delivery to particular warehouses where families could collect it with their ration cards. From 1999 on, however, food rations became distributed every week (Ravallion and Wodon 1998: 8) through private food retailers, mainly in order to save teaching time for the members of the school management committee (Meng and Ryan 2003: 3; see also Ahmed and del

11 Again the information provided by evaluation reports (e.g. Meng and Ryan 2003: 3) and by government officials from Bangladesh differ. Thus, Tapan Kumar Chakravorty, Deputy Director of the PESP, claimed in an interview that households owning land up to 1.5 acres would be eligible to participate in the program (interview Tapan Kumar Chakravorty, ibid, Deputy Director, 17 July 2008).

12 See also interview Tapan Kumar Chakravorty, ibid.

Ninno 2002: 4). Due to a rise and subsequent instability in food prices, but also due to time constraints and the harmful influence of corruption,[13] the FFE programs turned into the PESP in 2002. Eligible students now receive a stipend of 100 BDT per month or 125 monthly altogether if more than one child attends school on a regular basis. The stipend money is taken from the government revenue fund without any external donor contribution. Students' mothers administer the bank accounts and obtain the cards needed to collect the money. Just like the former FFE programs, the has broad coverage; at the moment, about 5.5 million students in 62,000 schools are benefiting from it.[14] Management and targeting procedures in the PESP remain basically the same as in the preceding project; hence, the change is limited to a transition from an in-kind to a cash provision.

The regular receipt of the cash stipend is based upon certain conditions the students have to fully comply with. They need to attend school regularly, at least 85 percent of the classes, and they have to attain at least 40 percent pass marks to receive the subsidy in that particular month. In addition to that, respective FFE or PESP schools have to sustain a 60 percent attendance rate of all enrolled students. Furthermore, based on their performance, schools receive an A, B, C or D classification. Schools graded with a D are exempt from food-grain allocation until their achievements have improved. Among the criteria are that at least ten percent of the school's grade five students have to qualify for the annual scholarship examination and students in grade three, four, and five have to receive at least 40 percent correct results in exams (Ahmed and del Ninno 2002: 9–10). Due to the need for program participants to comply with these conditions, the FFE and PESP projects are also called "demand-side interventions" demanding a behavioral change of their beneficiaries. In contrast, "supply-side interventions" simply supply additional infrastructure, such as new schools or health centers (Ahmed and Babu 2007: 1) without imposing any conditions. Compliance with the FFE and PESP Programs is monitored by the school management committee which is supervised by the Upazila Education Officer and the Monitoring Officer of that particular division.[15] Although evaluation studies point to an attitudinal

13 Private food retailers did not distribute the whole prescribed amount of wheat or rice to the program participants but kept part of it for themselves so that too much food got lost on the way to the beneficiaries in need (Ahmed and Babu 2007: 7). However, a local government official, the Upazila Education Officer in Savar, claims in an informal interview that even the chairmen of the school management committees have peculated about 1.5 out of 10 kilograms of food stuff. The chairmen, in turn, stated that all of the incentives they took were invested in school equipment (Informal interview Md. Abdul Aziz, Upazila Education Officer, 19 July 2008 and author's notes from field visit: FFE/PESP with Md. Abdul Aziz (Upazila Education Officer, Savar) and Nahar Sultana (Dhaka Division Monitoring Officer, Dhaka) Gorad Government Primary School, Savar Upazila, 19 July 2008.

14 Interview Tapan Kumar Chakravorty, MoPME, PESP, Deputy Director, 17 July 2008.

15 Author's notes from field visit: FFE/PESP with Md. Abdul Aziz (Upazila Education Officer, Savar) and Nahar Sultana (Dhaka Division Monitoring Officer, Dhaka) Gorad Government Primary School, Savar Upazila, 19 July 2008.

change towards schooling and education as one result of enhanced school attendance, no explicit awareness raising or advocacy component were part of these programs (Ahmed and Babu 2007: 2).

The World Food Program (WFP) has supported the FFE Programs from 2002 on with its own project called School-Feeding-Program. Its main intervention strategy is to offer a mid-morning snack, usually high-nutrition biscuits, to children regularly attending primary school (Ahmed and Babu 2007: 5). Hence, continuing the larger idea of providing food for education, the WFP supplements the main FFE/PESP project components. This indicates a particular form of cooperation between the national, i.e. Bangladesh's government, and the international level, i.e. the WFP. Another form of inter-organizational cooperation, in this case between the government and local NGOs, is found in the EHCL introduced below.

4.1.3 EHCL

Bangladesh's MoLE has launched an EHCL[16] which is implemented – predominantly in urban slums – with the help of local NGOs. Initially funded by the United States Agency for International Development (USAID), the second phase, from 2005 through 2009, and the third phase, from 2010 on, have been financed by the government's own revenue fund – turning it into an exclusively governmental undertaking.[17] In its third phase of project execution, between 2010 and 2013, EHCL has extended its target areas and has become operational in five of the six regional divisions in Bangladesh, namely Dhaka, Chittagong, Khulna, Barisal and Sylhet (Masud 2011). Compared to the other projects considered here, it can be described as a middle-range program aiming at integrating 50,000 children between ten and 14 years old who are occupied in hazardous working arrangements. Local project realization was carried out by 76 domestic NGOs during the second phase.[18] In the course of project implementation, the following regulative mechanisms are utilized for promoting children's rights in the urban target communities.

Before realizing the single program components, the MoLE funded a survey to identify child laborers and their families. Surveying was carried out by the

16 Data and information pertaining to this project are scarce; there are no project documents or evaluation reports available except for one annual report made by the NGO Eco-Social Development Organization (ESDO) (Mostofa 2008), some newspaper articles published by *The Daily Star* and implementation tenders (addressed at NGOs) announced on the MoLE's website.

17 "14 lakh children engaged in hazardous jobs" in *The Daily Star* (internet edition), 19 May 2008, Dhaka, Bangladesh: http://www.thedailystar.net/story.php?nid=37168 [retrieved 4 March 2010].

18 See also: "14 lakh children engaged in hazardous jobs" in *The Daily Star* (internet edition), 19 May 2008, Dhaka, Bangladesh: http://www.thedailystar.net/story.php?nid=37168 [retrieved 4 March 2010]. There are no data available on how many NGOs were contracted to implement the third phase.

implementing local non-state organizations.[19] The targeting process involved selecting urban areas with a heavy child labor problem, usually slums in major cities that belong to the five regional divisions mentioned above. The concept applied includes the withdrawal of the children in these areas from the worst forms of child labor and providing them with education alternatives. To coordinate the delivery of rights-related services, center management committees (CMC) were called into life. These are responsible for raising awareness among parents and convincing them to not send their children to workplaces that are detrimental to their physical and mental well-being and to their development. Local NGOs coordinate the awareness-raising activities and try to integrate the entire community into the program.

After the CMCs were formed, 11,550 learning centers were established nation-wide during the second phase. From 2010 on, another 1,667 of these centers are planned to be set up (Masud 2011). They serve as local infrastructure for providing non-formal primary education to the targeted beneficiaries. In the case of this project, NFE services are supplied for a time period of two years (IRIN 2008). Non-formal learning is conducted in flexible three-hour shifts either in the morning or in the evening, according to the schedule of the working children. Teaching is limited to very basic subjects like reading and writing Bengali and elementary mathematics.

Before the skills training component could be introduced, a basic needs assessment was undertaken in the target areas in order to find out more about prospective job placement opportunities. Vocational training is one of the modules that were not initially planned, but added in later phases. The skills development period commences after completion of the NFE phase and lasts for six months (Masud 2011).[20] About 21 trade courses can be chosen, depending on the interests of the students. Among them are hairdressing or radio and television mechanics for girls, and electrical work, house welding, carpentry, plumbing, and automobile repair for boys, as well as tailoring, block printing, and embroidery for children of both genders.

Throughout receiving NFE and vocational training, each student obtains a sum intended as income compensation, fixed at 75 BDT per month. This stipend is paid to the beneficiaries' parents on a quarterly basis. Within the framework of this project, implementing NGOs have earned 125 BDT per student per month as a so-called service charge covering the organization's rent and salary.[21]

19 Interview sources provide diverging information here; one interviewee states that the government, i.e. the MoLE, conducted the survey and another one states that the government funded it but NGOs carried it out.

20 At the time the interviews were conducted, the skills training development had been planned but not yet implemented. Nevertheless, it was to be arranged for the same children that received NFE through this project and for a period of six months starting in November 2008.

21 Meant is most probably the rent of the learning center that is covered with this amount.

During the second phase of the project, the MoLE had planned to channel most beneficiaries' parents, i.e. 20,000 mothers, fathers or guardians, into a bank or financial institute to provide them with some form of loan or micro-credit. By then, the government has argued that in cases in which children have received education and skills development training, the family will be able to use the granted money purposefully.[22] With a loan or micro-credit, children and their families should be able to become self-employed and to start their own small businesses. This strategic initiative marked the income generating component of the project.[23] In the third phase of EHCL implementation, however, the provision of micro-credits was suspended (Masud 2011).

This local policy initiative involves cooperation between the government and local non-state partners to reach out to children at the grassroots level. It introduces an approach that is pursued by a number of other projects in a similar way. Some of these were launched by IOs and, hence, are sufficiently funded to allow for operation at an even larger scale. Their objective is usually to foster conventions corresponding to their mandate and to promote one or more of the children's rights considered here. A program particularly focusing on promoting the CRC and the right to education is UNICEF's BEHTRUWC introduced in the following.

4.1.4 BEHTRUWC

BEHTRUWC is a wide-ranging policy initiative that was launched and funded by a constellation of diverse actors, including the Government of Bangladesh, the United Nations Children's Emergency Fund (UNICEF), the UK Department for International Development (DFID) and the Swedish International Development Agency (SIDA) (GoB/DNFE 2002: i). Replacing DFID, the Canadian International Development Agency (CIDA) took over funding during the second project phase which was planned to continue until 2012. From the governmental side, the MoPME with its Bureau of Non-Formal Education (BNFE) is responsible for project management, monitoring, coordination, and administration through a PIU. UNICEF – besides providing financial support – offers technical assistance to the BEHTRUWC project.

BEHTRUWC's implementation has been carried out in two phases, the first from 1997 to 2003 incorporating basically the provision of NFE, and the second phase between 2003 and 2012 with an extended concept.[24] During

22 "14 lakh children engaged in hazardous jobs" in *The Daily Star* (internet edition), 19 May 2008, Dhaka, Bangladesh: http://www.thedailystar.net/story.php?nid=37168 [retrieved 04 March 2010].

23 This mechanism had been planned but not yet installed by the time of data collection.

24 At the time of data collection, the second phase was still going on. In this section, all the project mechanisms applied during both phases will be introduced.

the latest phase of the Hard to Reach program, 20 local NGOs have provided rights-related services to the project beneficiaries. These were urban working children who were out of school – therefore hard to reach – and engaged in any type of hazardous or non-hazardous occupational activity. BEHTRUWC's activities have covered all six divisional cities of Bangladesh, i.e. Dhaka, Chittagong, Barisal, Khulna, Rajshahi, and Sylhet. Hence, it dealt with about 200,000 urban working children in its second phase (GoB/BNFE 2008: 13).

To identify the eligible project participants, a targeting process was conducted. Prior to planning the project, UNICEF surveyed all of Bangladesh's urban divisional cities. In a second step, the implementing NGOs carried out another survey taking account of any demographic changes in the targeted areas and preparing a preliminary learners' list. Selected children had to be engaged in any kind of hazardous or non-hazardous activity, they had to be completely out of school and between eight and 14 years old. Another selection criterion was to choose 60 percent of girls and 40 percent of boys for each learning center. With the support of the local community in the respective target areas, NGOs formed CMCs that tried to motivate children and employers to take part in the project, and that took over responsibilities in the monitoring system.

Local NGOs have engaged in social mobilization and awareness-raising. They organize activities, meetings, and extra-curricular events for children informing them about their rights, i.e. the importance of education and health care and the devastating effects hazardous child labor can have. Furthermore, NGOs take over management functions at the local level; they recruit coordinators, build up and administer learning centers in the target areas, hire teachers and supervisors, and coordinate all these activities with UNICEF and Bangladesh's MoPME. Within a considerable number of learning centers, 6,646 altogether in the last project phase,[25] NFE is provided to the child laborers. NFE is offered six days a week in flexible shifts of two and a half hours per day to make attendance possible, despite the tight working schedule of many participating children. Teaching includes basic literacy and numeracy, reading and writing Bengali, but also English. An additional module on livelihood or life skills is meant to educate students on how to communicate properly, on health and hygiene issues, as well as on environmental and societal themes.[26]

One of BEHTRUWC's project components aimed at building the capacities of the MoPME, the BNFE, the Ministry's PIU, and executing NGOs pertinent to their staff's planning, implementation, monitoring, and

25 At the time the interviews were conducted.

26 Interview Mohammad Golam Kibria, UNICEF, Education Section, Education Officer, 4 June 2008, Interview Rezaul Quader, MoPME, Project Director, 8 July 2008, Interview Hasina Habib, Gono Shahajja Sangstha (GSS), Coordinator Field Education Programme, 9 June 2008, Interview Musbah Alim, CATALYST, Executive Director, 19 June 2008, Interview Khandaker Asraful Islam, Bangladesh Development Service Center, Deputy Director, 24 May 2008.

evaluation competences. This component has been carried out through workshops and short training courses, incorporating sessions on financial management, observation techniques, data analysis and interpretation, gender analysis and sensitivity to children's rights (GoB/BNFE 2008: 46–7). In addition to that, a particular training was mandatory for all NFE teachers hired. It comprised sessions on appropriate teaching methods and prepared the instructors for the special situation of educating working children.[27]

Whereas UNICEF's project puts an emphasis on promoting the right to education, ILO/IPEC initiated programs focus on withdrawing child laborers from hazardous occupations in combination with providing them with viable alternatives, among them education and skills training. An introduction of the first ILO/IPEC project carried out in Bangladesh will disclose more about the varying implementation strategies IOs apply here for realizing children's rights.

4.1.5 ILO/IPEC USDoL

The overall objective of the ILO/IPEC USDoL project has been the systematic prevention and elimination of the worst forms of child labor in five prioritized formal and informal sectors of Bangladesh. Among them are the bidi industry, the construction sector, the leather tanneries, match factories, and domestic child labor. Funded by the United States Department of Labor (USDoL), the project intervention was carried out under the umbrella of the International Programme on the Elimination of Child Labour (IPEC), the ILO's largest technical assistance program, operational in Bangladesh since 1995 (Bannerman and Berghuys 2008: 1). The program targeted major cities in Bangladesh, namely Dhaka, Chittagong, Tangail, Rangpur, Kushtia, Narayanganj, and Munshiganj. Implementation was carried out between September 2000 and September 2004 (ILO/IPEC 2003b: iv) through social partners, mainly local NGOs, working under a sub-committee appointed by the National Steering Committee (NSC) of Bangladesh's MoLE. These partners implemented 24 action programs in the above-mentioned sectors and assisted the Bangladesh Bureau of Statistics (BBS) in conducting the National Child Labour Survey (NCLS) (ILO/IPEC 2003b: 1–2). The data of this survey are – until today – the only reliable source on child labor figures in the country (BBS 2003).

The project's scope can be described as middle-ranged compared to other initiatives considered here. Within its framework, almost 20,000 children, 93 percent of the initial target, were supplied with NFE services, over 30,000 children have received counseling, health or referral services, and almost 9,000 child laborers could be withdrawn from hazardous workplaces (ILO/IPEC 2003b: 16). Implementation took place in various sites, among them

27 Author's notes from field visit: GSS teachers' training for BEHTRUWC, in Tejgaon, Dhaka with Hasina Habib, GSS, Coordinator Field Education Programme and Harun ur Rashid, GSS, 9 June 2008.

NFE centers, young sibling centers, and health centers (ILO/IPEC 2003b: 4). The main target group consisted of child laborers between five and 17 years of age engaged in hazardous occupations. Their younger siblings were integrated in so-called pre-primary schools to prevent their engagement in child labor. Hence, these siblings can also be regarded as beneficiaries of the program. The various regulative mechanisms in use throughout project realization comprised the following.

With the help of ten baseline surveys covering the five sectors in which the project was meant to be operational a targeting process was carried out.[28] The baseline information covered eight geographical areas and served as a foundation for designing the respective action programs. At the same time, it helped to establish a database to identify and keep track of the progress of participating working children (ILO/IPEC 2003b: 12). This database contained a profile of each child, including information on the child's education, working conditions, health, socio-economic and family situation. Each implementing organization had the responsibility to update the database according to its own competencies, i.e. with respect to the services it delivered. The database became particularly significant for undertaking project monitoring and impact assessments later on. The target group comprised children engaged in hazardous occupations of the above-mentioned sectors who were between five and 17 years of age (ILO/IPEC 2003b: 12–13).

The gradual withdrawal of child laborers from their hazardous workplaces constituted another of the project's strategies. Whereas the children progressively left hazardous occupations, they were – simultaneously – already attending NFE classes and other social program activities (ILO/IPEC 2003b: 15). Child laborers did not have to change their working times but could attend flexible informal education classes for three hours a day during their time off. Such an approach made it easier for the employers to agree to the enrollment of their child employees.[29] ILO/IPEC USDoL's education programs were conducted by local NGOs, such as Lighthouse, the Bangladesh Development Service Centre (BDSC) or the Bangladesh Rural Advancement Committee (BRAC) (ILO/IPEC 2003b: iii, 16). In addition to offering primary and adolescent education, some pre-schooling facilities were set up for the younger siblings of the child laborers. These pre-primary schooling opportunities fostering educational opportunities at a very early age, constituted an important prevention mechanism for the siblings of the working children.[30] The overall objective of the NFE mechanism was to mainstream children up to 14 years of age into formal governmental schools, which was

28 The project was carried out in certain areas of the seven cities in which a particularly high number of child laborers were occupied in the target sectors.

29 Interview Md. Hamidul Islam, Bangladesh Development Service Centre (BDSC), Assistant Director, 24 May 2008.

30 Interview Profulla Chandra Barman, Bangladesh Rural Advancement Committee (BRAC), former Project Coordinator, 17 July 2008.

only possible after they had progressively terminated or substantially reduced their former working arrangements.

After having received NFE, children who were already too old to be integrated into formal primary schools were provided with skills development training. Among the trades taught were sewing, carpentry, embroidery, tailoring, cycle repairing, and shop or factory work. The provision of vocational training was conducted by local NGOs and aimed at qualifying children in light work activities that are neither hazardous to their physical nor to their mental development.[31] The provision of health care services to the children also belonged to the strategies pursued by this ILO/IPEC project. This comprised the delivery of immunizations, nutritious support, medicine, postnatal care and treatment, and a monthly health check.[32]

For the parents of the participants, several income-generating activities including entrepreneurship training and the provision of micro-credits for launching small business,[33] such as poultry and cow rearing,[34] were initiated. Alternative income opportunities were supposed to help parents to increase their own earnings and to allow for an ultimate withdrawal of their children from the worst forms of labor.[35] Another part of the income generation module was a savings scheme and group meetings to discuss problems pertaining to self-employment.

With the help of advocacy and awareness-raising, local NGOs addressed those who were part of child labor arrangements within a respective community, like the factory owners, the child laborers themselves but also the local Imam,[36] and other stakeholders. All of them were informed and educated about children's rights in general and the worst forms of child labor in particular.[37] This strategy involved counseling the entire community regarding various rights-related issues ranging from motivating local households to install and use sanitary latrines,[38] advising children and parents about health hazards in the bidi factories, and teaching employers about national child labor laws.[39] Important anti-child labor platforms became initiated with the formation of Programme Facilitating Committees and Community Watch Groups. These community organizations comprised local government authorities, employers, workers' representatives, and local elites. Together

31 Ibid. Interview Md. Hamidul Islam, Bangladesh Development Service Centre (BDSC), Assistant Director, 24 May 2008.

32 Interview Md. Harun-or Rashid, Lighthouse, Executive Director, 20 May 2008. Unfortunately, detailed data regarding these health provisions is neither available in ILO evaluation reports nor could it be obtained from the interviews conducted.

33 Interview Nazrul Islam Miah, ILO, Administrative and Finance Assistant, 24 June 2008.

34 Interview Profulla Chandra Barman, BRAC, former Project Coordinator, 17 July 2008.

35 Ibid.

36 Interview Md. Harun-or Rashid, Lighthouse, Executive Director, 20 May 2008.

37 Interview Md. Hamidul Islam, BDSC, Assistant Director, 24 May 2008.

38 Ibid.

39 Interview Profulla Chandra Barman, BRAC, former Project Coordinator, 17 July 2008.

with monitoring officers recruited from each executing NGO, the community groups themselves oversaw the operation of project activities and children's progress.[40] These committees remained active even after the project had terminated to monitor long-term achievements and to continue awareness-raising activities (ILO/IPEC 2003b: 19–20, 25).

Capacity building of governmental and non-governmental institutions constituted another of the ILO/IPEC USDoL's strategies. In particular, the MoLE was to be strengthened with support for the drafting process of a *National Child Labour Policy*, a requirement following the ratification of the *ILO Convention on the Worst Forms of Child Labour* (C182). The MoLE also received assistance for updating national statistics on the domestic child labor situation by the project (ILO/IPEC 2003b: 22). Additionally, local NGOs were trained on issues relating to children's rights to build up expertise, knowledge, and train professional staff. The development objective of this sub-component was to make these local NGOs capable of developing their own initiatives to keep promoting children's rights in Bangladesh (ILO/IPEC 2003b: 23–4). And indeed, not all of the social activities were terminated at the end of this ILO/IPEC project. Some capable NGOs, in particular BRAC, kept providing services and undertaking project activities, such as granting micro-credit loans, sustaining pre-primary schools or maintaining an ultra-poor program for poverty reduction. Gradually discontinuing social services provided for a bridging period for the beneficiaries and their families.[41]

ILO/IPEC projects usually work with the support of the domestic Labor Ministry and can – like in this case – incorporate local implementing partners. The project strategies applied by different ILO programs, however, may vary according to the objectives pursued. In the following, another ILO/IPEC program which focuses on abolishing the worst forms of child labor, first and foremost in Bangladesh's urban informal economy, will be outlined.

4.1.6 ILO/IPEC Net

The pilot project entitled *Prevention and Elimination of Selected Worst Forms of Child Labour in the Informal Economy in Dhaka City* (ILO/IPEC Net) sought to test a combination of integrated intervention strategies with the aim of withdrawing and rehabilitating child laborers engaged in the hazardous urban informal sector of Bangladesh. Estimates point out that 94 percent of Bangladesh's child labor force is to be found in the informal economy (ILO/IPEC 2003a: 8). These children are neither recognized nor protected by national legal and regulatory frameworks and remain in particularly vulnerable situations (Bannerman and Berghuys 2008: 1). As a policy response to Bangladesh's ratification of the C138 in 2001, the project became operational

40 Interview Nazrul Islam Miah, ILO, Administrative and Finance Assistant, 24 June 2008.
41 Interview Profulla Chandra Barman, BRAC, former Project Coordinator, 17 July 2008.

in the same year with funding from the Government of the Kingdom of the Netherlands (Bannerman and Berghuys 2008: i). It was also carried out by the ILO's technical assistance program IPEC (Bannerman and Berghuys 2008: 1). Compared to other projects assessed here, its scope was middle-ranged comprising about 30,000 children in hazardous work were enrolled in the NFE program and of whom 20,000 successfully completed the course. Moreover, about 9,500 guardians benefited from the micro-credit facilities offered through the project (Bannerman and Berghuys 2008: 42–3). During the pilot phase, the project became exclusively operational in Dhaka City.

Targeting in this project was conducted with the help of a baseline survey. To generate this survey, social monitors, teachers, and staff from the project's implementing partners identified children engaged in the worst forms of child labor at their respective workplaces. To discover children in hazardous working arrangements, they indeed went door to door in urban areas with a high prevalence of informal businesses. With these visits, they discovered more than 5,000 enterprises employing child laborers under hazardous conditions. Most of them were small-sized, lacked organizational structure, operated apart from the national tax system and were characterized by labor-intensive production. Surveying and targeting was focused on child laborers below 15 years of age engaged in the worst forms of work and occupied in the urban informal economy of Dhaka City (Bannerman and Berghuys 2008: 15). In a second household survey, data on the socio-economic conditions and the home environment of the working children were collected and cross verified with the data initially acquired. To ensure the accuracy of information, social monitors had to re-identify working children shortly before they established the project's infrastructure, i.e. the Multi Purpose Centers (MPCs), and prior to NFE enrollment (ILO/IPEC 2003a: 28).

For project implementation, 84 fully operational MPCs were set up for service delivery (Bannerman and Berghuys 2008: 46–7). These MPCs functioned as a focal point from which NFE was provided. The long-term objective of delivering NFE services as a transitional form of education was to (re-)integrate younger children into formal schools and to provide older children with basic literacy, numeracy, and life skills so they would be able to join a vocational school (Bannerman and Berghuys 2008: 24; ILO/IPEC 2006: 18). The NFE component was conducted by a local NGO named Dhaka Ahsania Mission (DAM) (ILO/IPEC 2003a: 21). Beneficiary children participated in daily two-hour sessions, undertaken in three shifts, for approximately one year. Next to literacy, arithmetic, and life skills teaching, the beneficiaries received information on health, hygiene and children's rights (Bannerman and Berghuys 2008: 25).

Skills development training (SDT) was initially also delivered utilizing the MPCs as the main infrastructure in Dhaka's urban slums. After a period of time, however, facilities and space were not sufficient anymore, and vocational training centers became established. These offered training in several marketable skills for the project participants, among them industrial electrics and electrics control, refrigeration and air conditioning, mechanical technology, motorcycle repair, signboard and banner writing, block and screen printing, embroidery and jori-chumki,[42] and tailoring and dress-making (Bannerman and Berghuys 2008: 26). Courses were supervised by a trained instructor and lasted between six and twelve months, depending on the trade. The trainees were provided with a monthly stipend for compensating transport costs and wages deducted from their employers due to the reduced time they were available for work. A job placement officer was responsible for placing the trained graduates in alternative, non-hazardous workplaces after they completed the program. All graduates were tracked by the project staff for the following six months, ensuring that they remained engaged in decent work. Implementation of the skills training component was mainly carried out by a local NGO, the Underprivileged Children's Educational Programs (UCEP) (ILO/IPEC 2003a: 23). In later phases of the program, DAM, initially engaged for providing basic educational services, took over the management and execution of vocational training (ILO/IPEC 2006: 24).

Guardians and parents of the beneficiary children were eligible to participate in a social and economic empowerment program (SEE) supporting income generating activities (IGA) through the provision of seed capital, i.e. micro-credits, and training on entrepreneurial skills. This strategic mechanism aimed at shifting the dependency away from the children and towards reliance on their parents' income (ILO/IPEC 2006: 7). Parents' eligibility to IGA initiatives was conditional upon their children's enrollment in the program's NFE and SDT modules. Micro-credits were usually granted to female borrowers who, according to the implementing NGO Resource Integration Centre (RIC), handled money more responsibly (ILO/IPEC 2003a: 24). Prior to receiving their loan, women formed so-called *samitees*, weekly group meetings, to coordinate repayments and discuss upcoming difficulties and progress. This secured women's orientation in the income-generation component and had the positive side effect that they could exchange information about health and hygiene issues and even the repercussions of child labor (Bannerman and Berghuys 2008: 27). These women used their micro-credits to establish cloth and sari businesses, grocery shops, and to purchase rickshaws and vans which they lend out to self-employed drivers. Other borrowers invested in fishery, tea stalls, candle making, sewing utensils, the stick business, scavenging, paying for a taxi license or other small business opportunities (ILO/IPEC 2003a: 24). Across the various components, a saving scheme was in place ensuring that money for children's educational purposes was regularly put aside (Bannerman and Berghuys 2008: 27). Half of the stipend vocational students had to receive, for instance, was immediately paid to the beneficiaries, the other half was saved and disbursed upon completion of the skills training

42 Jori-chumki is a special kind of glitter work on textiles from Bangladesh.

module (Bannerman and Berghuys 2008: 26). Micro-credit borrowers, the parents and guardians of the beneficiary children, were further encouraged to save small sums on a regular basis to cover the educational costs of their school children.

Several activities fostering advocacy and awareness-raising were initiated in the course of project implementation. These included the dissemination of material, announcements in daily newspapers, motivational meetings and activities, seminars, workshops, community theater performances, and media programs informing entire communities about children's rights (ILO/IPEC 2003a: 30). In the target communities, the MPCs served as focal points for this social mobilization program (ILO/IPEC 2006: 41).

Capacity building constituted a supplementary strategy, seeking to strengthen the capability of the various participating organizations to take concerted action in the fight against child labor. Therefore, implementing NGO representatives received training on financial management as well as on technical reporting and management matters. The formation of management committees for the MPCs comprised of community members and NGO field level staff was meant to increase the community's ownership of the program (ILO/IPEC 2003a: 31). Through their function in these committees, community members became particularly versed on children's rights issues.

A relatively new and unique component in this project is the workplace improvement program (WIP). With such a component, it is being acknowledged that there is not only the possibility to withdraw children from hazardous occupations but also to remove the respective hazards from their workplaces. In the context of Bangladesh, this is particularly relevant, since – in many cases – new child laborers were recruited for the same workplaces after their predecessors had been withdrawn. These risks could be decreased with the help of the WIP. Workplace improvement was mainly achieved by approaching the employers and convincing them that enhanced occupational safety and health often goes hand in hand with better productivity. Safety, health, and environment (SHE) committees were built that advocated relevant workplace innovations. And financial incentives were offered through the project for purchasing water filters, first aid boxes, improved ventilation, and protective equipment (Bannerman and Berghuys 2008: 27). In addition to the rights-related services delivered within the framework of this ILO project, strategic partnerships with other local providers could be established. This resulted in a much broader coverage of social and health services than the project alone could possibly offer. Among them were the delivery of high nutrition biscuits to the children attending NFE allocated by the WFP, and the provision of health care and other services offered by various Bangladeshi hospitals or local NGOs (ILO/IPEC 2006: 36). All of these additional services were provided using the infrastructure of the MPCs.

Experiences and lessons learned from the numerous components of this project became integrated into the five-year National Time Bound

Programme (TBP) towards the Elimination of Worst Forms of Child Labour in Bangladesh. The TBP Urban Informal Economy Programme was executed by the ILO between 2007 and 2011, administered by the MoLE and funded by the Kingdom of the Netherlands (ILO/IPEC 2007).

In addition to this pilot project, another ILO program – pursuing yet another different strategy – will be introduced in the following. It is exceptional among development programs, because it involves the cooperation of two international organizations, the ILO and UNICEF. Moreover, the private sector, i.e. a national employers' association, and several local NGOs participated in this program which became known as the South Asian role model for the elimination of industrial child labor.

4.1.7 BGMEA/ILO/UNICEF

Bangladesh's ready-made garment industry has constituted the country's main export sector for at least two decades now. In the early 1990s, the garment industry counted as the national motor of economic growth providing for 70 percent of exports and allocating a considerable number of employment opportunities. In 1992, 1,500 factories employed about 750,000 mainly female workers and 10 percent of the employees were below the legal minimum age of 14 years. During that time, international debates pointing to non-compliance with core labor standards in international trade agreements intensified, often centering on Bangladesh's garment manufacturers. As a result, in 1992, a Bill named the *Child Labor Deterrence Act* was introduced in the US Congress by Senator Tom Harkin, demanding a ban on any imports produced with the involvement of child labor. Although the so-called Harkin Bill was never passed, the Bangladesh Garment Manufacturers and Exporters Association (BGMEA) compelled its member factories to dismiss all workers below the age of 14 claiming the necessity to act in conformity with Bangladesh's 1965 *Factories Act* stipulating 14 as the minimum age for admission to employment. Consequently, from 1993 on, about 40,000 to 50,000 children were removed from the factories, whereas the reported figures differ considerably (ILO/UNICEF 2004: 5–6). These abrupt dismissals had serious consequences with laid-off children being pulled into even more hazardous work in the informal economy, including pornography and prostitution (ILO/UNICEF 2004: 6).

As a response to the removal of children from their initial workplaces and with the aim of providing viable alternatives for these discharged child laborers, the Government of Bangladesh, the garment industry through the BGMEA, and two IOs, UNICEF and the ILO, signed a Memorandum of Understanding (MoU) in 1995. In the same year, the *Bangladesh Garment Sector Projects* (BGMEA/ILO/UNICEF)[43] were launched. Five years later, in

43 The Bangladesh Garments Sector Projects comprise three phases and two additional components. Some of the applied mechanisms were repeated in the consecutive phases or were combined with other

2000, a second MoU was signed by the partners (ILO/IPEC 2004a: iv). This set of garment projects became a prototype of child labor elimination interventions in the manufacturing sector, and has been replicated in similar programs in other, predominantly South Asian, countries. In addition to that, it is known as the first large-scale collaborative project between the ILO and UNICEF pertaining to the abolishment of child labor (ILO/UNICEF 2004: 17). Whereas part of the project costs were jointly borne by the MoU partners, the USDoL served as the main donor for the first three phases and the two extended components were funded by the Norwegian Agency for Development Cooperation (NORAD) and the Italian Social Partners Initiative (ISPI) (ILO/IPEC 2004a: 50). Factories involved in any of the project components had to be registered BGMEA members (ILO/IPEC 2004a: 10). The target group of this comprehensive program intervention embraced former or current child laborers from BGMEA factories below the legal minimum age for employment. The total number of targeted beneficiaries encompassed 28,154 children (ILO/IPEC 2004a: 43). Major strategies applied in the entire framework of the project, throughout all three phases, will be introduced altogether and not separated by each phase in the following.

The first fundamental step taken was the collection of baseline information for targeting and fact-finding related to potential beneficiaries; these were either children under 14 years of age currently working in the factories or at risk of getting involved. The data were collected through two surveys conducted in 1993 and 1995 exploring the age of the child laborers, their working conditions, and information about the parents (ILO/UNICEF 2004: 8). Due to the US Embassy exerting pressure on the project partners, a large part of the withdrawal process of children below 14 years from the garment factories had to take place as a so-called intensive child collection drive (ICCD) during a time period of six weeks in 1996. Concentrated monitoring visits by a team of ILO, BGMEA and governmental monitors continued the removal of children from factories in the following years (ILO/IPEC 2004a: 2).

NFE was provided in a total of 336 so-called MoU schools, i.e. context-specific learning centers, set up in the time span between 1995 and 2001. Not only former garment workers but also their younger siblings were eligible to receive primary education services there (ILO/IPEC 2004b: 16). Overall, 8,588 children were enrolled in the BGMEA/ILO/UNICEF NFE program accounting for almost 30 percent of the children occupied in the factories during that period. The NFE module was directed by UNICEF but implemented through two major Bangladeshi NGOs, the BRAC and GSS (ILO/UNICEF 2004: 9; ILO/IPEC 2004b: 16). An Education Core Group including UNICEF, the ILO, BGMEA, the NGOs providing education services, and the Social Investment Bank Limited (SIBL) administering the stipend,

mechanisms. This brief delineation rather serves as a summary of intervention strategies in use than providing a detailed description of each single phase and its respective components.

coordinated upcoming implementation issues through this forum (ILO/IPEC 2004a: 18).

After a two-year MoU school education, former factory workers who were between 12 and 14 years of age had the opportunity to undertake a skills training appropriate to their age, level of education, and expressed interest. The BGMEA/ILO/UNICEF offered vocational training in tailoring, carpentry, auto repair, plumbing, handicrafts, food processing, and electronics with a training period varying from six months to one year. Whereas skills training took place under the direction of both ILO and UNICEF, local NGO partners were responsible for the actual implementation process (ILO/UNICEF 2004: 10). As part of the extended components of the projects, additional skills training opportunities, such as garment manufacturing, repairing of garment machines, wool knitting, embroidery, screen printing, and house-keeping (including basic cooking) were offered. Moreover, children engaged in these skills training components received a transport and a tiffin[44] allowance, not only covering their travel costs but also guaranteeing a complete meal per attendance day (ILO/IPEC 2004a: 29).

A monitoring and verification mechanism became operational in December 1996 and provided for the successful removal and prevention of child labor in the garment factories. This strategy involved the inspection of BGMEA factories by 12 monitoring teams. Each team was composed of two ILO monitors, one governmental and one BGMEA monitor. Due to its composition, it became known as the "Three Party Monitoring and Verification System" (ILO/IPEC 2004a: 23). The monitors' function ranged from factory inspection, identifying under-age workers, withdrawing and transferring them to the NFE program, to follow-up inspections and counseling of employers on child protection. According to the degree of labor law violations discovered in the respective factory, it was graded A, B or C, with A being the best rate. These categories predetermined the frequency of further monitoring; whereas C factories were inspected monthly, B factories were visited every second month and those with an A only once in four months. An upgrading of a respective factory to the next higher grade was possible after three clear inspections (ILO/UNICEF 2004: 10–11). The detection of any child laborers in the factories was fined with 100 US Dollars per infringement. The sum was to be paid to the BGMEA and used for the continuation of the project (ILO/IPEC 2004a: 23). One important aim of the monitoring and verification mechanism was to set up a self-audit scheme which could continue factory monitoring even beyond the scope of the project and without external assistance (ILO/IPEC 2004a: 37). In addition to that, an MoU Steering Committee was established comprising representatives of the BGMEA, UNICEF, the Government of Bangladesh, the ILO, and the US Embassy

44 The word "tiffin" is still commonly used in Bangladesh. It is an old term from former British India describing a light meal usually served with tea.

as an observer. The Committee supervised the activities agreed upon under the MoU, particularly with regard to every partner's role and responsibilities (ILO/IPEC 2004a: 17). Both of the extended project components provided for a tracking of the beneficiaries for at least six months up to a year after completion of the skills training. This helped to assess the children's living and working situation, to learn more about the difficulties they may encounter, and to further assist them in taking up decent employment opportunities (ILO/IPEC 2004a: 32).

Another project component facilitated an income compensation for the former child laborers and their families. It guaranteed that each working child employed in a garment factory was substituted by an adult family member. Moreover, a 300 BDT stipend was paid to those former garment workers who would enroll in a MoU school. The stipend money was managed and handed out through the SIBL (ILO/IPEC 2004b: 16). Simultaneously, an income generating mechanism was offered to the family of the beneficiaries. It comprised skills training and entrepreneurship development programs to support their way into self-employment. Small businesses established by families making use of income-generation services included selling saris, molasses, rice, vegetables, fish, sweetmeats, or oil from ships, as well as running restaurants, food joints, grocery shops, tea stalls, and rickshaw businesses (ILO/IPEC 2004a: 33). Access to micro-credit was granted to financially support the establishment of small family businesses geared towards the skills that had been developed (ILO/IPEC 2004a: 5).

Throughout the phases and extended components of the projects, several social mobilization interventions were executed. Among them was an awareness-raising element educating children about occupational safety and health, and workers' rights (ILO/IPEC 2004a: 16). After the child labor incidences in the factories went down, the monitoring teams' role shifted to carrying out motivational and preventative work pertinent to the employment of children with the managers and owners of the factories (ILO/IPEC 2004a: 22). Project monitors also engaged in counseling the beneficiary children themselves; they informed them about their rights and motivated them to continue with their education and skills training activities (ILO/IPEC 2004a: 31).

Table 4.1 summarizes the most relevant information pertaining to the seven projects introduced above. This summary is a useful tool for preparing the comparative assessment of all of these policy programs. Of particular significance for further analysis are the projects' outcomes relating to children's rights, the various regulative mechanisms in use, the actor constellations at work, and local infrastructure and institutions established by these initiatives.

4.2 Successful implementation and relevant configurations of mechanisms

All of the policy programs introduced above promote children's rights. Their purpose, historical background, social context, and objectives, however, differ (sometimes tremendously) from each other. Most of them were launched as a direct response to the ratification of international conventions, such as the governmental EHCL, the ILO/IPEC USDoL, and the ILO/IPEC Net. All three constitute a policy answer to Bangladesh's ratification of C182. UNICEF's primary obligation to promote the CRC with a special emphasis on fostering the right to education explains the establishment of the BEHTRUWC. The CLEP – the only non-state initiative examined here – promotes both the CRC and C182.

The FFE and their successor, the PESP, were embedded within the framework of UNESCO's EFA initiative and international efforts towards decreasing illiteracy and promoting primary education. Hence, FFE and PESP reflect Bangladesh's commitment to these demands. UNESCO's endeavors, of course, cannot be separated from the idea of promoting the CRC and in particular, the right to universal primary education.

Under US pressure exerted on the country's largest export industry and the threat of a ban on the import of garment products manufactured with the involvement of child labor, the BGMEA/ILO/UNICEF were born. At first sight, the BGMEA/ILO/UNICEF could appear like a policy response to the *ILO Minimum Age Convention*, since the international outcry resulting in these projects was mainly based on the employment of under-age workers in Bangladesh's garment factories. This convention, however, has not yet been ratified by the Government of Bangladesh although its labor legislation is largely in congruence with it. The garment programs were rather initiated in consequence of an extra-national instrument introduced but not passed in the US Senate, the Harkin Bill.

Due to these differences in context and background of the projects, their initial objectives vary considerably. In all evaluation reports utilized as primary sources for the empirical analysis, project success is measured according to these varying predetermined objectives. Diverse foci make it difficult to compare programs with each other and to assess which strategy has been more successful than the other. Significant differences in quantity add to the problem of comparability. Outcomes differ between a few thousand target children who were provided with rights-related services to several million children who benefitted from particular program components. Consequently, a problem-centered definition of success derived from the research question at stake needs to be developed.

4.2.1 Defining implementation success

The focus of this analysis is the local implementation of children's rights through policy programs. The quantitative number of program participants is not of primary significance here; rather, the configuration of regulative strategies applied for rights implementation is of interest. Nevertheless, at least a school class of children – in Bangladesh this would be between 30 and 100 students – had to be integrated into a program for it to be selected as a within-case. Hence, smaller projects, like the ones initiated by local NGOs, and bigger ones, such as broad-based International Organizations (IO) programs are part of the analysis. Making program mechanisms and combinations of mechanisms comparable, implementation is conceptualized along the dimensions of output and outcome (compare the dimensions of effectiveness according to Underdal 2004: 34). Hence, output describes measures offered through the projects (1) to protect children from hazardous child labor and/or (2) to promote the delivery of education and/or (3) health services for them. Outcome relates to the rights targets making use of the services offered. In this case, outcome does not differ from output because, as demonstrated in table 4.1 and 4.2 below, all of the components offered were also claimed by the respective beneficiaries. Hence, a program's success is defined according to its local implementation outcome relating to these three children's rights.

Table 4.2 summarizes the definition of implementation success according to program output and outcome. Outcome as the dependent variable in the qualitative comparative analysis (QCA) undertaken is determined by three major indicators derived from the CRC and the C138. These indicators comprise – at least a school class of (1) children who could be withdrawn from the worst forms of child labor and workplaces from which hazards could be removed, (2) children who could be provided with NFE and skills training, and (3) children who could be supplied with basic health care services.

To undertake the comparative analysis, an implementation success value has to be allocated to each case, i.e. to every single project. To conduct a crisp-set QCA, this value has to be expressed in a dichotomized way, as either zero or one. Table 4.1 summarizes how program success referring to children's rights implementation was defined along the output and the outcome dimensions. It not only presents success values in the form of binary data but additionally shows implementation success as a four value set (0/0.33/0.67/1). Four value sets are frequently used in fuzzy set analyses to not only demonstrate in a dichotomous way what is "in" and what is "out", but to be more precise in what is "more out than in", "neither fully in nor fully out" or "more in than out" (see also Rihoux and Ragin 2009: 91). This is also helpful for our purposes. Here, all the projects with an implementation value of 0.67 were added to the programs with an implementation value of [1] on the output/outcome dimension, recognizing that they are "more in than out". Or to express it in other words; if at least two of three implementation indicators are

Table 4.1 Summary of major project features

Project **Features**	**CLEP**	**FFE/PESP**	**EHCL**	**BEHTRUWC**	**ILO/IPEC USDoL**	**ILO/IPEC Net**	**BGMEA/ILO/ UNICEF**
Donors	LO/FTF Denmark	Government of Bangladesh/ USA (food aid)[1]	USAID/ Government of Bangladesh	UNICEF, DFID, SIDA, later: CIDA	USDoL	Government of the Kingdom of the Netherlands	USDoL, NORAD, ISPI, ILO, UNICEF, BGMEA
Local Structure/ Institutions	local community centers/ center development committee, children's rights forum	uses existing local governmental structures and institutions/ (school management committee)	learning centers/ center management committee	learning centers/ center management committee	NFE and health centers, young siblings centers (pre-primary schools)/ programme facilitating committees, community watch groups,	multi-purpose centers, vocational training centers, (WIP office)/ CMCs; SHE committees	NFE centers, (using already existing) skills training centers/ steering committee, education core group, joint technical advisory group, school management committee
Actors	NGOs	government	government and NGOs	IOs, government, NGOs	IOs, government, NGOs	IOs, government, NGOs	IOs, government, private sector, NGOs
Output pertinent to children's rights	NFE	fostering regular education	NFE	NFE	NFE	NFE	NFE
	skills training		skills training		skills training	skills training	skills training
	health care services				health care services	health care services	
			withdrawal		withdrawal		withdrawal

Mechanisms	targeting	targeting	targeting	targeting	targeting	targeting	targeting
	awareness raising and advocacy		awareness raising and motivation	awareness raising and social mobilization	awareness raising and advocacy	awareness raising and advocacy	awareness raising and social mobilization
	income generation (saving scheme/ provision of tools)		income generation (micro-credit)		income generation (training/ micro-credit)	income generation (saving scheme/ training/ micro-credit)	income generation (training/ micro-credit)
	monitoring	monitoring		monitoring	monitoring	monitoring	monitoring
	stipend	foodstuff/ stipend	stipend/ income compensation			stipend (for skills training students)	stipend/ income compensation
		conditionality					
				capacity building	capacity building	capacity building	

[1] Data sources provide divergent information; independent evaluation reports point to the receipt of food aid, whereas governmental officials claim that there is no donor involved in the FFE/PESP.

met, the project is considered to be successful. This decision has been made taking a human rights perspective into account. Due to the interrelatedness and mutually reinforcing character of human and children's rights, those projects that do not only withdraw children from hazardous occupations but also provide them with viable education alternatives are considered to be more successful. Furthermore, those programs that do not only deliver education services but also protect children from the worst forms of child labor and take care of basic health care at the same time, are treated to have the best effect on the children. Using four value sets helps to make more precise statements about the programs' success and allows for a more distinctive comparison.

Table 4.2 lists the project-specific output indicators, respective outcomes, and dichotomized as well as more fine-grained implementation values in a four value set.

All of the programs considered here promote at least one of these rights and therefore were accorded a minimum implementation value of {0.33}. The FFE programs and UNICEF's BEHTRUWC both solely foster the right to education and, therefore, are attributed with the lowest number in a four value set, i.e. {0.33}. Two projects, ILO/IPEC USDoL and ILO/IPEC Net, foster all three rights examined and, hence, receive an implementation value of {1}. The CLEP, the EHCL and the BGMEA/ILO/UNICEF were attributed a value of {0.67} implying that they are advancing two rights with their activities respectively.

4.2.2 Relevant configurations of mechanisms

The comprehensive introduction of all the policy programs above has shown that a project outcome pertinent to children's rights was usually supported by the application of several regulative mechanisms. Granting a stipend, for instance, served as an incentive measure and helped children in their gradual withdrawal from the worst forms of labor. Advocacy and awareness raising convinced parents of the value of education and encouraged them to agree to their child's participation in an NFE program. The question arising from that is: Which of these regulative mechanisms are necessary and which are sufficient for achieving rights implementation? Is it material factors, such as financial incentives in the form of a stipend or micro-credit, or immaterial factors like awareness raising that matters most? Or is it a combination of both?

The aim of this section is to identify the most successful configuration of regulative mechanisms in these programs. Therefore, a QCA of the mechanisms will be undertaken. The independent variables, i.e. the regulative mechanisms considered, are neither pre-determined nor deduced from theory; they are specified from the empirics and inductively generated. Nevertheless, most of these variables can be found in the theoretical literature as well, in particular relating to development or norm compliance approaches. From the empirical data under consideration here, seven independent variables were defined, namely targeting, incentives (subsuming the provision of stipends or food rations), advocacy and awareness raising, income generation, conditionality, capacity building, and monitoring (compare Table 4.2: Implementation outcome of policy programs).

To undertake a crisp-set QCA, the dependent as well as the explanatory variables have to be presented in a dichotomized way. Due to difficulties in measuring or allocating a quantitative value to some of the independent variables, such as targeting or advocacy and awareness raising, binary data are used from the outset simply categorizing whether a condition was present or absent in a particular project.

For the empirical data pertaining to the seven projects analyzed here, a general formal model consisting of the dependent and the explanatory variables can be deployed:

Outcome = f (Targeting, Incentives, Advocacy, Income, Condition, Capacity, Monitoring)

A dichotomized data table (Table 4.3) shows whether outcome and conditions are present or absent in each single case.

The dichotomized data tables already allow for drawing some preliminary conclusions. Targeting, for example, surely is a necessary condition present in all cases and even more importantly, in all cases leading to a [1] OUTCOME. Thus, targeting could theoretically be excluded from further analysis. Conditionality, on the other hand, is only present in one case leading to a [0] outcome. This means that conditionality is neither necessary nor sufficient for achieving implementation and the variable could as well be eliminated from further analytical proceedings. Altogether, there is no perfect "outcome" case in which the outcome [1] and all of the conditions are present. Neither is there a case with contradictory configurations in which the same combination of conditions leads to a different outcome. Cross-condition diversity is high; only two cases display the same configuration of conditions. From the dichotomized data table, as a first synthesis, a truth table can be derived. Table 4.4 summarizes identical configurations of conditions leading to the same outcome.

The truth table demonstrates that there are six different configurations of mechanisms present, that is, six combinations of conditions listed above. Two projects, the CLEP and the BGMEA/ILO/UNICEF, show exactly the same configuration of conditions and outcome. The rather slight reduction from seven cases to six combinations of mechanisms confirms that there is enough variation among the cases and that diversity across the conditions is ensured (see Rihoux and Ragin 2009: 52).

Table 4.2 Implementation outcome of policy programs

Project **Implementation Success**	**CLEP**	**FFE/PESP**	**EHCL**	**BEHTRUWC**	**ILO/IPEC USDoL**	**ILO/IPEC Net**	**BGMEA/ILO/ UNICEF**
Output (according to indicators)	(1) --- (2) provision of NFE and skills training (3) provision of basic health care services	(1) --- (2) regular provision of governmental primary education (3) ---	(1) withdrawal from hazardous child labor (2) provision of NFE and skills training (3) ---	(1) --- (2) provision of NFE and livelihood skills training (3) ---	(1) withdrawal from hazardous child labor (2) provision of NFE and skills training (3) provision of basic health care services	(1) withdrawal from hazardous child labor and workplace improvement to reduce hazards (2) provision of NFE and skills training (3) provision of basic health care services	(1) withdrawal from hazardous child labor (2) provision of NFE and skills training (3) ---
Outcome	(1) --- (2) between *2002–2008:* 1,386 graduates from NFE and 3,144 from SDT[1]	(1) --- (2) between *1993–2008*: FFE: 2.1 million beneficiary students (2002), PESP:	(1) indefinite number of children withdrawn from hazardous child labor (2) indefinite	(1) --- (2) between *1997–2009*: 517,150 children provided with NFE of which 166,150 received	(1) between *2000–2003*: 8,826 children withdrawn from hazardous work and 353 child domestic workers	(1) between *2001–2006*: 12,032 children withdrawn,[5],200 workplaces improved[6] (2) 20,000	(1) between *1995–2003*: 5,674 child laborers identified during child collection drive in 1996;[10] 3,290 children withdrawn

	(3) indefinite number of beneficiaries make use of health care services	5.5 million beneficiary students (2008);[2] increased school enrollment, attendance and duration, reduced drop outs (3) ---	number of children provided with NFE (3) ---	livelihood skills training[3] (3) ---	with safer working conditions (2) 19,191 children provided with NFE (3) 30,175 children have received counseling, health and referral services[4]	children successfully completed NFE,[7] 1,282 children graduated from the old and 180 children from the new SDT program[8] (3) health status and awareness of NFE and SDT graduates improved[9]	from garment industries (from 1998 on)[11] (2) 8,588 children enrolled in NFE[12] and about 2,035 children absolved skills training[13] (3) ---
Implementation Value (Outcome, dichotomized)	1	0	1	0	1	1	1
Implementation Value (Outcome, four value set)	0.67	0.33	0.67	0.33	1	1	0.67

1 Data obtained from personal e-mail correspondence with Sajjad Hossain (former Project Coordinator of the BILS/CLEP Project), 7 November 2009.
2 Ahmed and Babu 2007: 5, Interview Tapan Kumar Chakravorty, MoPME, PESP, Deputy Director, 17 July 2008.
3 GoB/BNFE 2008: 13.
4 ILO/IPEC 2003b: 16.
5 ILO/IPEC 2006: 23.
6 Bannerman and Berghuys 2008: 41.
7 Bannerman and Berghuys 2008: 30.
8 Bannerman and Berghuys 2008: 43. The old vocational training component was conducted by UCEP with considerable limitations in its concept. Of the 1,282 children who graduated from it, only 330 could be placed in wage-employment while 279 were listed for self-employment. The 673 children who could not be placed at all were left without future prospects. In 2003, a re-designed skills training module was set up (ILO/IPEC 2006: 24).
9 Bannerman and Berghuys 2008: 36, 42.
10 ILO/IPEC 2004a: 2.
11 ILO/IPEC 2004c: 22.
12 UNICEF/ILO 2004: 9.
13 ILO/IPEC 2004c: 29.

4.2.3 Successful configurations

There are five cases with a [1] value on the outcome variable indicating successful implementation of the three children's rights under consideration. These five cases are the CLEP and the BGMEA/ILO/UNICEF, the EHCL and both ILO/IPEC projects (ILO/IPEC USDoL, ILO/IPEC Net). The key operational step of a crisp-set QCA is Boolean minimization which makes it possible to identify conditions necessary to obtaining a certain outcome. Boolean minimization is the reduction of complex formulas or expressions that explain a certain outcome into shorter and more parsimonious ones (Rihoux and Ragin 2009: 35).

According to the truth table shown above, the following formula can be built representing a [1] OUTCOME (uppercase letters represent presence and lowercase letters absence of a certain condition). In Boolean algebra, multiplications imply a logical "and", whereas additions indicate a logical "or". In this case, multiplication means the combination of present and absent conditions that leads to a certain outcome (Ragin 1987: 91–2).

TARGETING * INCENTIVES * ADVOCACY * INCOME * condition * capacity * MONITORING +
TARGETING * INCENTIVES * ADVOCACY * INCOME * condition * capacity * monitoring +
TARGETING * incentives * ADVOCACY * INCOME * condition * CAPACITY * MONITORING +
TARGETING * INCENTIVES * ADVOCACY * INCOME * condition * CAPACITY * MONITORING → OUTCOME (1)

The most fundamental rule of Boolean minimization is to simplify the formal model by removing irrelevant conditions: "If two Boolean expressions differ in only one causal condition yet produce the same outcome, the causal condition that distinguishes the two expressions can be considered irrelevant and can be removed to create a simpler, combined expression" (Ragin 1987: 93).

Applying this Boolean minimization procedure, the first and second (sub-) formulas can be reduced, because they differ in only one condition, the presence and absence of monitoring, but still produce the same outcome. Hence, monitoring is not a necessary condition for achieving the outcome. The resulting minimized formula (a) is:

TARGETING * INCENTIVES * ADVOCACY * INCOME * condition * capacity → OUTCOME

The same procedure can be undertaken with the first and the fourth (sub-) formulas in which all elements except for the presence and absence of capacity building are identical resulting in the following minimized expression (b):

Table 4.3 Dichotomized data table

CaseID	Targeting	Incentives	Advocacy	Income	Condition	Capacity	Monitoring	Outcome
CLEP	1	1	1	1	0	0	1	1
FFE/ PESP	1	1	0	0	1	0	1	0
EHCL	1	1	1	1	0	0	0	1
BEHTRUWC	1	0	1	0	0	1	1	0
ILO/IPEC USDoL	1	0	1	1	0	1	1	1
ILO/IPEC Net	1	1	1	1	0	1	1	1
BGMEA/ ILO/ UNICEF	1	1	1	1	0	0	1	1

Table 4.4 Truth table of the Boolean configurations

CaseID	Targeting	Incentives	Advocacy	Income	Condition	Capacity	Monitoring	Outcome
CLEP, BGMEA/ILO/UNICEF	1	1	1	1	0	0	1	1
FFE/PESP	1	1	0	0	1	0	1	0
EHCL	1	1	1	1	0	0	0	1
BEHTRUWC	1	0	1	0	0	1	1	0
ILO/IPEC USDoL	1	0	1	1	0	1	1	1
ILO/IPEC Net	1	1	1	1	0	1	1	1

TARGETING * INCENTIVES * ADVOCACY * INCOME * condition * MONITORING → OUTCOME

Furthermore, the third and the fourth (sub-)expressions differ solely on the presence and absence of incentives, and can be reduced to the formula (c):

TARGETING * ADVOCACY * INCOME * conditions * CAPACITY * MONITORING → OUTCOME

Models (a) and (b) can be further minimized due to the fact that they again only differ on one condition, the absence of capacity building and the presence of monitoring although leading to the same outcome. Hence, the absence or presence of these two conditions is not necessary for the outcome as long as the other conditions are present (or absent). After further minimization, the resulting model (d) is the following:

TARGETING * INCENTIVES * ADVOCACY * INCOME * condition → OUTCOME

Another minimization can be undertaken reconsidering expression (b) and (c) with their only difference being the presence of incentives in model (b) and capacity building in model (c) but apart from that leading to the same outcome. This produces the minimized formula (e):

TARGETING * ADVOCACY * INCOME * condition * MONITORING → OUTCOME

Model (d) and (e) can again be further minimized. Both lead to the same outcome with only one differing condition, the presence of incentives in formula (d) and the presence of monitoring in expression (e). Eliminating these leads to the final model (f):

TARGETING * ADVOCACY * INCOME * condition → OUTCOME

Consequently, the presence of targeting combined with the presence of advocacy and awareness raising, and measures for income generation, as well as the absence of conditionalities lead to the outcome.

4.2.4 Necessary and sufficient conditions

The Boolean approach considers the relation between results obtained from Boolean minimization and necessary and sufficient conditions. Necessary conditions must be present for a particular outcome. They might appear in various combinations with sufficient conditions, but have to be present in all of these configurations. Sufficient conditions are capable of producing a certain result but they are not the only conditions with this capability (Ragin 1987: 99). For the final outcome in this analysis, the following formula remains:

OUTCOME = TARGETING * ADVOCACY * INCOME * condition

It cannot be further minimized and reflects the most parsimonious result possible. From this result, some statements can be made regarding the combination of conditions needed for successful programs with respect to children's rights implementation. The presence of targeting, advocacy, and income generation mechanisms can be highlighted as necessary conditions for obtaining implementation. In other words; in all of the successful cases, a combination of targeting, advocacy, and income generation was present. Both outcomes additionally require the absence of conditions. Conditionality as a project strategy was only present in a single case, the FFE and its consecutive PESP. In all other cases, including the successful ones, conditions were absent. This can most probably be explained with the FFE and PESP constituting demand-side interventions. In return for paying a stipend to poor students, both projects "demand" compliance with conditions, such as regular school attendance and certain achievement rates. Whereas conditionality seems to be a successful mechanism in the FFE project, the programs analyzed here – of which most focused on the elimination of the worst forms of child labor – refrained from imposing conditions. This means that applying conditionalities most probably works well in programs fostering education and less in projects eliminating child labor. Hence, if implementation success is defined as fostering both rights simultaneously (and the right to health care), conditions have to be absent.

The other variables included in this analysis that are not necessary for producing the outcome, i.e. incentives, capacity building, and monitoring, can be described as sufficient conditions. They contribute to the implementation success but they are not the only conditions capable of doing so (see also Ragin 1987: 99).

4.3 Cross-checking the results with the empirical cases

The results obtained match perfectly with the background information on causes leading to the denial of children's rights in Bangladesh elaborated above (see Chapter 3). Illustrations from the empirical cases help in understanding how these regulative mechanisms take effect in tackling the root causes of hazardous child labor and deficits in the provision of education and health rights.

Targeting was identified as a necessary condition since it was present in every single case or program observed here. It constitutes a significant mechanism that is usually applied prior to project implementation. In some cases, a two-step targeting procedure was utilized, selecting particularly poor and disadvantaged intervention areas on the one hand and exceptionally poor households or children engaged in the worst forms of child labor on the other hand. In other programs, the targeted areas were pre-selected depending on the respective objectives and actors involved. The CLEP initiated by the BILS, for instance, was traditionally involved in areas belonging to Dhaka's industrial belt that have strong ties to the trade union movement. The ILO/IPEC USDoL aimed at tackling the worst forms of child labor, among others, in the bidi industry. This implied that certain factories with a high prevalence of child labor in Rangpur, Northern Bangladesh, were the focus of project intervention. Baseline or household surveys are the main instruments used for targeting procedures, often carried out by the implementing partners or the field staff of IOs. Sometimes targeting implies some kind of fact-finding or collecting information about the children and their work places, their entire socio-economic situation, home environment, and family data. Altogether, the goal of targeting is to find the most disadvantaged children whose rights have so far been denied, and to provide them with basic protection and social services.

All of the projects leading to a positive outcome include an advocacy and awareness-raising mechanism. Providing information on children's rights and making beneficiaries aware of their entitlements as right-holders takes place for the target group, usually within the framework of NFE programs. Beyond that, they are also directed at the entire community. This includes addressing various stakeholders, among them employers, the Imam, government authorities or local elites. Some grass-roots initiatives emphasize the importance of preventive activities, for instance through informing the siblings of child laborers of the negative consequences of working instead of attending school. Depending on the scope of the particular project, awareness raising might also be framed as a social mobilization component, sometimes even reaching out to an international public. Hence, some projects conduct rallies and other motivational activities, roundtable discussions, press conferences, theater performances, media programs, and workshops or disseminate leaflets, brochures, and posters. The implementing NGOs, project monitors or management committees of particular learning centers often function as advocacy facilitators, and engage in dialogue with children and their families.

The third necessary condition, the presence of IGAs, has also been an integral component of all programs resulting in a [1] OUTCOME. Fostering income generation takes various forms in the projects' context, ranging from the provision of saving schemes that enable beneficiaries to acquire tools and become self-employed after project termination, granting loans and micro-credits for establishing small businesses, to skills training and entrepreneurship development. These initiatives are usually targeted at the parents of working children or other adult family members with the objective of gradually withdrawing under-age children from occupational activities and substituting their income loss with the help of adult labor. Due to a lack of employment opportunities, the promotion of self-employment is a recurring scheme in these projects. Self-employment concepts usually imply micro-credits, probably Bangladesh's most popular regulative mechanism for development programs. Additionally, some projects foster the formation of community groups and meetings in the intervention areas for paying back loans, discussing upcoming problems pertinent to small-scale businesses, and exchanging perspectives on children's rights.

All of the above-mentioned regulatory mechanisms need infrastructure and coordinating institutions to come into effect. Whereas awareness raising is usually undertaken as an integral part of NFE programs in learning centers, IGAs (like the provision of micro-credits), are mostly administered by local committees. In a way, the existence of infrastructure and institutions can also be described as necessary conditions, because they were present in every single case examined here. How exactly both were realized, and what specific function they had within the scope of the programs will be elaborated in the following.

Chapter 5

Local infrastructure, institutions and actors

> [...] there [are] no governmental schools in the urban slums and the education opportunity is less so that's why the accessibility is less so that's how the enrollment rate is less and there is no good opportunities [...].[1]

This chapter investigates the second part of the local implementation process of children's rights by focusing on structures, institutions and actors. The previous introduction of local programs showed that in all seven cases some sort of infrastructure, institutional arrangements and actor partnerships were necessary to carry out project activities, i.e. to deliver rights-related social services to the norm targets. An in-depth description on how these come about helps to develop a comprehensive understanding on the evolvement of an implementation process at the local level. Next to evaluation reports and existing interview material, this thick description is based on field notes from visits to respective project sites.

One important result from field research in Bangladesh is that whereas the infrastructure in use, e.g. education and health centers, frequently have a quite provisional character, institutions are launched on a more permanent basis. Institutions involving community members have the potential to remain in place and to spread the message of children's rights even beyond the temporary framework of externally funded projects. A second outcome relates to partnerships between actors at different levels that institutionalize on a temporary basis. Here, international organizations IOs, the national government and local non-governmental organizations (NGOs) bale their strengths and share expertise, resources and capacities to compensate governmental implementation deficits. These multi-level actor partnerships will be examined in greater detail in the second section of this chapter.

1 Interview Mohammad Golam Kibria, United Nations Internation Children's Emergency Fund (UNICEF), Education Section, Education Officer, 4 June 2008.

5.1 Context-specific infrastructure and institutions

With the funding of the Danish Trade Union Council (LO/FTF), the *Child Labour Elimination Project* (CLEP) of the Bangladesh Institute of Labour Studies (BILS) set up local community centers hosting non-formal schools and skills training facilities in three areas, Tongi, Mirpur, and Keranigonj. Within these centers, not only educational but also health services were provided. In each of the community centers, a coordinator responsible for ensuring smooth project operation and for hiring teachers as well as vocational trainers was employed. A Center Development Committee, composed of community leaders, local government and trade union representatives, social activists, teachers, guardians, parents, and employers, monitors and evaluates the project (Hossain 2008: 13). This committee motivates the entire community to comply with children's rights and assists in solving problems hampering implementation. Each Center Development Committee has one chairperson functioning as a commissioner. A peculiar institutional arrangement of CLEP is its Child Rights Forum. It organizes children in a group to advocate children's rights related to the *UN Convention on the Rights of the Child* among their peers.[2]

Visiting the Tongi center provided valuable insights into how children learn here. The center was accommodated in an old building in which, due to humidity, the paint was coming off the wall. Occupying five small and rather dark rooms and one office, the project seemed to run productively. In one of the rooms, in which vocational training was provided, girls sat on the floor to stitch or at desks learning how to use antiquated sewing machines. The boys were located in a separate classroom and received training on house welding, while others learned the names of tools and had a motorcycle to be used as equipment for instruction. Non-formal education (NFE) was provided in a full-fledged classroom with school benches, chairs, and even self-painted pictures and banners on the walls. The girls seemed to be particularly active in class, performing a dance, singing a song, and reciting a poem for the visitors. For NFE and skills training courses, high quality school materials seemed to be available. Schoolbooks were partly provided from Dhaka Ahsania Mission (DAM), another domestic NGO, or developed by BILS itself, such as a book about hygiene intended to educate children on health issues and themes not usually publicly discussed in Bangladesh's society, such as diseases, but also female menstruation and HIV/AIDS prevention.[3]

The governmental *Food for Education* (FFE) program and the consecutive *Primary Education Stipend Project* (PESP) reverted to an already existing local

2 Interview Sajjad Hossain, BILS, CLEP Project Coordinator, 21 May 2008.

3 Author's own notes from field visit: BILS: CLEP with Sajjad Hossain (Project Coordinator), Tongi area, Dhaka, 7 June 2008.

infrastructure.[4] Both projects are usually carried out in governmental primary schools and, in fewer cases, in non-governmental and religious schools. Thus, no new schools or learning centers have to be built. Government officials at the lower administrative levels, the Thana Nirbahi (Executive) Officer and the Thana Education Officer, execute the programs with the support of the school management committee (SMC) and take over monitoring and supervisory functions (Ahmed and del Ninno 2002: 8). These SMCs are an inherent part of Bangladesh's school system, whether in governmental or non-governmental institutions, and in this case, consist of the headmaster and teachers of the respective school as well as the Compulsory Primary Education Ward Committee.[5] Whereas the FFE's grain distribution had initially been conducted through the school management committees, later on private retailers and warehouses were assigned to deliver wheat and grain to the beneficiary families. Mainly due to corruption in this conveyor chain, the former food incentive got converted into a cash stipend and thereby, the PESP came into existence. This program transition led to charging state-owned commercial banks with distributing the money to the participants' mothers taking away this responsibility from the SMCs.

Gorad Government Primary School in Savar Upazila, District Dhaka, was one of Bangladesh's first governmental schools to receive the FFE incentive and has remained a PESP school until today. When visiting this primary school, it appeared to be relatively well-equipped with school benches, chairs, and materials – in spite of the overcrowded classrooms in which children traditionally sat separated; girls on one side and boys on the other. Almost all of the students wore school uniforms; some additionally were in the possession of flip-flops or even shoes, while most of them ran around barefoot. New local structures had not been established; the project ran rather invisibly and made use of whatever schooling infrastructure was already in existence. Counting all of the children who were present revealed an enlightening result: One of the two first-grade classes had a total size of 92 students with 71 of them being present. In this class, 30 children, 29 of whom attended school that day, received the stipend. In other classrooms, similar numbers could be detected,[6] which suggests that the stipend project indeed seems to increase attendance rates.[7]

4 This means that no new structures had to be established at the local level. On the national scale, however, administrative units were created for project management.

5 Another administrative institution at the ward level.

6 Nevertheless, attendance rates seem to decrease with the increasing age of the students most probably due to older children taking up employment; in class five of this school, total class sizes were much smaller with only 50 students of which merely 58 percent were present. 11 out of 14 project beneficiaries attended school that particular day.

7 Author's own notes from field visit: FFE/PESP with Md. Abdul Aziz (Upazila Education Officer, Savar) and Nahar Sultana (Dhaka Division Monitoring Officer, Dhaka) Gorad Government Primary School, Savar Upazila, 19 July 2008.

Within the framework of the *Eradication of Hazardous Child Labour Project* (EHCL), funded by the Government of Bangladesh, several learning centers were established in the urban slums of Chittagong and Dhaka. These were used to provide children, who were formerly engaged in hazardous occupations, with NFE in flexible three-hour shifts of schooling, either in the morning or in the evening of their work days. Skills training, another project component, is also offered in these community centers. A center management committee (CMC), comprising NFE instructors and parents, oversees these learning centers and undertakes monitoring, management, and problem-solving functions.

Visiting four of these community centers in the slums of Hazaribagh in Dhaka revealed how minimal and provisional a schooling infrastructure for NFE can be. Due to a lack of space in the urban slum, the so-called learning centers either were damp and dark little single-room houses or shabby bamboo huts fixed above the Buriganga river. In one of the centers, lots of flies were sitting on the children and were flying into everyone's face while the students tried to concentrate on studying. Provisionary planks almost collapsed when one entered the learning hut attached above the river. The children, almost all of them migrants from Barisal, sat on the floor cramped together on the tiniest space. Some of them had even brought younger siblings that they had to watch during their time in the NFE center and most probably, while earning their income as well. And learning indeed took place; the children were able to write words in their notepads and some school material, such as chalk and a board, as well as a few books, were available.[8]

For the *Basic Education for Hard to Reach Urban Working Children Project* (BEHTRUWC), launched by UNICEF in cooperation with the Ministry of Primary and Mass Education (MoPME) and local non-state organizations, a completely new infrastructure had to be set up.[9] About 6,646 learning centers became established and operative during the second project phase. Most of them are situated in the urban slums of Dhaka and Chittagong, but also in Khulna, Barisal, Rashjahi, and Sylhet. Whereas project coordination and administration is handled by the governmental Project Implementation Unit (PIU), the actual implementation process on the ground is conducted by

8 Author's own notes from field visit: Eco-Social Development Organization (ESDO): Eradication of Hazardous Child Labour (EHCL) Project with Md. Golam Mostofa, Non-Formal Education Centers, Hazaribagh, Dhaka, 10 July 2008.

9 Several institutions established for project supervision and management are in place at the national level, among them a Project Steering Committee, a Project Working Committee, and a City Implementation and Monitoring Unit led by the City Corporation (Interview Mohammad Golam Kibria, UNICEF, Education Section, Education Officer, 4 June 2008). These are exclusively governmental institutions without community involvement. Project personnel from the governmental side involve a project director, deputy director, assistant directors, program and monitoring officers who all serve administrative, monitoring, and planning functions and are employed by the MoPME. Program officers are closest to the local level and coordinate the executive work of NGOs (interview Rezaul Quader, MoPME, Project Director, 8 July 2008).

local NGOs.[10] Teaching and learning takes place on a daily basis for two and a half hours.[11] NGO coordinators formed CMCs – one for each community center – with the help of local people from the target areas themselves. The CMCs are teams of seven members representing parents, employers, local schoolteachers, and influential community people of whom one is nominated as the chairperson. Committee members try to motivate children and their employers to join BEHTRUWC's non-formal schooling program. They come together every three months to monitor the learning centers and supervise the participants' progress. Furthermore, they pay visits to certain employers, beneficiary children or their families, especially whenever problems pertinent to center operations develop.[12] In some cases, CMC representatives undertake their own initiatives beyond the project's objectives even if additional costs are involved that have to be borne by the community. In one BEHTRUWC center, for instance, the CMC decided to endow their center with electricity[13] and collected the money needed from supportive members of the community. Overall, CMCs work towards increasing the centers' retention rates and decreasing students' dropout rates.[14] Usually only one teacher per center, mostly a woman, will be hired and instructs 25 participating students. Each supervisor, in turn, oversees the functioning of ten learning centers.

A field visit to a CATALYST[15] learning center in Mirpur, a shanty town area in Dhaka, was again enlightening with respect to how provisional a NFE infrastructure can be. Due to the very low fixed sum that NGOs receive for center rental, namely 1,800 BDT monthly in Dhaka and 1,500 BDT in other divisional cities, there is very little space for the 25 students who learn here. The small budget provision, about 100 BDT, for center maintenance and operation costs contributes to their poor quality and makes them appear shabby and scanty.[16] CATALYST's single-room-center in Mirpur is not even endowed with a glass window. The children who learn here are of quite different ages; some seem to be primary school children, while others are adolescents. In official terms, the participants should be between ten and 14 years old, several of them, however, look much younger than that. Another issue is more than obvious; all of the children in this room are laborers; they look very serious, they don't smile, and they seem to be grown-ups. They tell us about their 12-hour workdays starting at seven or eight in the morning, lasting until just

10 Interview Mohammad Golam Kibria, UNICEF, Education Section, Education Officer, 4 June 2008.

11 Interview Rezaul Quader, MoPME, Project Director, 8 July 2008.

12 Interview Mohammad Golam Kibria, UNICEF, Education Section, Education Officer, 4 June 2008.

13 Interview Hasina Habib, Gono Shahajja Sangstha (GSS), Coordinator Field Education Programme, 9 June 2008.

14 Interview Mohammad Golam Kibria, UNICEF, Education Section, Education Officer, 4 June 2008.

15 CATALYST is one of the 20 local implementing NGOs.

16 Interview Hasina Habib, GSS, Coordinator Field Education Programme, 9 June 2008, Interview Musbah Alim, CATALYST, Executive Director, 19 June 2008 and Interview Khandaker Asraful Islam, Bangladesh Development Service Center (BDSC), Deputy Director, 24 May 2008.

about the same time in the evening. In between, they are now becoming literate in this NFE center for a few hours per day. Sometimes, they even bring their younger siblings to the center. Next to all of the responsibilities they have to bear, watching younger sisters and brothers is another duty which is taken for granted. Of course, studying is only possible for them if the employers of these domestic workers or shop helpers give their permission. But in the end, this learning center is their only chance to get in touch with basic education.[17]

Various local arrangements, in terms of infrastructure and institutions, have been developed within the framework of the ILO/IPEC project *Preventing and Eliminating the Worst Forms of Child Labour in Selected Formal and Informal Sectors in Bangladesh* (ILO/IPEC USDoL).[18] Municipal centers were set up to deliver various services at once; among them NFE, but also primary health care which includes the provision of immunizations and medicine, nutritious support, post-natal care, and monthly health check-ups.[19] One implementing NGO, the Bangladesh Rural Advancement Committee (BRAC), even arranged day-care centers and play groups, known as pre-primary schools, for the younger siblings of the participating child laborers. These pre-primary schools hosted all children from three years of age, who initially had to be watched by their older siblings during NFE attendance or in some cases, even while they were working.[20] Within each locality, Programme Facilitating Committees and Community Watch Groups were formed and comprised local government authorities, community members, and leaders, teachers, workers' representatives, employers, businessmen, and factory owners of whom one, usually the Union Parishad Chairperson, was the head of the committee. These committees arrange meetings with the NGO field workers and International Labour Organization (ILO) monitors to discuss emerging problems related to project operation.[21] During their quarterly meetings, they decide on community initiatives and on agreements with employers for combating child labor immediately and in the long run. Such institutions at the community level are meant to function as anti-child labor platforms to sustain the project's impact and spread the message of children's rights protection even after its termination (ILO/IPEC 2003b: 19).

Visiting one of BRAC's pre-primary schools in Mohakhali in Dhaka was rewarding with respect to seeing an at least dry and roofed hut in which

17 Author's own notes from field visit: CATALYST: BEHTRUWC Project, learning center in Mirpur, with Musbah Alim and CATALYST's field coordinator, 19 June 2008.

18 Within the framework of this project, some national administrative structures were established, such as a National Steering Committee (NSC) or its sub-committee reporting to the NSC and the *International Programme on the Elimination of Child Labour* (IPEC) and functioning as the central project advisory committee (ILO/IPEC 2003b: 7). The focus here, however, is on the installation of local infrastructure and institutions.

19 Interview Md. Harun-or Rashid, Lighthouse, Executive Director, 20 May 2008.

20 Interview Profulla Chandra Barman, BRAC, former Project Coordinator, 17 July 2008.

21 Interview Nazrul Islam Miah, ILO, Administrative and Finance Assistant, 24 June 2008.

children learn in the middle of a deteriorated, wet, and muddy slum during Monsoon time. The single-room learning center was astonishingly well-equipped with school materials, toys, a board and chalk, and even a floor cover. Children of different ages, who indeed could have been primary school children already, were engaging in learning games including singing, dancing, and rhyming, which they proudly presented to the visitors. This center offered a much more spacious, healthier, and cleaner atmosphere than these children were used to from their own homes in the urban slum.[22]

The establishment of so-called multi-purpose centers (MPCs) constituted an integral part of ILO/IPEC's policy initiative *Prevention and Elimination of Selected Worst Forms of Child Labour in the Informal Economy in Dhaka City* (ILO/IPEC Net) and went hand in hand with the development of a new local infrastructure. Within this project's framework, 92 MPCs served as the focal point for the delivery of various services, among them NFE, skills training, micro-credit provision, workplace improvement, supplementary nutrition, and health services. Apart from that, the MPCs were also perceived as a community platform and, for instance, hosted regular meetings of women's groups or female loan takers. Thereby, the centers did not only operate at the heart of service delivery, but also facilitated social mobilization, awareness raising, and community participation. Skills development training, however, had only initially been conducted in these MPCs. Later on, as a response to space and facility constraints, full-fledged vocational training centers became established in which these services could be delivered without any hindrances. Respective CMCs were composed of NGO representatives and the local community, including beneficiary parents and guardians, the Mullah, i.e. the religious leader, local government authorities, community elites, schoolteachers, social workers, and employers. Their role encompassed the daily supervision of program activities, center maintenance, coordination of strategic partnerships, and possibly the allocation of additional financial resources to ensure each MPCs' sustainability (Bannerman and Berghuys 2008: 46–7).[23] The project's Workplace Improvement Programme (WIP) implied the establishment of safety, health and environment (SHE) committees in charge of making feasible suggestions for improving work conditions among children occupied in Dhaka's informal economy. A WIP office near an agglomeration of informal businesses in Old Dhaka served as a focal point and exchange platform for this module (Bannerman and Berghuys 2008: 41).

22 This field visit was conducted to comprehensively understand BRAC's concept of pre-primary schools. A visit to an actual project site could not be undertaken since the program was already terminated in 2004. Nevertheless, some of these pre-primary schools initiated in the course of project implementation are still operating in Rangpur (Interview Profulla Chandra Barman, BRAC, former Project Coordinator, 17 July 2008 and author's own notes and photos from field visit: BRAC Pre-primary School, Mohakhali, Dhaka, 20 July 2008).

23 Interview Ronald E. Berghuys, ILO/IPEC, Chief Technical Advisor, 19 May 2008 and Interview Abul Haseeb Khan, Resource Integration Centre (RIC), Director, 26 May 2008.

Visiting one of the women's groups[24] originating from this project was revealing in terms of observing easily set-up institutions that have an enormous empowering effect. The group visited here has emerged from the program's micro-credit component and comprises 22 female loan takers of Lalbagh's slums who are all mothers of former child laborers. Their meetings take place on a weekly basis in one of their tiny shanty homes, in which they hardly fit altogether. Once a week, they do not only come together to pay back their dues to an NGO project monitor, but they also discuss upcoming problems related to their newly established small businesses. These encompass lending out rickshaws, buying and selling garments and dishes on the market or doing prints and block batiks. If one of the women faces any obstacles, the others are there to help with suggestions and advice, but also with financial support. Today, none of their children work anymore; after completing NFE, they all became integrated into governmental schools and a considerable number even enrolled in secondary education institutions. An additional program effect was that these women – with their new role as breadwinning family members – reported to have gained respect and bargaining power at home and in their communities.[25]

For the Bangladesh *Garment Sector Projects* (BGMEA/ILO/UNICEF), local infrastructure only partly had to be developed because some already existing premises could be utilized, in particular, for conducting the program's vocational training. In the course of project realization, more than 300 NFE centers became established and staffed with trained teachers. These were situated in locations that could be easily accessed by the target children (ILO/UNICEF 2004: 7). Skills training, however, was carried out in the implementing partners' own training facilities. This means the program reverted to an infrastructure already in place at minimal costs (ILO/IPEC 2004e: 15). From an institutional perspective, the BGMEA/ILO/UNICEF were coordinated by an informal steering committee, comprised of representatives of the relevant stakeholders, among them the BGMEA, the Government of Bangladesh, the ILO, UNICEF, and a deputy of the US Embassy with an observational function. An education core group that included staff members from UNICEF, the ILO, Bangladesh Garments Manufacturers and Exporters Association (BGMEA), local NGOs in their role as education providers, and the Social Investment Bank Limited (SIBL) met regularly to coordinate upcoming

24 By the time of data collection, due to the termination of the project's pilot phase and its transition towards a subsequent comprehensive Time Bound Program (TBP) – Urban Informal Economy (UIE), the established local infrastructure was no longer in place, and consequently, could not be included in the field visit. An institution, i.e. this women's group, that has remained even beyond this project's temporary frame could be visited.

25 Author's own notes from field visit: ILO/IPEC project: ILO/IPEC Net, Hazaribagh and Lalbagh area with a field coordinator from RIC, ILO/IPEC project field and social workers and Anna Ensing (Senior Researcher from the Foundation for International Research on Working Children (IREWOC), Netherlands), Dhaka, 8 June 2008.

implementation issues and provide a project discussion forum for the various partners (ILO/IPEC 2004c: 12). Towards the end of the project, UNICEF and the ILO formed a joint technical advisory group (JTAG) to prepare an assessment framework of the separate components and common programs (ILO/UNICEF 2004: 7). Just like in most of Bangladesh's other projects involving a setup of NFE facilities, SMCs were initiated in each community's Memorandum of Understanding (MoU) Schools.[26]

Today, the child labor ratio in Bangladesh's garment industry is almost at zero. Nevertheless, it was worth investigating children's former workplaces during a field visit to one of the country's numerous garment factories in Gazipur, Dhaka. This helped to gain a better understanding of what child labor in the garment industry was like. The facility visited, "Unique Dyeing and Washing Ltd.", specialized in washing and dyeing clothes but also engaged in ready-made garments production. Its factory management has signed several codes of conduct to ensure compliance with certain social and labor standards. The factory is a subcontractor of various well-known garment buyers, among them H&M, Gap, Zara, Walmart, and others. Working conditions in this big and modern business seemed to be decent. During an announced visit to the production site, almost all of the workers wore mouth protection and gloves; signs with emergency plans and exits could be found all over the production section. Although the factory's staff and management were not very keen on talking about child labor, they showed sections in which children would have been engaged if they were still working here. According to a staff member, child labor was mainly concentrated in the packing division.[27]

A crucial result of these descriptive elaborations is the existence of local infrastructure and institutions enabling the provision of rights-related services in the implementation process. Both can be considered to be necessary conditions for implementing children's rights at the grassroots level. With the help of the field notes presented above, it became clear that educational infrastructure does not have to be costly; it can be informal, simple, and by all means provisional. In addition, the FFE and the PESP demonstrate how already existing schools, local governmental institutions and authorities, and even state-owned banks can be utilized to contribute to rights realization. Vocational training in the BCMEA/ILO/UNICEF could be undertaken in facilities once set up by the respective service-providing NGO. Hence, both are examples of the cost-effective sharing of an infrastructure that is already existent. Whereas, non-formal schools or learning centers established within

26 Interview Md. Monwer Hossain Khandker, BRAC, Programme Manager, Field Operations BRAC Education Programme, 8 June 2008.

27 As an independent researcher, it is almost impossible to gain access to Bangladesh's garment factories. This field visit was made possible by David Ambadar, project manager at the German Gesellschaft für Technische Zusammenarbeit (GTZ). The condition for a factory visit, however, was that a factory with decent work conditions had to be chosen. Author's own notes from field visit: Unique Dyeing and Washing Ltd in Gazipur, Dhaka with David Ambadar (GTZ), 23 July 2008.

the framework of a transnational development project might be dismantled with its termination, an infrastructure utilized by several partners is more likely to remain in place.

The buildup of such structures comes together with the establishment of administrative, supervisory, and coordinating institutions, which usually took the form of center or school management committees. On the one hand, these constitute a typical feature of community involvement in Bangladesh's educational landscape, also found in most governmental schools. On the other hand, management committees in NFE centers face a number of diverging problems. Their attendees are working children living in poor communities with illiterate parents who insist on their children's income contribution. These children are much more at risk of dropping out of school. Under these circumstances, committees in NFE centers take on different responsibilities, such as motivating children to enroll into a program, attend it on a regular basis, not leave before completion, and if possible, to continue their education. Beyond persuading the children, they have to convince entire communities of the meaning of education. Issues to be dealt with are not limited to the educational sphere but also comprise the prevailing beliefs regarding gender roles, family concerns, and child labor. Furthermore, SMCs in NFE centers monitor, evaluate, and supervise program implementation. They maintain the respective center, solve daily problems, eventually create their own initiatives or allocate additional financial resources. Each projects' SMCs are composed differently including local government officials, religious leaders, community elites, employers, social workers and parents. In a hierarchical society like Bangladesh, it is of particular relevance to integrate local authorities in disseminating a project's message. Dependent on the particular program's focus, additional rights-promoting institutions might be set-up. Examples are CLEP's *Child Rights Forum* or the *Safety, Health, and Environment Committees* of the ILO/IPEC project.

Table 5.1 summarizes each project's infrastructure and pertinent institutions.

Having discussed the need for a context-specific infrastructure and relevant institutions to realize children's rights in weak states, the involvement of specific actors and actor constellations in the implementation process is now examined in more detail. An emphasis is placed on investigating the emergence of multi-level partnerships that compensate governmental implementation deficits.

5.2 Multi-level actor partnerships

In the seven cases under consideration, several actor partnerships, including governmental and private players come into existence to promote children's rights realization. Such forms of cooperation, however, does not only comprise diverse types of actors, but also protagonists from various levels,

Table 5.1 Local infrastructure and institutions

Project Features	CLEP	FFE/PESP	EHCL	BEHTRUWC	ILO/IPEC USDoL	ILO/IPEC Net	BGMEA/ILO/ UNICEF
Local Infrastructure	local community centers	uses existing local governmental structures (and institutions)	learning centers	learning centers	non-formal education and health centers, young siblings centers (pre-primary schools)	multi-purpose centers, vocational training centers, (WIP office)	NFE centers, (used existing) skills training centers
Institutions	center development committee, child rights forum	SMC	CMC	CMC	program facilitating committees, community watch groups	CMCs, safety, health, and environment committees	steering committee, education core group, joint technical advisory group, SMC

among them international organizations, the national government, a domestic employers' association, and local non-governmental organizations. These cooperative relations between such a variety of actors are termed multi-level actor partnerships here.

Actor partnerships have been addressed in International Relations' scholarship mainly under the heading of global policy networks (Reinicke and Deng 1999; Dingwerth 2004), public-private partnerships (Börzel and Risse 2005; Huckel, Rieth and Zimmer 2007; Beisheim, Liese and Ulbert 2007; Schäferhoff 2009) or inclusive multipartite institutions (Rittberger 2009). The partnerships investigated here have some common characteristics with all of these kinds of actor arrangements. Like public-private partnerships and policy networks, they are institutionalized forms of cooperative relations between the public and the private engaging in norm implementation (Börzel and Risse 2005: 198; Reinicke and Deng 1999: vii, ix–x; Dingwerth 2004). To pursue a common objective, they mutually provide material resources, i.e. money, goods, and infrastructure, as well as immaterial ones, including knowledge, information, and experience (Brühl and Liese 2004: 166; Huckel, Rieth and Zimmer 2007: 118; Beisheim, Liese and Ulbert 2007: 253).

Nevertheless, multi-level actor partnerships are also distinct from policy networks, public-private partnerships, and inclusive institutions. Their partners, for instance, are not equal in agenda-setting and conducting a policy process like in public-private partnerships (compare Huckel, Rieth and Zimmer 2007: 116). Stakeholders in Bangladesh's partnerships do not have the same decision-making powers like in inclusive institutions (Huckel, Rieth and Zimmer 2007: 116) and the actors' cooperation cannot be described as non-hierarchical like in policy networks (compare Reinicke and Deng 1999; Huckel, Rieth and Zimmer 2007: 117). In addition, the partnerships examined here are not necessarily of a trans-boundary nature comprising several state governments (Reinicke and Deng 1999: vii; Beisheim, Liese and Ulbert 2007: 247). They are rather characterized by their multi-level character. This vertical outreach makes them indispensable for transporting norms from the global to the local, whenever governmental capacities are lacking. Meaning and functioning of these transnational actor arrangements, in particular with respect to participating local partners, however, have been neglected and under-researched in International Relations scholarship (compare Liese 2009: 194).

This section concentrates on partnerships that have evolved around children's rights implementation. Therefore, experiences made by solely governmental undertakings, such as FFE and PESP, and by exclusively non-governmental projects like CLEP will be left aside in this part. The objective here is to investigate actor partnerships that were discovered in the empirical analysis. The focus of this investigation is on the types of cooperating actors, the responsibilities and functions they take in a partnership and the regulatory level at which they operate. Inductively derived from the evidence at hand, three different groups of partnerships can be identified.[28] These are (1) partnerships between the national government and local NGOs, (2) partnerships between IOs, the national government and local NGOs, and (3) partnerships between IOs, the national government, the domestic private sector and local NGOs. In the following, examples of such partnerships – derived from the seven cases considered – will be further investigated. The analysis is based on evaluation reports and expert interviews undertaken; it focuses on the emergence and functioning of these partnerships as well as on the roles and responsibilities actors take therein.

5.2.1 Partnerships between the government and local NGOs

Within the framework of the EHCL project, a partnership between the government of Bangladesh and local non-state organizations evolved. Due to a lack of governmental infrastructure and staff in the targeted urban slum areas, the Ministry of Labour and Employment (MoLE) has engaged NGOs to take over implementation activities at the grassroots level. In this partnership, the government provides necessary financial and other required resources, among them school books and learning materials, stipend money, and additional funds needed to conduct the baseline survey, to rent the center facilities, and to pay the salary of teachers.[29] It also offers management and administrative support through its PIU.[30]

With the help of governmental funds, non-state organizations have commenced program realization by conducting a survey to identify children in hazardous occupations that are out of school. First contacts are usually established through house-to-house visits and calling community meetings. Implementing NGOs motivate and convince targeted children to participate in the project, they gradually withdraw children from hazardous occupations, maintain good relations with the beneficiaries' parents, and establish local institutions, such as the CMCs. In addition, non-state organizations set up the required infrastructure, like education and training centers, and hire teachers from within each community to instruct the working children.[31] In general, NGOs also communicate with the employers persuading them to let child laborers employed in their businesses participate in educational programs,

28 Due to the limited number of cases and the great variety of actor constellations present, the elaboration of a typology or rather – since the classification is empirical and not conceptual – a taxonomy, does not seem appropriate or methodologically sound. Therefore, what is undertaken here is merely called a uni-dimensional classification (Bailey 1994: 4) resulting in the establishment of three groups comprising seven cases. This implies that although these groups are both exhaustive and mutually exclusive (Bailey 1994: 3), some of them contain unique actor constellations. Nevertheless, this highlights the emergence of partnerships that might be worth further qualitative exploration.

29 Interview Sanwar Moni, Padakhep, Coordinator Executive Director's Secretariat, 1 July 2008.

30 Interview Shahid Uz Zaman, ESDO, Executive Director, 6 July 2008.

31 Interview Sanwar Moni, Padakhep, Coordinator Executive Director's Secretariat, 1 July 2008.

initially only for a few hours per day. Equally important, they urge them not to hire any children who are below the age of 14 in the future.[32]

An integral function of local NGO partners can be described as maintaining a dialogue with entire communities on children's rights issues, usually leading to an awareness process among them. To counsel a neighborhood on rights related to children, local organizations frequently engage respected community members to act as multipliers.[33] The overall aim of the counseling process is to ensure that community ownership for the skills training and NFE centers is emerging: "[...] that is the schools of the community so [...] that means, that is the ownership of the community".[34] This fosters a project's long-term impact and sustainability. For the delivery of their implementation services, NGOs receive a monthly service charge of 125 BDT per student attending the program. This sum is allocated by the MoLE.[35]

To execute the EHCL project, local non-state organizations like Padakhep, Jano Seba Kendra (JSK), and the ESDO were selected as grassroots partners. Selection criteria required an NGOs' proper registration with the governmental NGO Affairs Bureau, a department of the Prime Minister's office, their expertise pertinent to NFE and the elimination of hazardous child labor, their existing management capacities, their liability, reputation, relations to the government, and previous experience in implementing similar projects.[36] NGOs themselves applied for the implementation assignment through an open bidding process. They claim to pursue the objective of assisting the poor and vulnerable. Overall, they see themselves in the role of a facilitating agency towards the project beneficiaries.[37]

5.2.2 *Partnerships between an IO, the government and local NGOs*

A different kind of partnership emerges in cases in which an IO is the initiator of the undertaking, and project realization is carried out in cooperation with the national government and implementing local NGOs. Among the cases considered here, there are several examples of collaboration between these diverse actors, such as BEHTRUWC and both ILO/IPEC (DoL and Net) projects. With an international actor at stake, the distribution of roles and responsibilities in project implementation turns out to be different from what was observed in the previous case.

BEHTRUWC, for instance, was designed by two major stakeholders, UNICEF and Bangladesh's MoPME. Its realization on the ground is

32 Interview Shahid Uz Zaman, ESDO, Executive Director, 6 July 2008.

33 Ibid.

34 Ibid.

35 Interview A.N.M. Shamsuddin Dewan, JSK, Director, 26 June 2008.

36 Interview Sanwar Moni, Padakhep, Coordinator Executive Director's Secretariat, 1 July 2008.

37 Ibid; interview A.N.M. Shamsuddin Dewan, JSK, Director, 26 June 2008, Interview Shahid Uz Zaman, ESDO, Executive Director, 6 July 2008.

undertaken by a number of local NGOs. Here, the Ministry's own PIU, which draws on its divisional staff, is responsible for field coordination and administration from the governmental side involving supervision, monitoring, evaluation, management, and planning.[38] Next to its role as a donor, which is shared with the Canadian and Swedish International Development Agencies, CIDA and SIDA, UNICEF provides technical assistance and builds capacities not only through the delivery of financial resources, but also with technical assistance like the delivery of school materials or the establishment of a financial management system. Further capacity-building measures involve training of executing NGOs' staff and project teachers.

Implementation at the grassroots level is, again, conducted by 20 non-state organizations chosen through an open bidding process.[39] Local implementation in this case implies establishing and opening learning centers, selecting students according to certain predetermined criteria, training teaching staff, trying to mainstream NFE graduates into formal schools,[40] and convincing employers to let their child employees participate in the NFE program. To legally commit the implementing partners to all of these responsibilities, contractual agreements between them and the government exist. These document that:

> [...] NGOs' main responsibility is to, through some survey, identify the learners [...] and then they select the learning centers, they rent the learning center, they organize the learning center, they form a center management committee with the help of the, the participation of the community people, the influential people around the learning center and they recruit teachers, they recruit the supervisors and they recruit also their coordinator[41] who will be exclusively looking after this project [...] so these are the main actors at the field level so they are responsible for [learner] selection, learning center organization and to provide basic education to the children through teachers and supervisors. [...] the NGO is also involved to organize the social mobilization events; [...] mobilization and advocacy [...] awareness raising activities planned under this project, so NGOs are extensively used [...].[42]

This statement highlights the broad range of assignments that local partners are supposed to carry out. At the local level, they are recognized as the main actors who take over all of the vital responsibilities in the rights implementation process. Overall, the role that NGOs play as local implementers can be summarized as that of a social agent:

38 See also: interview Rezaul Quader, MoPME, Project Director, 8 July 2008.

39 Interview Hasina Habib, GSS, Coordinator Field Education Programme, 9 June 2008.

40 See also: interview Musbah Alim, CATALYST, Executive Director, 19 June 2008.

41 The coordinator, however, is a representative of the implementing NGO itself (interview Rezaul Quader, MoPME, Project Director, 8 July 2008).

42 Interview Mohammad Golam Kibria, UNICEF, Education Section, Education Officer, 4 June 2008.

> Social agent is one of the role they are playing, I mean, social agent to changing the society, the attitude, behavior of the society from one stage to another stage, I mean, the overall attitude and behavior of the community, I mean, to change [behavior] towards education and child rights and all other development issues as a social agent and at the same time, they play the role of a promoter of child rights issues and other issues related to children, they are always trying to promote and also they are like key actor for social development in the country [...].[43]

These key actors for social development are selected by UNICEF and Bangladesh's government after an official announcement in the daily newspapers has been made. With this call for tenders, a bidding process commences from which a number of applying NGOs is chosen in an evaluation process according to their implementation proposal, their economic viability, administrative functioning, their expertise and project experience, and their capability to provide qualitative NFE.[44] Other relevant selection criteria are their organizational capacity, their human resources, their network within the country, their recognition and acceptance in the respective locality, and their access to the targeted communities.[45] These eligibility measures were developed by the government in cooperation with UNICEF and are based upon previous project experience with local partners. Governmental committees scrutinize NGOs' submissions and prepare a list of appropriate implementers that are then passed on to the Prime Minister's office for approval. In the first phase of BEHTRUWC, 150 NGOs conducted the project on the ground. To improve the quality of the program, the government decided to work with a more manageable number of implementing agencies in the second round and, therefore, appointed only 20 NGOs.

Different types of actors who cooperate at various levels in a tripartite constellation are to be found within both ILO/IPEC projects as well. In the case of ILO/IPEC USDoL, however, not only project initiation was taken on by an IO in cooperation with Bangladesh's MoLE. Administrative functions, including financial monitoring and controlling, were also mainly carried out by the ILO field level staff. It was a team of ILO field workers who conducted the baseline survey in the targeted areas[46] to identify the beneficiaries. Moreover, the ILO provided the funding for this project channeled by one main donor, the US Department of Labor (USDoL). Support from the national ministry was very limited compared to the government's engagement in BEHTRUWC. This ILO/IPEC project also constitutes the only case in which local project

43 Ibid.

44 Interview Rezaul Quader, MoPME, Project Director, 8 July 2008, Interview Hasina Habib, GSS, Coordinator Field Education Programme, 9 June 2008.

45 Interview Rezaul Quader, MoPME, Project Director, 8 July 2008.

46 Interview Md. Hamidul Islam, BDSC, Assistant Director, 24 May 2008.

realization is being shared. NGOs, on the one hand, take over home visits, all forms of direct interaction with the children, their parents and employers, and they form the required community committees. ILO field workers, on the other hand, organize area-based meetings and seminars.[47] This means that not only non-state organizations, but also field staff hired by the ILO, engage as actors at the grassroots level. However, NGOs take over major parts of project realization by integrating their own context-based ideas, especially within the framework of the advocacy and awareness-raising component:

> [...] there are a lot of advocacy programs we had there like popular theater we took this issue [...] and by the drama we tried to make awareness among the people. There sometimes of rally, [...] meetings, seminars, workshops leaflets, and billboard some [...?] thing also.[48]

Altogether, in this project, NGOs themselves described their role as that of a mediator who takes over primary responsibilities in a process that transports norms of international conventions to the local sphere and relevant rights-holders: "[...] our main assignment is to promote the sense of human rights and child rights in the community".[49] Within the framework of their action programs, local NGOs withdraw children from hazardous occupations in different work sectors, arrange learning centers for NFE, and empower adolescents and family members through income-generating activities and the provision of micro-credits. Non-state organizations also take care of the delivery of health care and nutrition services and conduct advocacy and awareness-raising activities. In cooperation with ILO field workers, NGOs try to bale their influence on the community through the involvement of local government officials and religious leaders.

To conduct this program, local NGOs had to submit technical proposals according to the respective terms of reference prepared by ILO/IPEC. Selection criteria were determined by the ILO and included previous project performance, professional expertise in supporting working children or children who have dropped out of school, and capabilities for providing NFE and skills training. Access to micro-credit facilities and experiences in loan management additionally played a role. On that basis, the ILO contracted NGOs to execute action programs on the ground. Hence, similar to the role that local NGOs took in EHCL, these non-state actors have become active as local implementers.[50] From the perspective of one of the non-governmental implementing partners, NGOs chose to take over executive responsibilities in

47 See also: interview Profulla Chandra Barman, Bangladesh Rural Advancement Committee (BRAC), former Project Coordinator, 17 July 2008.

48 Ibid.

49 Interview Md. Hamidul Islam, BDSC, Assistant Director, 24 May 2008.

50 Interview Nazrul Islam Miah, ILO, Administrative and Finance Assistant, 24 June 2008.

this project, because they disposed of the necessary capacities and envisioned the empowerment of the poor.[51]

The remaining ILO/IPEC Net constitutes a project initiative planned by an IO in cooperation with Bangladesh's MoLE and with financial support from the Kingdom of the Netherlands. After governmental approval, the ILO entered into a contractual arrangement with selected NGOs. The content of these contracts spelled out the implementation of one or more of the project's action programs. Within the framework of ILO/IPEC Net, pre-selected NGOs were involved in designing the action programs that they were supposed to conduct. This ensured each NGO's project ownership and the availability of necessary capacities and resources. Whereas NGOs executed particular program activities, the ILO, at the same time, tried to further strengthen their capacities with the help of trainings closely related to their work. From IPEC's perspective, the role of implementing NGOs included the involvement of the entire community in target areas, to create accountability towards the project beneficiaries, and to manage their programs in a transparent and solution-oriented way.[52] In this project, again, local level activities were divided between ILO field workers who, for instance, collected the data necessary for the baseline survey and for identifying children, and local NGOs who took over the bulk of program execution at the grassroots level.[53] The procedure in which the implementing partners engaged is quite similar to what was described for the other two projects in this section: local NGOs identify beneficiary children usually at their workplaces, they try to build a relationship of trust with relevant employers and parents or even the religious leader, and they convince them to let the child laborers take part in NFE and vocational training programs, which gradually leads to their withdrawal from hazardous workplaces.[54] Awareness about children's rights issues is additionally raised among the entire targeted community through the initiation of social activities, such as street dramas or rallies.[55] For the parents of beneficiaries, opportunities for alternative income sources and empowerment are offered and managed by the NGOs as well.[56] These comprise microcredit and training in income generating activities. One NGO representative summarized these tasks as conveying all necessary field activities:

> And our role was mobilizing the community, sensitizing the parents, working with the employers to help the children to get out of hazardous work. As it was all field level activities we have been doing.[57]

51 Interview Profulla Chandra Barman, BRAC, former Project Coordinator, 17 July 2008.

52 Ibid.

53 Interview M. Ehsanur Rahman, DAM, Deputy Executive Director, 25 May 2008.

54 Interview Ronald E. Berghuys, ILO/IPEC Chief Technical Advisor, 19 May 2008.

55 Interview Aftab Uddin Ahmad, Underprivileged Children's Educational Programs (UCEP), Executive Director, 25 June 2008.

56 Interview Ronald E. Berghuys, ILO/IPEC Chief Technical Advisor, 19 May 2008.

57 Interview M. Ehsanur Rahman, DAM, Deputy Executive Director, 25 May 2008.

Here again, NGOs describe their own role as one of a catalyst or a facilitating institution that simultaneously tackles various issues such as education, livelihood, and health. Responsibilities of local NGOs within one program, however, can vary. Whereas some implementers are concerned with persuading children, parents, and employers simultaneously of the importance of letting child laborers take part in NFE; other NGOs, especially those delivering micro-credit services, only deal with the parents of beneficiary children. For this task-sharing to run smoothly, inter-organizational coordination has to function.[58] Executing NGOs' assignments include the establishment of local infrastructure and corresponding institutions, such as MPCs and CMCs in which they constitute one group of representatives.[59] Other stakeholders, like parents, teachers, the local government, elite community members, and social workers, however, are equally involved.[60]

The project management recruited cooperating local non-state partners according to the program's mandate and following United Nations and, more specifically, the International Programme on the Elimination of Child Labour (IPEC) rules. An open bidding process was initiated through ILO/IPEC, which published corresponding terms of references in daily newspapers. As a response to the bidding process, NGOs submitted their proposals for project implementation. This was followed by a scrutinizing process on the basis of a whole set of pre-determined criteria established by the ILO. To be eligible for implementation, the existing capacities of applying NGOs play an important role, such as a specialization in offering NFE and vocational skills training. Of further relevance were their outreach and the existence of an appropriate administration system besides their image, reputation, and overall profile.[61] The responsible ministry had to approve of both the selection criteria applied and the organizations chosen by ILO/IPEC to conduct the program. To bale their strengths, NGOs in this project established strategic partnerships with individual actors to provide certain services that were difficult for them to cover. Examples are health services offered by welfare hospitals and high-nutrition biscuits that were delivered by the World Food Program (WFP). Both, the hospitals and the WFP, were not initially contracted by the ILO but joined the project at a later stage to contribute to an additional program outcome.[62]

Considering these partnerships between an IO, a governmental ministry and local NGOs, two major observations need to be highlighted. First of all, various actors complement each other. This explains why usually diverse types of actors collaborate. If the government lacks local staff and infrastructure, it

58 Ibid.

59 Interview Ronald E. Berghuys, ILO/IPEC Chief Technical Advisor, 19 May 2008.

60 Interview Abul Haseeb Khan, RIC, Director, 26 May 2008.

61 Ibid, and interview Aftab Uddin Ahmad, UCEP, Executive Director, 25 June 2008, interview Ronald E. Berghuys, ILO/IPEC Chief Technical Advisor, 19 May 2008.

62 Interview M. Ehsanur Rahman, DAM, Deputy Executive Director, 25 May 2008.

engages NGOs to work with the communities and to establish learning centers and administrating committees. Many of these non-state partners are well acquainted with certain areas of Bangladesh and their local residents, which makes it easier for them to convey the message of children's rights.

Second, there are cases in which governmental involvement is higher, such as in EHCL and in BEHTRUWC. Here, the MoLE and the MoPME are closely involved in project management, administration, and supervising implementation. In both ILO projects, however, the government plays a less significant role which is limited to approving the most important decisions in scope and design of the project. Instead of engaging in field coordination and management, administration, supervision, and monitoring, like in EHCL and BEHTRUWC, the MoLE assigns an IO, the ILO, to take over these functions. Hence, multi-level actor partnerships with lower and higher governmental involvement can come into existence.

Only very rarely, more than three types of actors are involved in a policy program. In Bangladesh, such a partnership emerged when the private sector, the BGMEA, decided to co-engage in the realization of children's rights in the garment sector. As a consequence, responsibilities were again allotted differently between the various partners. An example of a multi-level actor partnership that comprised four diverse kinds of actors, the BGMEA/ILO/UNICEF, is introduced below.

5.2.3 Partnerships between IOs, the private sector, the government and local NGOs

Another project initiative under consideration in this set of cases took advantage of combining the various strengths of the entire range of actors. The BGMEA/ILO/UNICEF *Garment Sector Projects* comprised two IOs simultaneously, the ILO and UNICEF,[63] in addition to the national MoLE and local non-state organizations. It also involved considerable initiative from the private sector, the BGMEA. Project costs and planning, in this case, were divided between the signatories of the MoU, namely the ILO and UNICEF, the government, and BGMEA. The first three phases of this multilateral undertaking were financially supported by the USDoL, whereas the two extended components received funding from the Norwegian Agency for Development Cooperation (NORAD) and the Italian Social Partners Initiative (ISPI) (ILO/IPEC 2004a: 50).

Prior to project implementation, an initial survey was conducted by the ILO, UNICEF, and BGMEA to identify underage children in Bangladesh's

63 This project has become a regional and international role model and constitutes the first technical cooperation project in which the ILO and UNICEF culminate their endeavors in the fight against child labor (ILO/UNICEF 2004: 17).

garment factories (ILO/IPEC 2004a: 1).[64] Educational endeavors in this project were – for the most part – directed and financed by UNICEF. Non-state partners with a specialization in providing NFE set up the required local infrastructure by establishing learning centers and initiating relevant institutions like the SMCs. Moreover, they recruited and trained necessary teaching personnel and provided the required learning materials (ILO/UNICEF 2004: 9; ILO/IPEC 2004b: 16).[65] NGOs also interacted with the parents to convince them to let their underage children leave the factory and join alternative education programs instead. They counseled entire communities, among them the employers, and discussed various issues relevant to children's rights.[66] In this project, teachers were trained to not only pass on basic education and vocational skills, but also to function as some kind of social worker to counsel the target communities:

> If any student does not come to our school consecutive two days, then teachers has to go to the community, what are the reasons for not coming to the schools and they try to motivate their parents, if their parents disagree with their suggestion that they should go to the school, then what they do is, they go to the community leader to make them convince to send their children in the schools. And we just always organized a parents/guardian meeting [...] and we try to disseminate the information relating to the importance of education and relating to the importance of health, hygiene, relating to the importance of behavioral change.[67]

Throughout project realization, NGOs remained in close contact and communication with the community members, engaged in social mobilization and awareness raising, delivered vocational training services to the project beneficiaries and assisted their graduates in finding decent workplaces according to their qualifications acquired in the course of the program.[68] UNICEF and the ILO, for their part, concertedly guided and supervised the skills development training. In a joint effort, the BGMEA, together with the ILO and the MoLE conducted the withdrawal process of underage children from the garment factories (ILO/IPEC 2004a: 2). This team of three partners also recruited and trained monitors with the aim of establishing a garment factory labor inspection system within the framework of the "Three Party Monitoring and Verification System" (ILO/IPEC 2004a: 23).

64 However, information on surveying differs; some NGOs claim to also have collected data (for example: interview Md. Monwer Hossain Khandker, BRAC; Programme Manager, Field Operations BRAC Education Programme, 8 June 2008). It might be the case that initial data had to be verified by the implementing partners.

65 See also Interview Md. Monwer Hossain Khandker, ibid.

66 Ibid, see also interview M. Mohiuzzaman, UCEP, Manager Technical Education, 2 June 2008.

67 Interview M. Mohiuzzaman, UCEP, Manager Technical Education, 2 June 2008.

68 Ibid.

After submitting project proposals in an open bidding process, local non-state organizations had been selected as implementers mainly according to their past experiences in project realization. Non-governmental partners were chosen with respect to their organizational strengths, capacities, transparency, and openness. Most of them had a strong reputation for their teaching methodology, the quality of their non-formal or vocational education models[69] and the achievement rates of their students.[70] Local NGOs took the role of complementing governmental work, especially in areas in which the government's capabilities and human resources were limited.[71] They describe themselves as the main and direct implementers[72] in this policy program. According to their own assessment, they pursue the aim of making a difference in the lives of urban working children and of creating intergenerational change.[73]

5.3 Actor partnerships as governance institutions

More is not always better. It cannot simply be assumed that a multi-level actor partnership baling the multitude of strengths and resources of a large number of actors is necessarily the most successful in fostering children's rights at the local level. Key to the local implementation process, instead, are local NGOs. They act as transmitting agents between IOs, the government and the rights-holders.

Whereas an NGO, the government or an IO can function as the initiator, designer or planner of a policy program and can engage in supervision, monitoring, and administration, local actors are always needed for successful implementation on the ground. This is particularly the case whenever the government lacks resources, expertise and capacities to comprehensively implement the rights it has ratified and to provide for pertinent rights-related services. If local government officials cannot take over certain functions, such as establishing infrastructure and administrating institutions, non-state partners have to be contracted in order to do so. In the case of children's rights implementation in Bangladesh, all of these contracted non-governmental partners were local NGOs.

Within the framework of the transnational rights promoting projects investigated, IOs, the national government and local NGOs institutionalize on a

69 Ibid, see also: Ali Hossain Sarder, GSS, Regional Coordinator Monitoring and Evaluation, Education Programme, 22 June 2008.

70 Interview Ali Hossain Sarder, GSS, Regional Coordinator Monitoring and Evaluation, Education Programme, 22 June 2008.

71 Interview Rafique Uddin Ahmed, ILO/IPEC/UNICEF/BGMEA garment sector projects; former ILO National Project Coordinator, 18 June 2008.

72 Interview Md. Monwer Hossain Khandker, BRAC; Programme Manager, Field Operations BRAC Education Programme, 8 June 2008.

73 Interview M. Mohiuzzaman, UCEP, Manager Technical Education, 2 June 2008.

temporary basis. By taking over traditionally governmental implementation responsibilities, multi-level actor partnerships build a governance institution. These are characterized by a vertical diversification – due to integrating international and local actors – and by a horizontal diversification – through the involvement of civil society and private business actors. Governing human rights with the help of multi-level actor partnerships is an ambiguous undertaking. On the one hand, it means that governmental implementation deficits can be compensated in weak state contexts in which a state government has ratified human rights and does not lack the willingness – but rather resources and capacities – to realize them for the respective rights targets. These governance institutions usually have, on the other hand, a temporary character. This means that they can initiate a local rights implementing process during the time period in which a project is operative. In the course of that time, an IO in cooperation with a governmental ministry can plan a policy initiative and local NGOs can establish an infrastructure, respective institutions and can take care of the provision of rights-related services. After the project has terminated, however, the initiative has to be upheld to continue rights implementation for the societal target group. The next chapter provides some more critical thoughts on what happens beyond project outcomes.

In most projects, funding and technical assistance is allocated by external donors. These could be trade union councils for international development cooperation, as in the case of CLEP, donor countries or their ministries, like the Kingdom of the Netherlands or the USDoL in the *ILO/IPEC Net* and *ILO/IPEC DoL*, or partial funding from private employers' associations, such as the BGMEA in the *Garment Sector Projects*. In this analysis, external donors were not explicitly treated as actors unless they took an additional role in project design, planning, supervision, monitoring or administration. The large amounts of donor money involved, however, made it difficult to distinguish local non-governmental implementers from small private companies. The empirical reality often proved that these forms of contracted service delivery turned out to become commercial. This is not entirely surprising if one considers how implementation proposals are evaluated according to certain pre-determined criteria following an open bidding process. This, in many cases, leads to competition between the contractors, considering the fact that there is a substantial amount of money invested by the donors of such programs. These sums were managed by the selected NGOs in the course of the implementation process. In order to strengthen their own capacities – one important criterion for being selected by an IO – NGOs hired additional personnel and tried to strengthen their own administrative knowledge and financial resources. In the end, they competed like entrepreneurs for gaining the next lucrative development contract.

Table 5.2 summarizes the entire classification of actor constellations, which includes the groups described, the types of actors, and the sharing of responsibilities among the various partners in the projects under consideration.

Characteristic of these partnerships is their multi-level character. In contrast to what was described in IOs scholarship on global policy networks, these actor constellations are PPPs that are hierarchically organized. Responsibilities are usually divided between actors of the higher levels, i.e. IOs and the government, that undertake policy planning and supervisory functions. Actors at the lower level, i.e. NGOs, are responsible for all implementation activities on the ground. Despite their incremental growth, particularly in developing countries and in weak state contexts, multi-level actor partnerships, and the responsibilities involved actors take therein, have – until today – not yet been closely investigated in IRs. In Bangladesh, these partnerships, without a doubt, take a crucial role in temporarily compensating governmental implementation deficits and in transporting norms from the global to the local level.

Table 5.2 A classification of multi-level actor partnerships implementing children's rights in Bangladesh

Actor constellations	**Single actor initiatives**		**Partnerships between the government and local NGOs**	**Partnerships between IOs, the government and local NGOs**		**Partnerships between IOs, the private sector, the government and local NGOs**
Type of actors	***Solely non-governmental***	***Solely governmental***		***Higher governmental involvement***	***Lower governmental involvement***	
Local NGOs	planning, supervision, monitoring, administration, local implementation (setting up infrastructure and institutions, providing social services)		local implementation (setting up infrastructure and institutions, providing social services)	local implementation (setting up infrastructure and institutions, providing social services)		local implementation (setting up infrastructure and institutions, providing social services)
Government		planning, supervision, monitoring, administration, local implementation (setting up infrastructure and institutions, providing social services)	providing financial and other resources, planning, supervision, monitoring, administration, implementation support	planning, supervision, monitoring, administration	initiation and approval	providing financial resources, capacity building, monitoring, field assistance

Table 5.2 (Continued)

IOs	providing financial and other resources, technical assistance, capacity building	providing financial resources, administration, technical assistance, capacity building, field assistance	providing financial and other resources, planning, supervision, monitoring, capacity building, field assistance
Private actors			providing financial resources, monitoring, capacity building, field assistance, guaranteeing access

Chapter 6

Beyond project outcomes: reflections upon local children's rights change

> [...] but if the project is withdrawn, just as per completion of this phase, then [...] the impact of the project will not be sustained.[1]

Most of the cases considered here are development projects characterized by temporary effects and funded with the help of external donor money. Although all of these policy initiatives were successful in implementing at least one of the children's rights principles examined in this case study, their impermanency and aid-reliance raise a number of questions relating to sustainability. Particularly relevant are the following: What exactly happens after project termination? Does the established infrastructure remain in place? Are services continuously provided and if so, by whom, using what resources? Do children and their communities at the grassroots level experience persistent change regarding their rights and are they able to multiply what they have learned or been made aware of?

This chapter is an attempt to tackle some of these questions and concerns. Of significance here is whether indicators pointing to a long-term impact can be identified in the policy activities analyzed. This study has been careful about estimating program impact as the third dimension of effectiveness (compare Underdal 2004: 34). It has been argued that the temporary nature of the projects, the scarcity of accurate data at hand and the unavailability of follow-up reports make an impact evaluation a difficult endeavor. According to Underdal (2004: 34), an impact is visible whenever the problem at stake (i.e. deficiencies in protection from the worst forms of child labor and insufficient provisions of education and health services), has been significantly reduced. Due to the obstacles named above, such a significant reduction could not be comprehensively demonstrated in this study. The Children's rights change observed was rather limited within the temporary and target area-based frame of the projects investigated.

1 Interview M. Ehsanur Rahman, DAM, Deputy Executive Director, 25 May 2008.

In this research, outcome has been defined as norm targets making use of the protection measures and provisional services offered through policy programs. Some indicators discovered in this study, however, point to achievements initiated by these project activities that reach beyond a mere program outcome. Hence, one goal of this chapter is to describe indicators that suggest a development towards impact and to group the programs considered according to the sustainability indicators detected. The indicators identified are based on empirical evidence that: younger siblings of former child laborers are sent to school (6.1), increased governmental education investments can be observed (6.2), children start to claim their own rights (6.3), awareness raising can be sustained within the target communities (6.4), income generation is continued among the groups concerned (6.5), and that a governmental monitoring system could be established (6.6). For all of these indicators, project examples will be outlined.

Additionally, this chapter places an emphasis on infrastructure, institutions, and services that do remain in place after the respective project has phased out. If something lasts, it is important to identify who is operating it and with what kind of funding – another descriptive step undertaken here. Moreover, the interview partners' reflections on possible long-term impacts pertinent to children's rights realization and sustainable local change are presented. Perspectives of the implementing partners will be particularly highlighted, since they have been the closest to the beneficiaries themselves. Opinions from representatives of international organizations (IOs) or the government, on the other hand, will also be emphasized to critically reflect the performance of local non-governmental organizations (NGOs).

The objective of this chapter is to create a mixture of "hard facts", the measurable quantitative outcome, and "soft facts", a non-measurable impact that can only be assumed at this point. This combination of sustainability indicators, outcome figures, and soft facts (including the experiences and reflections from stakeholders collected) aims at drawing a picture that goes beyond outcome, a picture that comes closest to an impact evaluation.

6.1 Siblings are sent to school

An important indicator pointing to an impact beyond the framework of a project is that siblings of former child laborers are sent to formal governmental schools although their families do not receive additional incentives. If parents and children are making such a decision, the awareness that education is important could be decoupled from receiving material incentives. In such cases, families have realized the importance of education and have explored ways to make primary schooling feasible without the support of a project or a facilitating NGO. This also means that the younger siblings either do not work at all or combine work and school. If this practice can be habitualized, child labor will be further decreased and an increase in primary education can be achieved. Both point to an impact with respect to children's rights implementation, an impact that is observable beyond a temporary project outcome.

One example for siblings' formal school enrollment is the Bangladesh Institute of Labour Studies (BILS') *Child Labour Elimination Project* (CLEP). In the course of its operation between 2002 and 2008, CLEP has reached out to 1,386 non-formal education (NFE) graduates, while 3,144 beneficiaries profited from skills training.[2] A quantitative evaluation surveying the initial 480 vocational school graduates between January and December 2007 found that 36.46 percent of the former students were self-employed in the trade they had been qualified for, whereas 1.66 percent engaged in a different trade. Another 27.29 percent found employment in the profession they had learned, while 8.54 percent were occupied elsewhere, and 5 percent remained unemployed. A few children, 7.08 percent, moved away to other places, 6.04 percent entered continuing education programs, and 5.62 percent dropped out. Early marriages still occurred, albeit affecting only a small number of 2.29 percent girls (Hossain 2008: 14). With the provision of NFE, skills training and health services for these children, two of the three indicators for implementation success applied in this study have been met.

After project termination, established institutions like the center development committees composed of government representatives, trade union delegates, and other community people are supposed to remain in place as a counseling body that multiplies the message of children's rights protection and promotion. These committees and substantiated ties to the local trade union movement are considered aspects of a long-term impact lasting beyond CLEP's termination. According to CLEP's former project coordinator, children are, as a consequence of project participation, aware of their basic rights including protection from hazardous occupations and the right to education and to health. Their teachers had – prior to project implementation – received a special children's rights training. Thus, rights consciousness could be included into the NFE curriculum and passed on to the project beneficiaries. Awareness was also fostered through workshops, games, and cultural activities in which children were engaged.[3]

Since CLEP has still been ongoing at the time of data collection, it is not entirely clear whether the center development committees will indeed remain in place as a counseling body on children's rights. Besides these institutions, it seems like none of the infrastructure or service providing components will be continued after project termination. However, beneficiary families send the siblings of former program participants to school, indicating that awareness of the right to education could be raised. Considering that the

2 Recent data from personal e-mail correspondence with Sajjad Hossain (former Project Coordinator of the BILS/CLEP Project), 7 November 2009.

3 Interview Sajjad Hossain, BILS, CLEP Project Coordinator, 21 May 2008.

enrollment of siblings is not rewarded with any beneficial provisions such as a stipend or any other incentives, this indicates that parents are aware of the meaning of education.[4] And most probably, there will be a long-term impact on the individual future of those children who have received education and skills training, and their families.

6.2 Increased governmental education investments

The significant increase of investments in education indicates that Bangladesh's government is taking more and more responsibility for implementing the right to education. By enabling a growing number of children to attend formal basic education, an impact with respect to strengthening primary schooling, eliminating illiteracy, and possibly reducing hazardous child labor could already be achieved. In the framework of the *Food for Education* (FFE) Programs, the governmental expenditure on primary education has increased from 4.7 percent in 1993/94 to 19.9 percent in 1997/98. Governmental spending on education has continuously grown since then, attaining a peak in investments on primary education at the time the *Primary Education Stipend Project* (PESP) was introduced in 2002 (Rahman, Kabir and Alam 2005: 8). The PESP's budget for the project period between 2002 and 2008 accounted for 60 percent of Bangladesh's total development budget available for primary education (Tietjen 2003: 31). Governmental investments in primary education have demonstrably resulted in considerable enrollment increases and gender parity in primary education in Bangladesh. Hence, in this case, a program impact with respect to fostering universal primary education for both genders and reducing the problem of illiteracy could be ensured. Escaping the intergenerational cycle of illiteracy will most probably result in a change of the rights situation among target children and their families.

At the moment, the PESP is reaching out to 5.5 million beneficiary children in 62,000 primary schools. Most of the students who have received food or stipend benefits have continued their education to the high school level. Girls in particular were at risk of dropping out prior to finishing secondary school. Due to poverty, they often had to get married at an early age. School survey results reveal that over a period of two years, from the year prior to FFE's introduction to the year after, students' enrollment had increased by 35 percent, with a remarkable increase for girls by 44 percent (Ahmed and del Ninno 2002: 16). Other evaluation studies point to reduced drop-out rates, which are at 6 percent among FFE beneficiaries compared to 15 percent among non-beneficiary students (Ahmed and del Ninno 2002: 18). School duration has also increased for program participants; different evaluations reports indicate that children spent between 0.56 and 0.7 more years in

4 Ibid.

educational institutions (Meng and Ryan 2003: 25; Meng and Ryan 2007: 21). Additionally, food consumption by beneficiary households could significantly be enhanced (Ahmed and Babu 2007: 6). The increase in school enrollment, attendance, and duration, as well as the reduction of drop-out rates lead to a higher number of children receiving primary education and being encouraged to continue education. Due to the programs' educational focus, only one of the initially defined implementation indicators has been met.

Although the project's concept did not comprise any advocacy or awareness-raising component, students as well as their families and teachers have learned from the FFE and PESP initiative. Whereas basic children's rights are being taught in primary schools to stipend receivers and non-receivers likewise, social gatherings around the programs support the entire community's learning about civil and social rights. During project implementation, seminars involving all school management committee (SMC) members including teachers, local elites, government officials, parents, and guardians are being held. Explaining the project's design to community people underlines important issues relating to basic human rights, such as the right to education, and the promotion of gender equality. Mothers, for instance, are the ones who receive the bank cards needed to collect the stipend money. This helps to empower their role within the family. Whereas initially, parents might start sending their children, particularly the girls, to school to receive material benefits, they gradually realize the positive effect of school education on their children and start assigning meaning to it. The Deputy Director of the PESP describes this awareness process in the following way:

> [...] through this project, particularly the stipend project, we are providing seminars and symposiums at Upazila level, seminars and at that seminar, school teachers, guardians [...] local elites, school managing committee members, they are coming and they are listening, what has to be done and [...] what should be avoided [...] and through this they are learning, they are listening and it is the total process from which they are being enlightened, they are learning the children's right, women's right, the social rights, their citizen's rights.[5]

Due to the FFE's and PESP's wide outreach – in combination with the effects of other educational provisions from various policy initiatives – girls' and boys' school enrollment is at par in Bangladesh today. This leads to a change in common expectations about societal gender roles among both women and men. Girls are decreasingly getting married below the age of eighteen and therefore are not bound to remain in private as housewives and mothers anymore. They are expected to be at least basically literate and to contribute

5 Interview Tapan Kumar Chakravorty, Ministry of Primary and Mass Education, Primary Education Stipend Project, Deputy Director, 17 July 2008.

to the family income accordingly. Completing the secondary education level qualifies them to take positions in the governmental sector, allowing for young women to be emancipated from working in garment factories and breaking the reproduction of traditional gender roles. With more and more women on the labor market, their decision-making power in the public sphere is considerably increased. This constitutes a long-term impact and a change in Bangladesh's society summarized by the Deputy Director of the PESP as follows:

> And after that, a good mother never keeps her children illiterate. If I am SSC [Secondary School Certificate holder, A.S.], I'll try my best to keep my daughter or my son at least graduate, it is the common expectation of a guardian. I am literate, I don't want to be, to keep my son illiterate [...]. He or she must be literate and must go to the, to the [ideal] level. So it is the long-term benefit and they are also providing long-term contribution to the society.[6]

The PESP Deputy Director describes the project as effective at the local level, mainly because the rights holders – identified through a two-step targeting procedure – directly receive their stipend benefits. This helps maintain the whole family properly. Pre-determined conditions, such as regular school attendance and certain achievement rates, make the project a demand-side intervention and contribute to the program's success.

Although FFE and its successive PESP have only promoted one of the children's rights examined here, the right to education, both have had (and PESP still has) a considerable outcome. The programs have reached out to a significant number of children and fostered their school enrollment and attendance. As a demand-side intervention based on certain conditions, they utilize already existing infrastructure and institutions for service delivery. Hence, instead of supplying new schools or any kind of service centers, they demand compliance with certain conditions, such as regular school attendance, and educational achievements. This also means that the infrastructure will most probably remain in place even after project termination and students might be able to continue schooling there even though their stipend cannot be delivered anymore. There is also a chance that school management committees continue awareness-raising activities.

There are several indicators pointing to a program impact beyond its outcome. First of all, the government of Bangladesh provides the funding of this initiative; the programs even led to a general increase in governmental expenditures on primary education. Hence, the government takes responsibility for promoting the right to primary education in accordance with the UN *Convention on the Rights of the Child* (CRC). FFE and PESP furthermore

6 Ibid.

contribute to a significant increase in enrollment and a decrease of drop-out rates, while at the same time promoting gender equality among enrolled students. This not only enhances literacy rates in the country but results in breaking with traditional gender roles. The PESP is one of very few long-term, government-funded initiatives independent of external donor money. Therefore, chances are good that it might sustain until major problems relating to primary education in Bangladesh are resolved. This, indeed, points to an educational impact beyond a mere program outcome.

6.3 Sustained awareness raising

In some cases considered here, awareness on protecting children and promoting their rights could become so deeply anchored within the target communities that they continue to spread this message beyond the program's limited frame. Community support is valuable for keeping this awareness alive after the executing NGOs have left the areas they have supported. Since most of the children are simply too young – and still too uneducated – to claim their rights without assistance, they need backing from their social environment. This often goes hand in hand with an attitudinal change; instead of viewing them as mere income-earners, they become respected in their role as school children. If communities manage to keep multiplying the message of children's rights beyond a project's scope, families will – even without external financial and material provisions – find ways to make education possible for their descendants. Whenever children still need to work to contribute to the household income, they will most likely not be forced to perform the worst forms of child labor. And in some cases, when health services are available to them, increased rights awareness will lead to a situation in which these will be used extensively. This indicates that even beyond the programs' scope, a further implementation impact can be expected.

In two of the projects considered here, significant evidence for sustained awareness-raising activities could be established by the interview material at hand. Since the *Preventing and Eliminating the Worst Forms of Child Labour in Selected Formal and Informal Sectors in Bangladesh* Project (ILO/IPEC USDoL) also featured a number of additional impact indicators, it will be discussed elsewhere. The governmental *Eradication of Hazardous Child Labour Project* (EHCL) outcome data, in the form of impact assessments or evaluation reports, are not (yet) published. Nevertheless, in its third phase between 2010 and 2013, the project's objective was to reach out to 50,000 child laborers engaged in hazardous occupations, to withdraw them, and to provide them with NFE and skills training. Since precise data are not available, it is difficult to estimate the extent of the program's actual outcome. Nevertheless, on the basis of a field visit to four learning centers in Hazaribagh, Dhaka, and the annual report of one of the implementing NGOs during the second phase of project implementation (the Eco-Social Development Organization (ESDO), supplying 300 students with NFE[7]), it can at least be claimed that some kind of – quantitatively indeterminate – outcome can be observed. An unknown number of children have been withdrawn from hazardous workplaces and provided with basic education and skills training.[8] Hence, two of the three initially defined implementation indicators have been successfully met.

After project termination, children will most probably not return to the worst forms of child labor as stated by representatives of the implementing local NGOs, Padakhep, Jano Seba Kendra (JSK) and the ESDO. They are expected to be in an improved economic and social position and aware of the health risks related to some occupations. Micro-credit opportunities and skills development will enhance chances of former child laborers to become employed at safer workplaces.[9] Due to the fact that other options have evolved and their rights consciousness could be strengthened, parents will prevent their children from entering risky jobs.[10] Enabling a community dialogue that is responsive to children's concerns encourages the whole environment to multiply the message of rights protection.[11] This is an important indicator for global children's rights principles reaching the local level:

> Now all the community people, they are highly positive to provide their all support from their heart-felt realization about the issue of hazardous child labor. [...] So they are continuing the process, now they realized and provide a lot of support to the issues of children, save the children to the non-formal education center, have regular follow-up in the community level; that is one of the major successes and my observation.[12]

This comprehensive assistance leads to a changing role for children and adolescents within their families and communities. Their empowerment, based on literacy and vocational education, enables them to participate in decision-making.[13] The concept of rights, however, remains abstract for most of the families. What definitely changes with the project cannot be described as detailed knowledge on certain conventions but some kind of awareness on

7 Mostofa 2008: 1.

8 The field visit, however, revealed that not all of the children in the education centers have been withdrawn from hazardous workplaces. Short interviews with them uncovered that a few of them were still occupied in the leather tanneries of Hazaribagh, where working conditions were particularly risky (see also: own notes from field visit EHCL with Golam Mostofa (Programme Officer), learning centers of the ESDO in Hazaribagh, Dhaka, 10 July 2008). But observing that the project is operating and providing services to the beneficiaries suggests that there is an outcome even though its extent remains unclear.

9 At the time the interviews were conducted, the program was still in the two-year NFE phase and skills training as well as the micro-credit component had not started yet.

10 Interview Sanwar Moni, Padakhep, Coordinator Executive Director's Secretariat, 1 July 2008.

11 Ibid.

12 Interview Shahid Uz Zaman, ESDO[, Executive Director, 6 July 2008.

13 Interview Sanwar Moni, Padakhep, Coordinator Executive Director's Secretariat, 1 July 2008.

fundamental rights principles through information provided by the center management committee (CMC) and NGO staff.[14]

Representatives of the implementing partners reckon that the eradication or at least the reduction of hazardous child labor constitutes a long-term impact of the EHCL project. The provision of information and education will change children's attitudes and possibly lead to shifting priorities and to making different choices.[15] Apart from families' changed perceptions on children's rights, employers' position on recruiting under-age workers could be altered, leading to a decreased use of child laborers in their businesses.[16] A coordinator of Padakhep, one of the implementing partner organizations, revealed that local change was made possible by directly addressing the local people involved and by accompanying them on their way to claim their rights:

> [...] this is the root of the sustainability, I think, because if we don't involve the local people, we are the outsider, [...] but they are the people, their area; [...], if we aware them, [...] then they are the actual factors to sustain the project.[17]

This means that besides the program's outcome, which cannot yet be grasped in concrete figures, an implementation impact through the participation of the target communities in awareness-raising activities can be observed. This impact is expected to sustain beyond the EHCL's scope.

Even though EHCL's outcome is observable in the communities, its precise extent cannot (yet) be measured or quantified due to a lack of available data. Nevertheless, an indefinite number of children are being withdrawn from hazardous occupations and supplied with NFE. At least one of the implementing NGOs, ESDO, claims that it will continue providing social services to the families in respective target areas, even beyond program termination. Since the project is still ongoing, it remains unclear whether this will indeed take place after the third phase has run out. The interviews conducted point to significant community support when it comes to disseminating the message of children's rights protection and promotion. This indicates that the awareness raised in the social environment of these child laborers might indeed sustain and contribute to an implementation impact beyond EHCL's scope.

6.4 Children claim their rights

Another impact indicator is closely interlinked with a sustained awareness on children's rights in the target communities but relates more to the rights-holders, i.e. the children, themselves. If children are aware of their

14 Ibid.

15 Ibid.

16 Interview Shahid Uz Zaman, ESDO, Executive Director, 6 July 2008.

17 Interview Sanwar Moni, Padakhep, Coordinator Executive Director's Secretariat, 1 July 2008.

rights and if institutions facilitating rights protection are available, these children may start claiming their own rights. In Bangladesh, children have – in some cases – addressed CMCs, executing NGOs, and teachers whenever they felt that basic entitlements pertinent to their work, education, and health have been denied by their social environment. Children also directly referred to their rights when they complained about violations. As a consequence, committees and actors could systematically intervene and provide for children's protection. The fact that children actively demand compliance points to an increased understanding of their own rights. This consciousness will spread among entire communities and it will, most probably, last beyond the project's scope. Hence, an empirical situation in which children claim their own rights indicates that an implementation impact could be achieved.

An example of this scenario is the *Basic Education for Hard to Reach Urban Working Children* (BEHTRUWC) program. It provided 517,150 children with basic NFE and 166,150 of them with livelihood skills training between 1997 and 2009. For these students, 6,646 learning centers were established during the second project phase, mostly in urban disadvantaged or slum areas (GoB/BNFE 2008: 13).[18] The project's main purpose was to provide education services to urban working children, an aim that could be achieved in accordance with the education indicator determined above. By focusing on a target group between ten and 14 years of age, it additionally fosters a minimum age for admission to employment of 14 years. Although under-age children are not being withdrawn from hazardous occupations, they work less during their participation in the NFE program and receive support from the teachers and of the learning centers. With such a strategy, the United Nations International Children's Emergency Fund (UNICEF) implements the so-called learn-and-earn approach. With the help of a life skills component and separate skills training elements offered by NGOs, children and adolescents are being prepared to (re-)enter the employment market at the age of 14, preferably under improved working conditions or in more decent jobs.

Although, at the time of data collection, BEHTRUWC's long-term impact had not yet been examined by any kind of long-term assessment, interviewees from UNICEF, the ministerial Bureau of Non-Formal Education (BNFE), and local implementing partners provided their expert evaluation on the future activities of the children. Mohammad Golam Kibria, education officer at UNICEF, stated that most of the children will continue to work in the jobs they had been engaged in from the inception of the program on.[19] This could be confirmed by representatives of the implementing organizations.[20] Only in some cases did parents insist that their children should continue education, usually in governmental primary schools.

18 Ultimate figures from the outcome of the second phase which lasted until 2012 are not yet available.

19 There was no withdrawal component at work in this project.

20 Interview Musbah Alim, CATALYST, Executive Director, 19 June 2008.

Nevertheless, some effort was put into advocating for children's rights. The provision of supplementary school materials and the initiation of interactive popular theaters, street dramas, group works, and plays helped bringing fundamental rights principles closer to the children and their families. As a consequence, change is obvious in local people's attitude and awareness:

> [...] the changes we found that their attitude, their behavior, the way they talk, they think, their imagination [...] and their awareness level and their attitude in the workplace. That kind of changes happened actually and that, basically, that was the benefit of the beneficiaries.[21]

Increased awareness about their workplace situations, including the risk of exploitation or hazards, strengthened children's bargaining power towards their employers. In many cases, this led to negotiated improvements in working conditions.[22] Members of CMCs can be approached for help by BEHTRUWC's participants whenever their rights at the place of employment or in their social environment are denied. This has led to children gaining confidence about their own entitlements and enables them to claim their rights.[23] The fact that children demand help from the CMC or from teachers and refer to their rights when issues are discussed, indicates that their actual level of awareness of basic rights principles has been raised.[24]

The provision of NFE enhances students' opportunities to receive vocational training or to mainstream into formal schools.[25] Beneficiaries pursuing an education program start attaching a certain value to learning opportunities. The empowering effect education has on children also becomes visible in their increased participation in decision making. Children's roles within their own families are starting to change. Valuing education is usually passed on to the next generation and eventually leads to breaking the cycle of illiteracy and poverty in the long run.

After finishing BEHTRUWC's education program, some children decided to join vocational trainings offered by the implementing NGOs in the respective target area, that were carried out apart from the main project. Children who participated in it could indeed change their workplaces afterwards due to the new skills they had acquired.[26] The importance of vocational training,

21 Interview Mohammad Golam Kibria, UNICEF, Education Section, Education Officer, 4 June 2008.

22 Interview Musbah Alim, CATALYST, Executive Director, 19 June 2008, see also: interview Rezaul Quader, MoPME, Project Director, 8 July 2008.

23 Interview Hasina Habib, Gono Shahajja Sangstha (GSS), Coordinator Field Education Programme, 9 June 2008.

24 Interview Khandaker Asraful Islam, Bangladesh Development Service Center (BDSC), Deputy Director, 24 May 2008.

25 Interview Mohammad Golam Kibria, UNICEF, Education Section, Education Officer, 4 June 2008.

26 Ibid.

a component which was not part of this program until 2008, has been emphasized by implementing organizations as crucial for achieving a long-term impact with respect to abolishing child labor.[27] Nevertheless, employment opportunities are still rare, in particular, decent ones. If decent workplaces would increase, chances for BEHTRUWC and other projects to have sustainable effects would improve.[28]

A few NGOs maintain their learning centers in target areas with the support of separate external funding, even though the project phase has already terminated. In these cases, they uphold close ties to the local community and convince siblings of former beneficiaries to join their education program.[29] BEHTRUWC's governmental project director, based at the Ministry of Primary and Mass Education (MoPME), confirms that a long-term impact can only be sustained if the government increases its support and comprehensively engages entire local communities:

> [...] not only aware, to involve all these people; we'll also have to involve all these people. Without the government servant support, in our country it is difficult to sustain anything. It needs government support in each and every sphere. This is our mentality in our country. If government never supports anything, then that will die. Those thing will totally die.[30]

This statement makes reference not only to the need for more governmental backing and more initiatives reaching out to the local level but also to integrating people at the margin of society. NFE for working children, for instance, has only been offered within the framework of specific projects or through NGOs' services, often involving external funds. This is in sharp contrast to Bangladesh's reality, with 7.4 million economically active children, among them almost 3.2 million child laborers (BBS 2003: 63).

In order to achieve sustainable local change pertinent to children's rights, a permanent infrastructure for the delivery of educational and social services has to be established.[31] These services need to comprehensively reach all members of the society, including working children. UNICEF's representative, Mohammad Golam Kibria, confirmed that transnational development programs like BEHTRUWC are a way of transporting key principles of children's rights from the international to the grassroots level, an assessment that is shared by the local implementing partners as well.[32] Regulative mechanisms

27 Interview Musbah Alim, CATALYST, Executive Director, 19 June 2008.

28 Ibid.

29 Interview Hasina Habib, GSS, Coordinator Field Education Programme, 9 June 2008.

30 Interview Rezaul Quader, MoPME, Project Director, 8 July 2008.

31 Ibid.

32 Interview Hasina Habib, GSS, Coordinator Field Education Programme, 9 June 2008.

used in these projects, according to Kibria, constitute instruments of local change:

> [...] we are promoting not maybe the convention as a whole but the main, basic ingredients, the core things, [...] based on these articles, we are trying to put those issues in the curriculum, in the life skills component, in the social mobilization activities, I mean, whatever the way, [...] we are trying to promote these things just to make them, educate them about the child rights issues, to promote child rights issues.[33]

Hence, major principles of international children's rights conventions are called into life at the grassroots level through social mobilization, life skills training, and NFE.

Next to the provision of NFE services to 517,150 children, this project promotes the legal minimum age of 14 years for admission to employment in Bangladesh. After the first project phase ran out, a few implementing NGOs were able to maintain their infrastructure, i.e. the learning centers, in the target areas and offered skills training opportunities to the former BEHTRUWC beneficiaries. Due to a strong advocacy and awareness-raising component in this program, children started demanding help from local CMCs in cases where they felt that their rights had been denied – an indication of an impact that might last beyond the project termination. With the maintenance of infrastructure and services by the non-governmental partners, the siblings of former project participants were provided with non-formal schooling and could enjoy their right to education as well. This has led to a strengthening of ties between NGOs and local communities. Eventually, the integration of siblings, established interaction channels with affected communities, and the fact that children are in a position to claim their rights suggests that a program impact will take effect even after the project implementation phases have run out. This impact relates to reducing illiteracy among children engaged in all forms of child labor in Bangladesh's poor urban areas.

6.5 Employers refrain from recruiting children

Another relevant impact indicator is that employers' rights awareness could be raised to an extent that makes them refrain from recruiting children. As elaborated in earlier sections of this book, especially informal businesses operating at the edge of economic survival rely on child labor. Many business owners are not aware of the fact that recruiting underage children into hazardous forms of labor is prohibited by international and national law. If these employers are successfully integrated into program strategies that

33 Interview Mohammad Golam Kibria, UNICEF, Education Section, Education Officer, 4 June 2008.

reveal economic alternatives to them and that convince them of the devastating effects that child labor might have on young workers, they will – in the long-run – try to rely on adult employees. Hence, children will simply not be recruited into certain forms of occupation anymore. If the employers' awareness in this respect can be upheld, an impact towards reducing hazardous child labor beyond the outcome of local policy initiatives can be observed.

In two of the projects considered here, ILO/IPEC USDoL and the *Garment Sector Projects* (BGMEA/ILO/UNICEF), such awareness among employers could be observed. Both have, to a large extent, intervened in formal working sectors, e.g. the bidi and the garment factories. This suggests that persuading owners of formal businesses to refrain from recruiting child labor is much more feasible. At the same time, Bangladesh's governmental monitoring system is evolving and employers most probably also hesitate to recruit children in fear of sanctions and penalties. The development of a functioning governmental monitoring system is another indicator of effectiveness considered here; it can most evidently be observed with the implementation of the BGMEA/ILO/UNICEF. Hence, ILO/IPEC USDoL is elaborated in greater detail as an example of employers refraining from recruiting underage children.

Despite a comparatively short project implementation period of only four years,[34] the USDoL-funded ILO/IPEC USDoL achieved considerable outcome rates. Overall, 8,826 children could be withdrawn from hazardous workplaces and 353 domestic child workers were provided with safer working conditions. About 19,191 child laborers received NFE and 30,175 of them participated in some form of counseling, health, and referral services offered with the support of local partners. Between 2000 and 2003, 7,305 children could be mainstreamed to formal education and 6,550 families were supplied with income-generation training and/or a micro-credit (ILO/IPEC 2003b: 16). Taking account of the number of children withdrawn from hazardous workplaces and their provision with NFE and health services, all three implementation indicators were met. Interviewed project stakeholders unanimously agreed that most of the targeted working children were ultimately withdrawn from hazardous occupations. Many of these former child laborers could be integrated in formal primary or secondary government schools after a bridging period in which they received NFE.[35]

34 The project duration had been extended to four years in 2003; this means, the implementation phase was going on until 2004. All the figures mentioned here are taken from the mid-term evaluation and relate to the period between 2000 and 2003 (see also ILO/IPEC 2003b).

35 Interview Md. Harun-or Rashid, Lighthouse, Executive Director, 20 May 2008, Interview Profulla Chandra Barman, Bangladesh Rural Advancement Committee (BRAC), former Project Coordinator, 17 July 2008.

Afterwards, their opportunities to engage in decent employment were considerably increased.[36]

Before ILO/IPEC USDoL became initiated, no government officials monitored the bidi factories or knew in detail what the situation there was like. Nowadays, government inspections take place regularly.[37] Another important program effect suggesting a continuous program impact is that former child laborers' siblings in the target areas immediately join formal primary schools, usually after they have attended the project's own pre-schooling institutions. Awareness has been raised not only among direct beneficiaries who now seek to be educated and are concerned about their own health.[38] Even the bidi factory owners consciously refrain from recruiting workers below the age limit of 14 years.[39] They are also increasingly sensitized about children's rights and they know about the national legal provision for admission to employment as well as the detrimental effects that working in bidi factories might imply for children.[40]

Visible changes – the establishment of schools or the provision of educational materials and micro-credits – contribute to a change in people's minds and attitudes.[41] Parents, in particular, begin to consciously review their own responsibilities towards their children and towards protecting their rights:

> [...] they came to know these children have rights to go to school for education, no? And for parents came to know, "we have rights to protect them from that types of activities, that types of harmful activities" and they came to know, "we need to send my children to their school for education for future [...] for his or her good positions, no?" So for this reasons we were about to raise awareness among the parents and local community also.[42]

Parents' and children's roles were modified with this project initiative. Whereas parents incrementally take on their responsibility to protect children and provide for the bulk of household income on their own,[43] children regularly attend school and do not work in factories anymore.[44] Nevertheless, children keep contributing to their family's earning by undertaking light and non-hazardous occupational activities.[45]

36 Interview Md. Hamidul Islam, BDSC, Assistant Director, 24 May 2008.

37 Interview Profulla Chandra Barman, BRAC, former Project Coordinator, 17 July 2008.

38 Interview Md. Hamidul Islam, BDSC, Assistant Director, 24 May 2008.

39 Interview Profulla Chandra Barman, BRAC, former Project Coordinator, 17 July 2008.

40 Ibid.

41 Ibid.

42 Interview Nazrul Islam Miah, International Labour Organization (ILO), Administrative and Finance Assistant, 24 June 2008.

43 Ibid.

44 Interview Profulla Chandra Barman, BRAC, former Project Coordinator, 17 July 2008.

45 Interview Md. Hamidul Islam, BDSC, Assistant Director, 24 May 2008.

Not only children's roles and responsibilities have altered; their own awareness can be observed in the way they raise their voices towards their families and demand to be educated.[46] Another important indicator pointing to the meaning that children's rights have gained is that community members and elites have started own initiatives like awareness-raising workshops[47] in the target areas.

Learning about the worst forms of child labor and predominant sectors in which these occur has also had a lasting effect on other relevant stakeholders. NGOs and even ILO staff themselves profited and gathered knowledge on hazardous child labor in Bangladesh and they can follow-up and multiply these experiences in their forthcoming programs. Thereby, capacity building, in terms of strengthening human resources and rights consciousness, belong to the project's impact and will most probably reduce the problems pertinent to the children's rights at stake.[48]

For transporting global norms to their local rights-holders, actors had to reach out to the people at the grassroots level and involve the employers of local businesses in the formal and the informal working sectors. Although NGOs can take the role of a transmitter here, increased governmental involvement is needed to make this change sustainable. However, until today, government officials lack the required expertise and capacities for starting a comprehensive and country-wide movement in support of children's rights. After donors withdraw from the projects and external funding expires, the government needs to take over and continue the effort initiated within the framework of a project.[49] Sustained change at the local level requires support beyond a pre-determined project period; support that needs to be backed by the government. Implementing partners disposing of larger capacities, such as BRAC, respond to this need for support by offering bridging programs with extended services to their beneficiaries:

> BRAC as the organization, we have lot, different types of activities [...] to engage them, to employ them in different [...] activities, by different income-generating program in the school, in the health program but if it was not possible to other organizations I think, the project will not be sustainable.[50]

Thereby, even after ILO/IPEC USDoL's expiration, pre-school facilities, micro-credit opportunities, and some income-generating training conducted by BRAC have remained in place.[51] This ongoing support creating links to

46 Ibid.

47 Ibid.

48 Interview Nazrul Islam Miah, ILO, Administrative and Finance Assistant, 24 June 2008.

49 Ibid.

50 Interview Profulla Chandra Barman, BRAC, former Project Coordinator, 17 July 2008.

51 Ibid; interview Md. Harun-or Rashid, Lighthouse, Executive Director, 20 May 2008.

alternative education and employment programs is even more important in areas lacking established industries and opportunities like the ones in which this ILO program was operative.[52] Hence, its outcome is not only in accordance with all three of the implementation indicators determined, it was also possible to maintain the infrastructure of the more capable NGOs, such as BRAC, which continue to provide rights-related services. Furthermore, the government started conducting monitoring visits to the bidi factories, which constitutes a program strategy that will remain in place beyond its termination. Other indicators for lasting change are that factory owners from now on refrain from recruiting underage children, siblings from the target areas immediately join formal primary schools, and that community members and elites independently initiate awareness-raising workshops.

6.6 Sustained income-generation

Throughout the projects considered here, various income-generating components have been assessed. Many of them work with micro-credits, a prominent regulative mechanism promoting self-reliance introduced in Bangladesh and copied in many other parts of the world. On a community basis, micro-credits can be used to help out one another through providing a loan to a member who aims to shift reliance on their children's contribution to the household income towards reliance on self-employment, e.g. in a family business. Whenever a micro-credit system runs smoothly, it can sustain itself from the dues and interest rates paid back by the other loan takers in the same community. Hence, it can continue even after the project that installed it has already terminated. In this way, an income-generation component can achieve an impact beyond the initial project objective and outcome. The only income-generation component that has ultimately sustained itself, among the range of programs considered here, is the *Prevention and Elimination of Selected Worst Forms of Child Labor in the Informal Economy in Dhaka City* Project's (ILO/IPEC Net's) micro-credit mechanism. With the help of this strategy, child labor could be reduced by 100 percent and school enrollment considerably increased in households that participated in multiple loan cycles (Bannerman and Berghuys 2008: 40). The micro-credit component has remained in place even after ILO/IPEC Net's pilot phase was terminated.

Sponsored by the Government of the Kingdom of the Netherlands, the ILO/IPEC Net helped to withdraw about 12,032 children from hazardous occupations (ILO/IPEC 2006: 23) and improved the conditions of 200 workplaces (Bannerman and Berghuys 2008: 41). The NFE program has been successfully completed by 20,000 children (Bannerman and Berghuys 2008: 30). Whereas 1,282 former child laborers graduated from the initial

52 Ibid.

vocational training module (ILO/IPEC 2006: 24),[53] only 180 students succeeded in the newly established skills development component (Bannerman and Berghuys 2008: 43). All of the graduates from NFE, as well as from vocational training, improved their health status and their awareness about health issues (Bannerman and Berghuys 2008: 36, 42). After accomplishing the educational courses offered, more than 50 percent of the children continued working. However, their status as employees had significantly changed:

> After completing the NFE programme, children at work were much less likely to be apprentices and much more likely to be wage employees or, in a significant minority of cases, self-employed. The wages these children earned had also increased substantially. (Bannerman and Berghuys 2008: 42)

With an increased awareness of hazards encountered at their workplaces, most beneficiary children were able to leave the worst forms of child labor (Bannerman and Berghuys 2008: 33).[54] In addition, about 9,500 guardians became supplied with micro-credits that were distributed in several loan cycles. Altogether, about 16,000 loans could be granted (Bannerman and Berghuys 2008: 28, 43).[55] Some implementing partner NGOs, such as DAM and the Resource Integration Centre (RIC), continued their support to the beneficiary children and their families even after the project had phased out. While DAM's own centers kept offering NFE,[56] the micro-credit component RIC has been conducting keeps running and sustains itself.[57] This, however, was only possible for these two service-providing NGOs that had built up considerable capacities even prior to program implementation.

A major deficit preventing a long-term impact of this policy project was that the overall infrastructure was not taken over by the government after the pilot phase as initially agreed upon:

53 The old vocational training component was conducted by the Underprivileged Children's Educational Programs (UCEP) with considerable limitations in its concept. Besides restraints in infrastructure, children did not have the choice of learning the skills they wanted to and prospective employers did not consider the training received as beneficial. Of the 1,282 children who graduated from the old program, only 330 could be placed in wage-employment, whereas 279 were listed as self-employed. All of the 673 children who could not be placed at all were left without future prospects. In 2003, a re-designed skills training module was set up for this project (ILO/IPEC 2006: 24).

54 Interview Ronald E. Berghuys, ILO/IPEC Chief Technical Advisor, 19 May 2008.

55 Parents and guardians participating in only one loan cycle, i.e. taking only a single credit and then trying to repay it, experienced a considerable decline of their economic situation, which led to a doubling of working children in their families. If multiple loans were taken, a 100 percent decrease of child labor could be observed (Bannerman and Berghuys 2008: 40).

56 Interview M. Ehsanur Rahman, DAM, Deputy Executive Director, 25 May 2008.

57 Interview Abul Haseeb Khan, RIC, Director, 26 May 2008.

> [...] we've been fighting like hell to, to bring the whole infrastructure over to the second phase and for bureaucracy, government bureaucracy and so, we seem to fail to do that, really, it was an incredible disappointment not only for us but in particular for these communities where we worked. They were very pissed, simply very, very pissed [...].[58]

The fact that the established multi-purpose centers could not be maintained says something important about the project's sustainability. Although the immediate objectives of the ILO/IPEC program have been achieved, and thereby, relevant children's rights were fostered, only a limited number of rights-holders could profit from this. Even after years of successful project implementation, the basic infrastructure for providing rights-related services to these children had to be dismantled and will, again, be re-established for the next project phase.

For the project beneficiaries at the local level, the concepts of rights and conventions remain to be abstract. In order to make them aware of basic children's rights principles, implementing NGOs usually start with explaining visible things such as injuries caused by hazardous working conditions:

> Rights is in the book, in the law book or conceptionally this is abstract, it cannot be touched. What people can touch, what can people feel is, what is visible is whether their income level is low or high whether their work the children engaged in, whether that affects their life or not, whether they become sick or whether, what is the direct effect of this hazardous work on the health of the child [...], what is the level of education of the parent [...] so we start talking on the visible things.[59]

This provides parents and guardians with a fundamental understanding of children's rights and convinces them to respect them. Children learn about rights issues with the help of cultural strategies; through acting, rhyming, and playing, rights gain meaning and become an integral part of their thinking.[60]

In the course of project realization, children start enjoying and valuing learning. Multi-purpose centers offer a child-friendly environment in which they are exposed to their peers and, in some cases, play for the first time in their lives. One important indicator of an increased awareness of children's rights is that most former child laborers enroll in government schools or other educational institutions after program termination.[61] Even three years after

58 Interview Ronald E. Berghuys, ILO/IPEC Chief Technical Advisor, 19 May 2008.

59 Interview M. Ehsanur Rahman, DAM, Deputy Executive Director, 25 May 2008.

60 Ibid.

61 Interview Abul Haseeb Khan, RIC, Director, 26 May 2008.

enrollment, 61 percent of the previous beneficiaries were attending school, of which 20 percent combined school and work (Bannerman and Berghuys 2008: 30). Another indicator that points to a program's impact and to a situation in which education is valued was that younger siblings of beneficiary children were sent to school instead of to work. This also demonstrates the multiplying effect advocacy initiatives can have:

> It's not only that you have been able to rehabilitate one child, but it has, it trickles down, the overall idea that education is, is more valued, has increased and also because [...] you have been able through other programs to increase their income level which also means that they don't need to send the siblings to work to survive as a household. But that in combination with simply valuing education better, seeing that your kids simply remain healthier and that they are happier.[62]

Ronald E. Berghuys, Chief Technical Adviser for this ILO/IPEC project, additionally mentioned two crucial aspects that come together with enjoying the right to education. He, first, emphasizes how education is the key to changing a society in which certain political elites dominate a "feudal system".[63] Education is indispensable for the development of a critical mass on the ground that starts breaking with hierarchical traditions, that participates in decision-making, and that shapes the change they envision. Second, he reminds us how increased awareness on education entitlements raises expectations that these are indeed provided:

> So that's why I was so incredibly disappointed that we had to cut down our infrastructure, that we had to dismantle it because we had raised expectation levels, we had raised value levels [...] which will sustain and then you can't provide it. It's like making people aware but don't give them the option to do anything with it.[64]

Although the initial plan and agreement with the government was that the established multi-purpose centers should keep running on a self-sustaining basis – financed by revenues from the micro-credit component – the centers had to be closed and abolished. For the upcoming national ILO/IPEC Time Bound Program (TBP),[65] the government has demanded a new open bidding

62 Interview Ronald E. Berghuys, ILO/IPEC Chief Technical Advisor, 19 May 2008.

63 Ibid.

64 Ibid.

65 A comprehensive TBP was started for a preparatory phase in March 2004. It involves a donor consortium of DFID, NORAD, USAID, the ILO, UNICEF, and the Asian Development Bank providing technical assistance to the Government of Bangladesh to generate a policy and action framework in the fight against the worst forms of child labor (ILO/IPEC 2006: 10).

process that draws in other implementing partners and entirely re-establishes the infrastructure.[66]

The ILO/IPEC project intervention promotes children's rights and initiates a shift in the roles and responsibilities that children take. With the help of various measures taken, they are protected from illicit activities[67] and the worst forms of child labor. Although they are going to school on a regular basis, are proud of learning, and have more time for playing, they might contribute to their family's income, but in less hazardous jobs and working fewer hours. After completing skills training, they engage in higher qualified occupations and earn more. Better salaries lead to improved living conditions and an increased decision-making power in family affairs. The latter mostly concerns adolescents and their mothers who might be receiving a micro-credit.[68] Even though improvements in the living, working, and educational situation do not immediately lead to breaking the cycle of poverty, these factors definitely contribute to the social and economic development of beneficiary families.[69]

To initiate local change, international conventions need to be applied contextually and require translation into the realities at the local level:

> So it has got a lot of dynamics from global human rights issue, customize it or contextualize in the local grassroots level and this, this is a big challenge for the human rights activists, development activists, and I think even government and other stakeholders. How they translate and how they relate with the [...] local context.[70]

With respect to child labor, local contextualization means that the focus of abolishment should be on the worst forms. Education provisions need to be flexible and tailored to working children's demands and time schedules; basic health care services should be affordable and accessible even for children living in the urban slums or remote rural areas. Not the comprehensive conventions itself, but a fundamental understanding of children's rights are promoted among the people at the grassroots.[71]

Despite the fact that this project has met most of its immediate objectives, its sustainability and influence on local change is limited, which is clearly indicated by the vanishing infrastructure and interrupted service provision. Ronald E. Berghuys, Chief Technical Adviser of that project, expresses this very bluntly:

66 Interview Ronald E. Berghuys, ILO/IPEC Chief Technical Advisor, 19 May 2008.

67 Interview Abul Haseeb Khan, RIC, Director, 26 May 2008.

68 Interview Ronald E. Berghuys, ILO/IPEC Chief Technical Advisor, 19 May 2008, Interview Aftab Uddin Ahmad, UCEP, Executive Director, 25 June 2008.

69 Interview Ronald E. Berghuys, ibid.

70 Interview Abul Haseeb Khan, RIC, Director, 26 May 2008.

71 Interview M. Ehsanur Rahman, DAM, Deputy Executive Director, 25 May 2008.

> Has the overall situation changed? No! I mean the 50,000 we were able to get out through the front door were filled in by another 50,000 from the back[door]. The overall child labor situation with all our efforts, with all the 100 centers that we were running, with all the 600 people and staff who were working their ass off [...]. The overall child labor situation has not decreased but increased.[72]

With this statement, Berghuys emphasizes that change can only sustain if the root causes for children's rights denial are addressed comprehensively. Considering the case of Bangladesh, this means that project initiatives establishing infrastructure, institutions, and effecting mechanisms, such as income-generating and awareness-raising components, need to be transferred into the national system. In addition, employment opportunities have to be created, the quality of primary education has to be improved, and laws, policies, and enforcement mechanisms have to be strengthened.[73]

ILO/IPEC Net has not only promoted children's rights according to all three implementation indicators examined here. A small number of services could be maintained by partner NGOs even after the project was phased out. DAM managed to continuously provide NFE in its own learning centers and RIC's micro-credit module sustains itself with incoming revenues. This self-sustaining income-generating component emphasizes an impact beyond the project's scope. With the reliance on self-employed parents and other adult family members to provide for the household income, children can attend school and need not engage in the worst forms of labor. Hence, problems pertinent to illiteracy and hazardous child labor are continually reduced. Other indicators pointing to an implementation impact relate to the large number of former child laborers enrolling in formal government schools and their younger siblings who are immediately sent to school and do not start working at all. Both indicate a persisting awareness of children's rights among the target communities.

6.7 Governmental monitoring

If the capacities of the government can be built towards the establishment of a functioning national monitoring system, child labor in the formal working sector can be progressively eradicated. Governmental monitoring, in contrast to monitoring undertaken by NGOs, IOs or the private sector itself, ensures that national labor regulations are enforced through the application of legal sanctions. Furthermore, a well-trained governmental labor inspection team can undertake unannounced visits on a permanent basis and can advise the factory management continuously on issues related to children's rights. This

72 Interview Ronald E. Berghuys, ILO/IPEC Chief Technical Advisor, 19 May 2008.

73 Ibid.

is much more effective for reducing hazardous child labor and observing a minimum age for admission to employment than a group of external monitors that solely imposes sanctions during a limited project period. Hence, if a functioning governmental monitoring system is in place, the problem at stake, i.e. child labor or non-attendance at school, can be significantly reduced and an impact can be observed.

Two projects considered here have introduced capacity-building mechanisms for establishing a governmental monitoring system. These labor inspection teams have, in both cases, been effectively installed and now contribute to the elimination of child labor, first and foremost in Bangladesh's garment and bidi factories. The labor inspection team that was established in the course of implementing BGMEA/ILO/UNICEF was particularly successful. Monitoring the entire range of factories led to a complete elimination of child labor in the garment industry. By the end of the project period, the rate of child labor in Bangladesh's garment factories was at 0.96 percent of the factories' workforce (ILO/IPEC 2004a: 22). With the help of a continuing monitoring process, this impact could be sustained until today.

Concrete outcomes pertinent to the Bangladesh BGMEA/ILO/UNICEF remain fuzzy from the evaluation reports at hand. The figures listed describe that 40,000 to 50,000 children were dismissed from Bangladesh's garment factories before 1995, when another 28,154 child laborers were identified by the project staff as engaged in factory work (ILO/IPEC 2004c: 29). Although aiming at withdrawing 10,000 children under 14 years of age from workplaces in the garment factories, exact numbers on how many indeed could be pulled out have not been listed. In the course of the "intensive child collection drive", 5,674 child workers could be "identified" within six weeks of the project's first phase in October 1996 (ILO/IPEC 2004a: 2). In the following years, between 1998 and 2003, another 3,290 child laborers were identified and withdrawn from the factories. During this period of five years, regular monitoring visits resulted in a continuously decreasing number of child laborers observed in the factories. Whereas in 1998, 1,240 children were found in the factories, in 2003, only 24 under-age workers could be detected (ILO/IPEC 2004c: 22). Altogether, 31 percent, 8,588 of the 28,154 children identified in the factories, became enrolled in the 336 so-called Memorandum of Understanding (MoU) schools established between 1995 and 2001 (ILO/UNICEF 2004: 9). However, none of the evaluation reports listed how many of these 8,588 children have indeed completed the NFE program and how many former child laborers have dropped out. Another 2,035 children, 7 percent of the ones identified, completed the skills training module by December 2003. Altogether, 451 families received loans in the form of micro-credits (ILO/IPEC 2004c: 29). Most of the pre-formulated objectives of this project have been met with the withdrawal of child laborers from the factories, the development of a monitoring and verification system, awareness raising in- and outside Bangladesh, capacity-strengthening of the national labor inspection system, and the provision of services including education, skills training, and income-generation support. But can an impact beyond this program outcome be observed?

Due to the lack of tracer studies, too little is known about what happened to the beneficiary children once the project terminated. Interviewed ILO staff point to the fact that NGOs with sufficient capacities tried to integrate these children into their own programs. These comprise additional education, health or income-generating modules. Local committees and institutions that were set up within the framework of this project assisted former child laborers in acquiring higher education.[74] Those who did not continue education, but returned to work were more aware of the hazards at their places of employment; they engaged in more decent work arrangements and received higher salaries.[75]

All of the stakeholders interviewed unanimously agreed on the changes in awareness concerning children's rights that could be initiated through the Bangladesh BGMEA/ILO/UNICEF. It supported children's interest in and demand for receiving education, which they – at the end of the project – could articulate towards parents or even employers. Many former child laborers became conscious about the fact that there is no alternative to education facing the high demand for skilled laborers.[76] Furthermore, children were increasingly aware of risks at their workplaces and tried to avoid hazardous tasks and low-paid, exploitative jobs.[77]

As a consequence of the BGMEA/ILO/UNICEF, rights consciousness and sensitivity have grown among former child laborers and their families. Knowledge about education, health, hygiene, and gender issues, including legal protection for girls from early marriages, reproductive rights, and contraception, could be enhanced.[78] Rafique Uddin Ahmed, the former national project coordinator, emphasized that the whole project could only be successfully conducted because children, parents, guardians, the factory management, and entire communities changed their attitudes pertinent to children's rights and roles:[79]

74 Interview Rafique Uddin Ahmed, ILO/IPEC/UNICEF/BGMEA Garment Sector Projects, former ILO National Project Coordinator, 18 June 2008.

75 Interview Ali Hossain Sarder, GSS, Regional Coordinator Monitoring and Evaluation, Education Programme, 22 June 2008; Interview Engr. M. Mohiuzzaman, UCEP, Manager Technical Education, 2 June 2008.

76 Interview Engr. M. Mohiuzzaman, UCEP, Manager Technical Education, 2 June 2008.

77 Interview Ali Hossain Sarder, GSS, Regional Coordinator Monitoring and Evaluation, Education Programme, 22 June 2008.

78 Interview Md. Monwer Hossain Khandker, BRAC, Programme Manager Field Operations, BRAC Education Programme, 8 June 2008.

79 Interview Rafique Uddin Ahmed, ILO/IPEC/UNICEF/BGMEA Garment Sector Projects, former ILO National Project Coordinator, 18 June 2008.

> [...] before the project actually, their parents, that is the community leaders and the community people, they do not know the impact of education, they did not know actually the lack of awareness in relation to child rights, human rights, then hazardous areas, then the impact of education, they did not know. But after the project they came to know all of the things which helped them to change their mind.[80]

With this attitudinal change, children started to experience more support from their guardians and communities,[81] and instead of simply following their parents' life paths, they could make educated decisions regarding their own future.[82]

Bangladesh's garment factories are virtually child labor-free today. Towards the end of the project period in 2003, within nine months, only 49 children were discovered in 24 factories, accounting for 0.96 percent of the entire countries' factories and 0.004 percent of the total workforce in the garment sector (ILO/IPEC 2004a: 22). This can indeed be described as an impact, i.e. a significant reduction of child labor in Bangladesh's garment sector. Due to continuous monitoring, the factory management is forced and – at the same time – encouraged to keep their facilities free of underage workers.

Considering the lack of impact assessments and tracer studies, evaluating the long-term effects of the BGMEA/ILO/UNICEF remains a challenging endeavor. According to the implementing non-state partners' estimation, obtaining education and skills itself can have lasting implications for the lives of the children and for the generations that follow. Families valuing literacy and vocational skills pay more attention to the education of their own children.[83] Girls, in particular, are going to profit from this change of a communal mindset that breaks with traditional gender roles.[84]

Representatives of the implementing NGOs have highlighted that it is possible to reach children at the grassroots and to achieve change relating to their rights through these kinds of policy projects. NGOs' engagement in the education sector, however, is not a permanent solution and NFE should be institutionalized by the government in the long run. In addition, the media could be more intensively utilized to spread the message of children's rights, through radio and television broadcasting or through magazines and comic

80 Interview Engr. M. Mohiuzzaman, UCEP, Manager Technical Education, 2 June 2008.

81 Interview Rafique Uddin Ahmed, ILO/IPEC/UNICEF/BGMEA Garment Sector Projects, former ILO National Project Coordinator, 18 June 2008.

82 Interview Md. Monwer Hossain Khandker, BRAC, Programme Manager Field Operations, BRAC Education Programme, 8 June 2008.

83 Ibid.

84 Interview Ali Hossain Sarder, GSS, Regional Coordinator Monitoring and Evaluation, Education Programme, 22 June 2008.

books, as the example of Meena showed.[85] Any kind of project that is launched needs to be of a sufficient duration with regular evaluations that are utilized to address upcoming constraints. Project staff should be well-informed about the immediate and about the long-term development objectives pursued with these initiatives.[86] Last but certainly not least, the program's ownership has to be clarified and transferred from external actors, such as IOs or donor countries[87] to internal ones, most probably the state government.

The BGMEA/ILO/UNICEF design has served as a role model for abolishing industrial child labor even beyond Bangladesh's borders, predominantly in the South Asian region. With various strategies involved, it has managed to withdraw a substantial number of children from the factories and made them virtually child labor-free. This, indeed, counts as an impact since it has reduced the problem of child labor in Bangladesh's garment factories to almost zero. Through building the capacities of a national governmental monitoring system, the impact of this project not only relates to making the factories child labor-free, but also to keeping them free of underage workers. From this perspective, an impact beyond the project's outcome can be observed.

Moreover, the programs supplied many of the former child laborers with non-formal basic education and some of them with vocational training. Direct beneficiaries were below 14 years of age, which implies that the national minimum age for admission to employment has been fostered with their withdrawal. However, after project termination, only a few NGOs with stronger capacities could maintain the provision of education and income-generating services. Capacities of the governmental monitoring system could be considerably strengthened and monitoring visits continue until today. Skills and knowledge attained, and the awareness raised within respective communities, will hopefully be passed on to coming generations.

6.8 Some reflections on the situation of the girl child

An old Bengali saying reveals that "caring for a daughter is like watering a neighbor's tree" (Raynor 2005: 83). It reflects parents' hesitation to invest in their daughter's education, health care or nutrition since she will – after her marriage – belong to another family. In Bangladesh, this was for a long

85 UNICEF developed Meena, a South Asian rural girl and famous comic figure, as a communication initiative to disseminate information about basic children's rights principles. In her comic books and stories, Meena experiences adventures relating to the rights of girls. The concept was developed to make particularly rural children learn about their own fundamental entitlements (see also: interview Md. Monwer Hossain Khandker, BRAC, Programme Manager Field Operations, BRAC Education Programme, 8 June 2008).

86 Interview Engr. M. Mohiuzzaman, UCEP, Manager Technical Education, 2 June 2008.

87 Interview Rafique Uddin Ahmed, ILO/IPEC/UNICEF/BGMEA Garment Sector Projects, former ILO National Project Coordinator, 18 June 2008.

time perceived as a waste of scarce resources (ibid). Today, the situation of the girl child has changed considerably but is not yet equal to that of its male counterpart. In this part of the chapter, I will present some facts and some thoughts on the situation of girls in Bangladesh. First, I will briefly provide a gendered analysis of the three children's rights investigated in this book. Following upon that, I want to take a closer look at the different effects the policy programs examined here have for girls and for boys.

Data from the last National Child Labor Survey (NCLS) of the Bangladesh Bureau of Statistics (BBS) reveal that 2.5 million boys are child laborers, compared to 718,000 girls. About 1.17 million of these boys and 120,000 girls are occupied in the worst forms of work (BBS 2003: 63). Gendered data on child labor, however, are particularly unreliable as girl children are predominantly engaged in domestic labor or home-based work which is invisible to the public eye and not considered in such surveys:

> "While a large number of women and children are employed as domestic workers, there are no statistics available on their actual numbers. Because of the nature of work they are isolated within the home and given their lack of bargaining power they cannot negotiate their wage" (Hossain 2007: 145).

This means that our knowledge pertinent to girls' work is very limited. Shoishab Bangladesh, a domestic NGO, brought to light that more than 300,000 child domestic workers are employed in Dhaka City alone. Usually, about 80 percent of them are female. These girls start working at the age of ten years, for about 15.5 hours a day and 6.99 days a week (Khair 2004: xv–xx). Child domestic labor, therefore, does not only take place in the informal working sector and under invisible working conditions of private homes, it also belongs to the worst forms of child labor. Sexual harassment, exploitation and abuse are among the hazards girls are confronted with as domestic workers:

Considering the education level among working children, the gender bias is obvious with significant differences between girls and boys, especially in rural areas. Here, 46.9 percent working girls are not educated at all compared to 39.7 percent of their male counterparts (BBS 2003: 66). Even though girls' enrollment has increased remarkably during the last decade being now at a net rate of 93 percent compared to 86 percent net primary enrollment of boys (UNICEF 2012: 104), drop-out rates among girls remain high and parents facing serious economic conditions try to marry off their daughters at a very young age, often not older than 15 or 16 (BSAF 2007: 14). The total rate of child marriage, referring to girls and boys under 18 years of age, is at 64 percent in Bangladesh, with 69 percent in rural areas (UNICEF 2008: 150). Early marriage of girls often happens at the expense of secondary school education:

"Unless rural poverty level can be reduced significantly, girls will keep leaving schools after reaching class 7 or 8" (BSAF 2007: 15). This was one of the reasons why the government of Bangladesh decided to make secondary education free for girls, in addition to primary education which, according to the CRC, is free for both, girls and boys. Girls' school education, however, does not necessarily reflect a transformation of gender roles. Ultimately, the purpose of education could again be driven by marriage (Blanchet 1996: 49) in order to find a husband who prefers to wed an educated wife.[88]

From an economic perspective, male children are preferred as future income earners – and therefore, allowed to receive more school education – whereas females usually remain without a salary as most of their duties are limited to the private sphere. In addition to girls' lacking income contribution, families have to spend considerable amounts of money for arranging their marriages and for paying their dowries (Maloney, Aziz and Sarker 1981: 107). After marriage, daughters are considered to belong to their husband's family (McNicoll and Cain 1990: 108), which often leads to parents' hesitance to invest in their education from childhood on. Another serious problem is the traditional practice of dowry demands to the bride's parents. The Government of Bangladesh has prohibited these payments with the *Dowry Prohibition Act* in 1980. Nevertheless, dowries are secretly demanded and frequently result in domestic violence. In 2006, according to Ain o Salish Kendra, a local human rights NGO, newspapers officially report 334 cases of dowry-related violence, including cases of acid burn, another forbidden habitual practice in Bangladesh, of which 259 led to death (Hossain 2007: 147). Forced marriage and rape of adolescent girls are alarming, particularly in the rural areas. These cases often are neither prosecuted, nor reported due the family's fear of their reputation (BSAF 2007: 17).

Female adolescents and women in Bangladesh frequently suffer from malnutrition, which can lead to stillbirth, premature delivery, low birth weight, and neonatal death. South Asia remains to be the only region in the world with clear evidence of gender discrimination in food distribution among female children and adolescent women (UNICEF 2008: 28). Discrimination in food distribution hampers the development of girls and results in the delivery of underweight infants. The risk of giving birth to a low-weight infant increases with early pregnancies – a consequence of early marriages – carried out by mothers under 18 years of age (Sultana and Ahmed 2001: 43).

Most of the programs investigated here had an astonishing effect on school enrollment and attendance of girl children. This was due to the fact that they worked with material incentives and income-generating opportunities, i.e. stipends and micro-credits, and consciousness-raising at the same time. The FFE and PESP programs, for instance, target rural areas in which girls' and

88 Interview Tapan Kumar Chakravorty, MoPME, PESP, Deputy Director, 17 July 2008.

adolescent women's discrimination is particularly pressing. As a consequence, the program effect, the increase in enrollment and attendance rates in primary schools, is significant for girls. A 2002 evaluation of the FFE revealed that between 1993 and 2002, school enrolment had increased by about 35 percent, particularly remarkably for girls with a 44 percent increase (Ahmed and del Ninno 2002: 16). In the PESP program, mothers receive the bank cards to collect the stipend. This changes their roles in the family and provides them with more bargaining power. With the help of both programs, parents and guardians start to change their views about early marriages. After they first are attracted by the material benefit, i.e. the cash stipend, they progressively start to believe that girl children should also be educated. Tapan Kumar Chakravorty of the MoPME explains how girls benefit the most from the PESP project: "[...] particularly the women, women students, the girl students that is, they became the honourable member of the society. In our society now a groom doesn't want to have the illiterate bride. So now they became the literate member of the society, a girl, so it is their status has already been changed".[89] This quote illustrates very well how – despite increasing education opportunities for girls – traditional gender models are perpetuated. Particularly alarming seems to be that uneducated girls have not yet been "honorable members of society" and how the bride depends on what the groom envisions her to be. Nevertheless, equal education opportunities, at least with respect to the primary education cycle, constitute an important impact the program had in the rural areas.

CLEP, a program that was operative in Dhaka's industrial belt, disposed of a particularly strong awareness-raising component which involved the establishment of Child Rights Forums. As a result, there are reported cases, in which girls prevent each other from being married off against their will at a very young age (Børnearbejde 2003: 17). Sajjad Hossain, Project Coordinator of the BILS project, reveals during an expert interview: "When we started in 2002, there were several early marriages, now it become so many decreases. In our center also, even for our children, our learners. Now they are more aware about these rights."[90] Rights consciousness was also developed by UNICEF with its Meena initiative. Meena is a South Asian rural girl and famous comic figure who – on television or in books – disseminates information about basic children's rights principles. In her stories, Meena experiences adventures relating to the rights of girls. Meena comics were developed to make particularly rural girl children learn about their own fundamental entitlements.[91]

Despite all of these efforts, in some of the projects' examined here, like ILO/IPEC Net, drop-outs among girls are particularly high, because many

89 Ibid, MoPME.

90 Interview Sajjad Hossain, Project Coordinator, BILS, 21 May 2008.

91 Interview Md. Monwer Hossain Khandker, BRAC, Programme Manager Field Operations, BRAC Education Programme, 8 June 2008.

of them get married during their NFE or skills development course. Against this background, it seems relevant to collect data on the girls' marriage status before they enter into the project, keep track of any changes and in particular, document the age at which these girls get married.

Another program effect pertinent to education is that predominantly young girls who participate in NFE components tend to visit primary school much more frequently than their male counterparts (ILO/IPEC 2006: 20). Hence, pre-primary schools like the ones offered by ILO/IPEC USDoL are very valuable for girl children and enhance their chances of attending a governmental primary school. Education is the key to girls' and women's empowerment in Bangladesh and can be seen as a major step on a long road towards gender equality.

The definition of hazardous child labor stipulated in the *ILO Worst Forms of Child Labour Convention* (C138) does not provide for any gender differences, although girls' and boys' physical development and vulnerability can vary (ILO/IPEC 2003a: 10). In programs that pulled child laborers from hazardous occupations to NFE modules like ILO/IPEC Net, fewer girls than boys could become enrolled. This happened because the target, i.e. reaching out to children in hazardous work, was not gender-segregated and more boys than girls are employed in the worst forms of child labor (ILO/IPEC 2003: 20). But – as argued above – girls often are engaged in domestic or home-based work and their working conditions could as well qualify as hazardous. Therefore, other programs, such as BEHTRUWC, determined that 60 percent of their participants should be girls, whereas the other 40 percent were boys.

Skills development components frequently offer gender-specific trades (ILO/IPEC 2003: 14) perpetuating existing employment opportunities and therewith, the roles girls take in society. This is explained as being sensitive to the Bangladeshi cultural context but hinders transformation and attitudinal change towards girls' empowerment. CLEP, for example, offers tailoring and embroidery or block-batik for girls, and electrical house wiring and motor mechanics (particularly for auto rickshaws and motorcycles) for boys.[92] Within ILO/IPEC Net's skills training element, only three of eight trades were "suitable" for the girls, namely food, tailoring and dress making, embroidery and block and screen printing. Consequently, only 38 percent of the Multi-Purpose Centers (MPCs) could actually offer skills development training for girls (ILO/IPEC 2003: 28). Taking into account that these were situated in various parts of Dhaka, the world's fastest growing Mega City, bearing many dangers especially for girls and female adolescents, this meant a severe constraint to girls' participation. Nevertheless, a large proportion of beneficiary girls, i.e. 69 percent, of the skills development graduates become self-employed and earn substantially more than the wage-employed boys and girls. This is mostly due to the

92 Interview Sajjad Hossain, BILS, CLEP Project Coordinator, 21 May 2008.

fact that self-employment in these cases means that they undertake home-based work on a piece-contract basis. Self-employed girls even save part of their earnings to support their mothers and families. These girls profit from higher income, reduced working hours, better health performance and improved recreation (ILO/IPEC 2006: 26).

Because of missing birth certificates, CLEP targets small children that are regarded as certainly too young to work. However, especially the girls report to have problems finding employment after they have graduated from NFE and skills development training, even though they have reached the legal age for admission to employment. They might simply be small and still look too young to be hired by a garment factory. Often, they lack equipment for self-employment, such as sewing machines. These two options, working in a garment factory or taking up self-employment, according to a qualitative evaluation study, seem to be most frequently chosen by the female project participants although they do not always manage to find an occupation that allows them to apply the skills they have developed (Børnearbejde 2003: 4–6).

From a feminist perspective, the re-construction of gender roles through the skills training modules has to be criticized. Bearing in mind that gender identities are socially constructed from early childhood on, such practices promote inequalities in entitlements and agency (Prügl 2008: 47). If a girl child is being trained in garments work, sewing, knitting and embroidery – which is the case in most of these programs – she will most probably end up working in one of Bangladesh's numerous garment factories. Recently, the working conditions in the garment factories, often characterized by dubious occupational safety and health standards and very low wages, have been made public by the international media. Channeling girls into the factories, therefore, means to reproduce a certain understanding of masculinity and femininity and pertinent power differentials (Prügl and Meyer 1999: 5). If children and adolescent women, for instance, will continue to earn less, their decision-making power within their families and communities will remain low. In Bangladesh's garment factories, a shift from child labor to female labor has taken place. This means that many of today's garments workers are yesterday's child laborers trained by the programs examined in this book.

6.9 Generating hypotheses on local children's rights implementation

In this last section of the chapter, the most important findings of the entire in-depth case study on the implementation of children's rights in Bangladesh will be summarized. While recalling the results obtained in a condensed form, hypotheses are formulated that seek to explain the local rights realization process in weak state contexts. These hypotheses are expected to be verifiable in empirical situations in which rights are *de jure* adopted, i.e. ratified and implemented at the national level, but *de facto* not entirely guaranteed, i.e. not in effect for a considerable number of local rights-holders.

In Bangladesh, implementation deficits at the local level are first and foremost due to poverty, adult unemployment, death or divorce of family members, natural disasters, and the poor quality of schooling, but they also originate in prevailing socio-cultural perceptions (see among others Bannerman and Berghuys 2008: 19; Hasan 2007: 84–5; Feldman and Larson 2004). Addressing these causes comprehensively requires the installation of complex regulatory measures. Many of these were revealed in greater detail in the case study presented above. In the following, hypotheses generated from major empirical findings are introduced stepwise with the objective of explaining the main characteristics of a local children's rights implementation process.

The Government of Bangladesh was among the first regimes to have committed themselves to the CRC in 1990, particularly embracing the right to education, but also to basic health care and protection from economic exploitation. Another convention ratified by Bangladesh in 2001 is the C138 focusing on immediate action to eliminate children's involvement in hazardous occupations. The *ILO Minimum Age Convention* has not yet been formally accepted by Bangladesh's government, although its main standard, providing for a minimum age for admission to employment, has already been anchored in national legislation, namely the 2006 *Bangladesh Labour Code*. The right to education and the right to health and nutrition, as well as protection from economic exploitation are reflected in the *Constitution of the People's Republic of Bangladesh*. A whole bulk of national policies, among them the recently adopted *National Child Labour Policy*, the *Poverty Reduction Strategy Paper*, a *National Children Policy*, several *National Plans of Action for Children*, the *National Education Policy*, and a *National Health Policy* as well as a *National Food Policy* reflect one or more, in some cases all of these children's rights.

Contrary to the multitude of these political declarations, empirical data has highlighted that – during the last point of data collection – 1.3 million children were engaged in hazardous child labor in the country (BBS 2003: 63). In addition, 46.9 percent of rural girls who work and 39.7 percent of rural working boys were not supplied with any educational opportunities at all (BBS 2003: 66). Furthermore, 41 percent of all Bangladeshi children were underweight in 2007 (National Institute of Population Research and Training, Mitra and Associates and Macro International 2009: 145–9) and with very limited access to basic health care services or to improved water and sanitation facilities (Sultana and Ahmed 2001: 41).

Within the framework of this study, site observations and interviews with local government authorities, NGOs and field level staff of IOs have revealed that rights principles had not trickled down to the local rights-holders within society. Mostly due to poverty, illiteracy among the parents, a lacking school infrastructure, limited access to social services, prevailing socio-cultural perceptions, and a lack of awareness, children's rights have not reached all of the children at the grassroots level. This has led to the assumption that, in particular weak state contexts, a national implementation process – in the sense of norm ratification and consequent legislative and policy changes – is necessary, but not sufficient for realizing children's rights. Here, it has been argued that a local implementation process is required to call these rights to life:

(1) *National and local human rights implementation are separate processes*. Whereas *national implementation* relates to the ratification of international norms and changing state legislation and domestic policies accordingly, *local implementation* refers to taking protective and provisional measures for the rights-targets at the grassroots level.
(2) *These protective and provisional measures need to be made available to the children, their families and entire communities in the form of rights-related services*. These social services are relevant for making rights effective among their holders within society. They can take context-specific forms like the provision of NFE or the gradual withdrawal of children from hazardous child labor in Bangladesh.
(3) *A permanent local infrastructure that is accessible to the rights-holders has to be in place for the delivery of social services*. This infrastructure is, again, dependent on the local context. It either has to be established, such as Bangladesh's provisional learning or MPCs, which sometimes were not more than little bamboo huts in the urban slums. Or it can already be in place or shared between different organizations and programs, as in the case of the FFE/PESP program operative in already existing governmental and non-governmental primary schools. It is indispensable that this infrastructure is accessible to all children, even the ones from remote areas, on a permanent basis. In Bangladesh, however, these learning centers usually become dismantled if they have been established in the framework of an externally funded project.
(4) *Local institutions involving community members need to be in place to coordinate the delivery of rights-related services, to protect children from re-engaging in the worst forms of child labor, to disseminate awareness about rights, and to resolve upcoming problems*. For administrating and monitoring the services provided, for counseling children and their families and maintaining the local infrastructure, functioning institutions have to be in existence at the grassroots level. In Bangladesh, these usually take the form of school management committees in the NFE centers in which representatives of the community, often local elites or religious leaders, parents and guardians, teachers, government authorities, but also employers and social workers participate. The multitude of actors engaged in local institutions

leads to a situation in which children's rights are effectively multiplied in respective communities.

(5) *Children whose rights are being denied have to be targeted, identified and directly addressed as the beneficiaries of protective measures and rights-related services.* Targeting is a regulatory mechanism that ensures that social services reach the ones whose rights have not yet been guaranteed. These disadvantaged children have to be directly addressed and protected. All of the projects fostering rights in Bangladesh examined here, have utilized targeting procedures and combined them with other regulatory strategies. Therefore, it constituted a necessary condition for the local realization of children's rights.

(6) *Increasing families' income in combination with raising their awareness about children's basic entitlements are necessary conditions for children's rights implementation.* Since deficient implementation can be explained with persistent poverty and prevailing socio-cultural perceptions, a combination of awareness raising on children's rights and income-generating measures for the entire family is needed to foster the rights of the child. Increasing families' income through creating employment opportunities and entrepreneurial training for parents leads them to make different choices about child labor and education. This has proved to be even truer if they, at the same time, are consciously aware of children's entitlements, the long-term impact of schooling, and the detrimental effects of hazardous child labor.

Altogether, a combination of targeting, awareness-raising and income-generation supports a situation in which the norm targets make use of the rights-related services and protective measures offered through the different policy programs. If the legal minimum age for admission to employment is considered, monitoring – as another regulatory mechanism – becomes more important and has to be added to the conditions that are necessary for achieving children's rights implementation. In Bangladesh, formal and informal work facilities have to be regularly monitored so that they do not hire laborers below the national legal minimum age of 14 years.

(7) *Local governmental or non-governmental actors are needed to conduct the implementation process on the ground.* These actors have to directly interact and communicate with the local norm targets. They establish the required infrastructure and manage service delivery at the grassroots level. Whenever governmental capacities, resources, expertise or local personnel are missing, non-governmental stakeholders – often supported by external donor money within the framework of transnational development projects – can take up these tasks. In Bangladesh, local NGOs with expertise in at least one of the local target areas and in not less than one of the rights-related issues were contracted by governmental ministries or IOs to undertake local implementation activities.

This means that they acted as a transmitter between the government (or governmental organizations) and society. In hierarchically organized multi-level actor partnerships, local NGOs bale their strengths with governmental actors and share responsibilities to initiate rights implementation processes.

Chapter 7

Conclusion

> Ideally, rights become full-bodied when they prove their worth in guiding everyday policy decision-making both locally and globally. Globally, they can build consensus about the place of children in the emerging political and economic order, yet allow sufficient room for local emphasis, refurbishing and interpretation.
>
> (Reynolds, Nieuwenhuys and Hanson 2006: 298)

This book investigated the implementation of global children's rights from a perspective that is yet relatively new to International Relations (IR): the local level. While examining the case of Bangladesh, the research question was *how* a local implementation process comes about *after* the national government has ratified international children's rights treaties. This implied that the endpoint of this process was not the transformation of international rights into domestic legislation and policies, a hitherto common definition of implementation. Here, implementing global children's rights has been understood as changing national laws and policies in accordance with global standards *and* improving the rights situation for their societal targets, i.e. the local children. To analyze this process, this book examined three non-controversial principles that represent a global consensus on children's rights. These are (1) the protection of children from the worst forms of child labor, (2) providing them with primary education, and (3) delivering basic health care services to them.

One significant assumption underlying this study was that meaningful answers to the research question could only be provided if two deficits in the IR treatise on human rights were addressed. As a consequence, this book – first of all – calls for paying closer attention to the local level within interwoven multi-level systems. Considering the local sphere and its relations to the national and the international level is something often preached and rarely practiced in IR. In this book, an emphasis on the local has broadened the analytical view towards a vertical governance dimension. This means that regulatory measures applied at the grassroots level for children's rights protection and promotion were investigated in greater detail. A second deficit regards contributions from non-state actors that complement governmental work and take over traditionally governmental responsibilities. This aspect has so far been neglected in research on human rights implementation. Earlier approaches, such as the Spiral Model of Human Rights Change, are based on the assumption that whatever the state ratifies leads to a governmental implementation responsibility. Considering non-governmental organizations (NGOs) as jointly responsible actors in human rights implementation stretches the horizontal governance dimension. Building upon these two points, partnerships between governmental and non-governmental actors at various levels, the international, the national and the local can emerge. In Bangladesh, international organizations (IOs) provide technical assistance to national governments and contract non-governmental actors to implement children's rights. These multi-level actor partnerships demonstrate that governing human rights became vertically and horizontally diversified.

In this book, it is argued that governance inspirations can enrich scholarship on human rights change, norm socialization, and compliance. Hence, the analytical framework applied here has integrated these three theoretical pillars. Considering governance concepts in the empirical analysis has led to the development of hypotheses filling the blank space between ratification of a children's rights treaty, i.e. transporting norms to the national political system, on the one hand, and children indeed being protected from hazardous labor, going to school, and receiving health care, i.e. transporting norms to their societal rights-holders, on the other hand. Governance considerations helped to answer the research question at hand and opened the door for an expanded understanding of children's and human rights implementation, the major theoretical contribution of this research.

Bangladesh, the case selected for a thick empirical analysis, displayed a children's rights situation that reflected the research problem at hand and, at the same time, implied several observations with a positive implementation outcome which could be further investigated. The national implementation dimension, bringing national legislation and domestic policies in accordance with the ratified conventions, could be traced by examining Bangladesh's constitution, the national *Labor Code*, the *Primary Education Act*, the *National Child Labour Elimination Policy* and various other policy papers. All of the children's rights under investigation here were reflected in these legislative texts and policy documents. Contrasting successful national implementation with the rights status in local communities *before* local policy activities became effective, however, revealed that anchoring rights in laws and policies had not led to an implementation outcome within society, per se. Although considered a necessary implementation step in scholarship on IR and in this book, harmonization of laws and policies is not enough to reach out to the local children. Hence, the first result of this study is that national and local implementation are processes that have to be distinguished from one another.

One major idea for an appropriate research design facilitating a comprehensive investigation of local implementation was to put the cart before the horse and to apply an outcome-oriented selection procedure. Using simple indicators for a successful outcome in a children's rights implementation process helped in identifying local policies through which at least one of the three principles considered had been implemented. These indicators were derived from implementation measures formulated in the *UN Convention on the Rights of the Child* (CRC) and the *ILO Worst Forms of Child Labour Convention* (C138) both ratified by Bangladesh's government. Hence, a policy program was assumed to successfully realize children's rights at the local level if at least one of the following indicators proved to be true (1) a number of children were withdrawn from the worst forms of child labor and/or the hazards of a number of workplaces were removed, (2) a number of children were provided with non-formal education (NFE) and/or vocational skills training, and a (3) number of beneficiaries were supplied with basic health care services. Through this outcome-oriented, or Y-centered, case selection procedure, relevant programs contributing to the transfer of global children's rights to the local level could be identified and comparatively analyzed. Seven of these policy programs displaying different case characteristics were investigated further. They were considered within-case observations, with limited variation on the dependent variable – all of them implemented at least one of the children's rights – and maximal variation on the explanatory factors – all of them were marked by different case characteristics. The within-cases framed this study's comparative design.

To inductively explore the local sphere of the implementation process, multiple sources of evidence pertinent to the seven programs investigated were combined with a variety of research and evaluation methods. Anthropological field research methods were used for analyzing grassroots phenomena (Merry 2006a: 28–9). During my field research in Bangladesh, I have conducted interviews with experts of multi-level actor partnerships that serve as transmitting agents in global, national and local processes and that are well aware of the social reality of Bangladesh's children, their families and entire communities (compare Merry 2006a: 29). With my comparison of norm implementation in these seven cases, I have engaged in what anthropologists call multi-sited ethnography (Marcus 1998: 79–104; see also Merry 2006a: 29). I have tried to learn more about these sites through field observation. My strategy was a combination of visiting the individual project components, particularly the existing infrastructure and respective institutions and observing the participants of these projects (see also Schapper 2009). Participant observation is a research method rooted in anthropology that allows the field worker to place individuals or communities in a certain context to gain a realistic picture of their behavioral dynamics (see Whyte 1984: 27).

Collecting primary and secondary documents, conducting problem-centered expert interviews, launching an expert focus group discussion, and carrying out field observations resulted in a body of empirical data that allowed for tracing the local implementation process. The success of the seven project initiatives in relation to children's rights was defined according to Underdal's (2004: 34) dimensions of effectiveness, predominantly the output and outcome dimensions. Whenever a program offered protection measures to withdraw children from the worst forms of child labor or to remove hazards from their workplaces, or whenever it provided education and health services, a certain output could be observed. If children and their families or communities made use of and benefitted from these protection measures and the services provided, a particular outcome became visible.

A qualitative content analysis of the evaluation reports helped in inductively exploring regulative mechanisms at work for achieving a successful project outcome. The most important ones, targeting, incentives, advocacy and awareness raising, income generation, conditionality, capacity building, and monitoring, were compared by applying a Qualitative Comparative Analysis (QCA). This led to a final formula suggesting that a combination of (1) targeting, (2) advocacy and awareness raising, and (3) income generation results in the implementation of the three children's rights principles investigated. Targeting, awareness raising and advocacy constitute socialization mechanisms that are addressed at society and, therefore, differ from the ones singled out in scholarship on norm socialization and compliance. Nevertheless, similarly to these studies, the strategies identified here reflect both, mechanisms that function according to a logic of consequences, i.e. income-generation, and mechanisms that function according to a logic of appropriateness, i.e. awareness raising.

The results of the empirical analysis strongly suggest that national implementation is an important indicator of governmental commitment following the ratification process, without which local policy programs are usually not initiated. It, however, does not imply that children's rights norms have reached their targets. The national and local implementation processes rather come about in different ways. Local children's rights implementation which is targeted at the societal rights-holders presupposes that a permanent local infrastructure and local institutions are in place. It also implies that local actors, governmental or non-governmental ones, actively manage the process in the target communities through installing protection measures for children in the worst forms of labor and providing them with education and health services. Rights-holders make use of these services whenever regulative mechanisms, such as income-generation and awareness raising, are in place.

7.1 Reiterating main results of the case study on children's rights in Bangladesh

In Bangladesh, the case under investigation, these results evolved in the following way. The establishment of a permanent local infrastructure can, in a very context-specific way, deviate from the conventional Western understanding of a school, in which children are provided with education, or a clinic, where they receive basic health care. Here, infrastructure often means not more than provisional learning or multi-purpose centers (MPCs); in some cases reduced to a little bamboo hut fixed above the Buriganga river. However, it can be assumed that a permanent infrastructure would indicate that education and health services will continuously be delivered, whereas a provisional infrastructure can easily become dismantled – as experienced in most of the projects considered here. This means that the indigence with which NFE centers are set up in Bangladesh indicates that the delivery of services there will not necessarily be sustainable. Of further importance is the infrastructure's accessibility. In particular for children from remote rural areas and urban slums, it needs to be reachable without security or transportation constraints.

The facilities established have to be administered. Therefore, local governing institutions consisting of members from respective communities are built. These center management committees (CMCs) comprise local elites, religious leaders, government authorities, social workers, children's employers as well as parents, teachers, and guardians themselves. Similar to Bangladesh's school management committees (SMCs) they take over supervisory and monitoring functions, but they also manage the delivery of social services and counsel children, families and the community on rights-related issues. Involving community members in these committees means to strengthen community ownership for a process of awareness-raising initiated by certain project activities. This also means that there is a chance that these institutions – after a project has terminated – remain in place and continue to multiply the message of children's rights protection.

In terms of regulatory mechanisms that govern the children's rights implementation process in Bangladesh, a significant insight of this study is that children whose rights had so far been denied have to be targeted. Especially since children and their families often lack knowledge and awareness about their own privileges and entitlements, rights-holders need to be identified and directly addressed with protective and provisional measures. Targeting has to be combined with income-generating and awareness-raising schemes for the entire family to comply with children's rights. Increasing a family's income by offering entrepreneurial training and employment opportunities for the parents leads to them making different choices about child labor and education. In many cases, it is easier to convince parents to let their children participate in the program if some kind of material benefit – very typical for Bangladesh are micro-credits – is involved. In later phases, families become more and more aware of the devastating effects hazardous labor might have on their child and of the remunerating long-term impact schooling usually implies for entire generations. This can lead to a situation in which they make different choices relating to their children even though no material benefits are involved anymore. In some programs, this became obvious when parents decided to send the siblings of former child laborers to school instead of to work. Hence, awareness raising usually has a lasting effect – even beyond the limited time frame of externally funded policy projects.

Although the (C138) has not yet been ratified by the Government of Bangladesh, its main provisions are already anchored in national legislation and have been promoted by many of the policy programs analyzed here. Monitoring was particularly important in Bangladesh's garment and bidi factories. It requires very detailed knowledge on what kind of work can be legally performed at what age with varying regulations for light, general, and hazardous labor according to the international standards put forward by the International Labour Organization (ILO). Since both workers and employers often lack this distinct information, external monitoring through governmental labor inspection teams or experts from IOs becomes indispensable.

Realizing rights for children requires the involvement of local actors. They are the ones interacting with the communities, establishing and maintaining an infrastructure at the grassroots level, installing institutions, and managing protective and provisional rights-related measures. Whenever governmental resources and implementation capacities are lacking, such as in weak state contexts, non-governmental actors can step in. They are contracted in externally funded policy projects and serve as transmitters between IOs, the national government and local society. Local NGOs usually are the only stakeholders with access to the targeted communities. Hence, they can draw them into the implementation process and engage them in multiplying the message of children's rights. The contracting of local NGOs by IOs or the government, however, can cause additional implementation costs and is usually only possible within a limited time frame, which leads to serious sustainability concerns. Local actors, whether governmental or non-governmental, take an executive role in a multi-level actor partnership. Here, they mostly conduct rights implementation on the ground whereas national and international partners hold the responsibility for planning the policy endeavor, undertaking supervisory, monitoring and administrative functions and providing for financial resources.

7.2 Human rights implementation reconsidered

These results lead to a reconsidered understanding of children's rights implementation. In this understanding the nation state, of course, plays a crucial role in governing the process; it actively participates in creating norms in international arenas, it decides to ratify them and takes the largest responsibility in deciding how to implement them. However, empirical research suggests a departure from the exclusive focus on state actors and an integration of societal actors in implementation policies. The case of Bangladesh illustrated how boundaries between the norm addressees, those who regulate, and the norm targets, those who are approached by regulations, become blurry (compare also Mayntz 2009a: 43). Community members in Bangladesh, for instance, are the targets of children's rights regulations and, at the same time, engage in further awareness-raising themselves. Hence, not only the distinction between government and society, but also the distinction between objects and subjects of control are increasingly fuzzy (compare Mayntz 2009a:46 and Olsen 2009: 198). This became particularly obvious in the policy programs investigated. Usually, the rationale behind these was to enable the participants to claim their rights and to take over project ownership. As a consequence, project beneficiaries themselves participated in the management committees of learning centers and initiated own awareness-raising modules. From a development perspective, this contributes to enhancing a project's sustainability. Taking a human rights view into account, this means that the rights-holders themselves participate in the implementation of the norms at stake: they learn about them, they learn to claim them, and they learn to multiply them.

Considering human rights, a stronger focus on the norm targets in implementation strategies seems to be plausible. Although human rights treaties are addressed at the state government, their regulations are targeted at each individual citizen. In this sense, human rights treaties are unique and can hardly be compared to other international agreements. Children's rights conventions are even more particular than other human rights agreements. While they address the respective national government, they are not only targeted at the children. Most of the time, it is not the children themselves, or certainly not the children alone, who make decisions about labor, education, and health. Since their situation is deeply woven into the net of their social environment, it is the whole community – the parents, guardians, employers, siblings and, in the case of Bangladesh, also local elites and religious leaders – who are the final targets of children's rights norms. All of them together have to change their behavior in accordance with international standards (compare Zürn and Joerges 2005: 26) and all of them together learn about them, learn to claim them, and learn to multiply them.

It is surprising that the emphasis on the national level and on governmental actors could be upheld in all strands of IR scholarship relevant for children's rights implementation: socialization and compliance research and the Spiral Model of Human Rights Change. Particularly the Spiral Model, which is expected to come closest to explaining the process of implementing children's rights, proved to be too narrow in several regards. The internalization of standards prescribing appropriate behavior, i.e. human rights, by governmental actors (compare Risse, Jetschke and Schmitz 2002: 19) is not only a challenging endeavor almost impossible to measure with the methodological toolkit of a political scientist. It should simply not be the endpoint of a human rights implementation process. Since it lacks the perspective of the norm targets completely, it can only describe the process partially. Additionally, it is based on an understanding in which the government alone takes the responsibility for norm realization without making reference to what exactly happens after the ratification process. Although this might be due to the model's scope of application, which is limited to repressive state governments denying personal integrity rights in domestic policies (compare Jetschke and Liese 2013), it leads to neglecting the role that non-governmental actors and the actual rights targets themselves can play (see also Schapper 2010). Transnational human rights networks are of primary importance in the Spiral Model. But their function is limited to influencing the behavior of state governments and IOs (Keck and Sikkink 1998). Hence, according to the model, non-governmental actors remain external to the implementation process itself – a fact that could be disproved in this case study.

The in-depth investigation of children's rights in Bangladesh has demonstrated that civil society and even private business actors participate in norm implementation. Whenever resources and capacities are lacking like in weak state contexts, international (governmental) organizations and national governments cooperate with local NGOs to build a multi-level actor partnership. These temporary governance institutions compensate governmental implementation deficits. Each partner in this constellation takes a role according to its particular strength and expertise. Local governmental and non-governmental actors are of primary importance here; they are the ones in direct interaction with the rights-holders at the grassroots level. They manage the implementation process on the ground, they install and deliver protective and provisional measures, and engage in awareness-raising activities targeted at the children and their families.

Finally, this research project departs from solely considering children's rights and moves a step further. It argues for abandoning conventional implementation conceptions when taking human rights into account and paying more attention to what is happening within a nation state after ratification. Human rights implementation requires the adoption of international principles into national schemes, legislation, and policies – but human rights are not implemented with only that. The process demands the initiation of different measures at various levels, but the local sphere is of utmost significance for calling these rights to life. Whereas national implementation emphasizes the norm addressee and socialization of state actors, local implementation focuses on the norm target and socialization of societal actors.

An interesting example demonstrating the importance of local rights realization is that of the C138, which has not yet been ratified by the government of Bangladesh. Long before regulations of this convention became anchored in the Bangladesh *Labour Code* in 2006, the minimum age principle was already implemented locally, within the framework of some of the programs considered here. This again suggests to moving away from the focus of the state as the norm addressee and paying closer attention to what is happening among the norm targets.[1] Here, a right might have already gained societal meaning without legal commitment.

Altogether, it can be assumed that all of the hypotheses developed in relation to local children's rights implementation, i.e. the need for a permanent context-specific infrastructure and institutions and the necessity to install regulative mechanisms that involve a combination of targeting, income-generation, and awareness raising are of relevance beyond Bangladesh's borders and beyond the case of children's rights. The scope conditions that would have to be met pertain to a cooperative state that has ratified international conventions and rather lacks resources, capacities and expertise – instead of political willingness (Chayes, Chayes and Mitchell 1998: 39) – to implement these. These are usually weak states in which the government exercises the monopoly of power but faces limitations in its welfare functions and in exercising the rule of law (Schneckener 2007: 107–109). Furthermore, the state must allow for external donors and IOs to plan and conduct policy programs on its territory. And finally, it has to agree to share responsibilities in the development and realization of policies with IOs and local non-governmental actors. In Table 7.1 a model delineating national rights implementation from local rights implementation that could be tested for other children's and human rights is suggested. It summarizes the hypotheses generated in this study with respect to each level, the implementation measures taken and the kinds of actors engaged.

This model displays the study's result that not only local civil society actors but also the rights-holders themselves play a role in taking over regulative functions, for instance through engaging in awareness raising in their respective community like in CLEP's *Child Rights Forum* or by preventing their peers from engaging in early marriages. Furthermore, the group of targets, which comprises parents, teachers, employers, and community leaders, can participate in protecting other targets from human rights violations, i.e. through preventing children from being hired in the worst forms of labor and securing their attendance in primary school. This raises interesting questions relating to the ways how global norms evolve. Is this always a top-down process – from the global to the local – or can rights-holders also influence how norm promoting policies are being shaped in the future? Are their ways for local ideas to also have repercussions at the national or even at the global level?

1 On the other hand, this does not mean that ratification becomes irrelevant. The *International Programme on the Elimination of Child Labour* (IPEC), the ILO's technical assistance program, for instance, only launches implementation projects in countries that have ratified the C138. Hence, if Bangladesh would not have ratified it, three of the seven projects investigated here would not have been operative. Other programs, such as CLEP and the *Eradication of Hazardous Child Labour* Project (EHCL), have explicitly been initiated in response to Bangladesh's C182 ratification and the *Basic Education for Hard to Reach Urban Working Children* (BEHTRUWC) and *Food for Education* Programs/*Primary Education Stipend Project* (FFE/PESP) are a direct policy response to adopting the CRC.

Table 7.1 A model of human rights implementation in weak state contexts

Level	Implementation measure	Actors	Addressee/ target
global	norm creation	IOs and governments	government
national	ratification, making norms effective in national legislation and domestic policies	government	government
local	establishing local infrastructure and institutions	local governmental and non-governmental actors	rights-holders
	installing regulative mechanisms (material mechanisms, i.e. income-generation and immaterial mechanisms, i.e. awareness raising)	local governmental and non-governmental actors and rights-holders	rights-holders
	effecting protective measures adn rights-related services	local governmental and non-governmental actors and rights-holders	rights-holders

Another crucial result of this study, which is highlighted in this model, is that the addressees of national human rights implementation are mainly governmental actors, whereas society is the target of a local human rights implementation process. The overall assumption is that this model is valid for civil and political as well as for economic, social, and cultural rights. Investigating both personal integrity rights, i.e. protection from hazardous child labor, and social rights, i.e. the right to education and health, in the framework of this study, suggests that this can hold true. Nevertheless, all of the hypotheses summarized here require further testing for human rights, in general, and for children's rights, in particular.

7.3 What else does this book contribute?

Besides reconsidering the hitherto common understanding of human rights implementation, this book shows that – with respect to governance research – it is worth it to practice what has been preached. In this case study, the local sphere was particularly relevant. James Rosenau's conception of governance embracing "[...] systems of rule at all levels of human activity – from the family to the international organization – [...]" (1995: 13) turned out to be a good slogan for this study. Global norms, created and promoted by IOs, were traced all the way through being anchored at the national level and gaining meaning for the families in a local environment. Opening a door beyond traditional socialization and compliance theorizing in IR and inductively exploring the implementation process from the perspective of the rights-holders not only pointed out solutions to the problem at hand, it also demonstrated that the local level features complex governance arrangements that are strongly interwoven with the domestic and the international levels. Neglecting the local sphere with its own complexity leaves the puzzle unresolved. Governance scholarship calls for considering interrelatedness in a multi-level system; it is the task of empirical researchers to follow the path of investigating how international politics affect its targets. The theoretical framework applied here is open to vertical and horizontal expansions beyond the state-centeredness of IR theory. It might need more distinct shaping, but can serve as a first step to discover old things anew. Enhanced attention to the local level and to ways in which government and society interweave will most probably secure a more prominent role for anthropological and sociological ideas and procedures within IR research.

Applying a governance framework of analysis to empirically explore a single case study in-depth led to the discovery of new developments in human rights politics that are worth further exploration. Not necessarily new is the notion of the "cooperative state" (Mayntz 2009a: 43) in which the government takes the role of "orchestrating" public and private actors who participate in regulatory activities (Abbott and Snidal 2009: 509–10). This becomes even more significant in countries that have not yet developed to their full potential and lack resources and capacities. Often, public expenditures are cut by the World Bank and International Monetary Fund's (IMF's) lending conditionalities imposed on developing countries, commonly called "fiscal discipline" in "structural adjustment policies" (compare Arat 2002: 190–1). Lacking material and immaterial resources and capacities can be compensated by different forms of cooperative partnerships. In the case of Bangladesh's children's rights policies, this means that the government has decided to cooperate with IOs, the private sector, and contracted NGOs. It is the government itself, however, that allows IOs' technical assistance programs in the country, that selects which NGOs can be sub-contracted, and that enters into a partnership with the private sector. Hence, it remains the main orchestrator in children's rights implementation.

The existing literature on actor arrangements concentrates on the influence and participation of international non-state actors in global policy networks, public-private partnerships (PPPs), and multipartite inclusive institutions. Although research on global public policy networks, for instance transnational human rights networks, also takes domestic NGOs into account, it is mostly their impact on the behavior of nation states and IOs that is considered. Insights about what functions actor partnerships can take within a nation state are yet limited. Correspondingly, very little systematic knowledge on multilevel actor partnerships is available, although these probably outnumber international partnerships by far. In the case study on the implementation of children's rights in Bangladesh, multi-level actor partnerships taking over governance functions have been identified. These partnerships are worth further investigation. In what other issue areas do they develop and implement policies? Do they have a sustainable impact on the problems they address or does their temporary nature impede with the achievement of long-term effects? What is the relationship between the various spheres; is it possible to typologize the tasks and responsibilities actors at one particular level undertake? And is the government going to remain the main orchestrator, i.e. the one who decides who is in and who is out of the cooperative network?

Another relevant aspect is that the regulative mechanisms inductively explored in this case study provide important hints to measures promoting norm socialization and compliance within society. IR scholarship focuses on mechanisms that international institutions employ to lead state actors towards accepting and adhering to the international community's rules of appropriate behavior (Checkel and Zürn 2005: 1049). Examples of socialization mechanisms deemed relevant in the literature are normative persuasion, external inducement, and internal reconstruction (Ikenberry and Kupchan 1990: 290–2), as well as material incentives (Ikenberry and Kupchan 1990: 314). Other scholars stress strategic calculation (Checkel 2005a: 808), social influence (Checkel and Zürn 2005: 1052), and role playing (Checkel 2005a: 810–12). Compliance research is the only strand of literature that points to mechanisms fostering compliance among state actors, i.e. monitoring and sanctioning, juridification, internalization (Zürn and Neyer 2005: 191–5), and capacity-building (Zürn and Joerges 2005: 30), as well as mechanisms fostering compliance within society, i.e. participation and social acceptance (Zürn and Joerges 2005: 26).

Socialization and compliance strategies observed in this study of children's rights implementation correspond to some of the mechanisms elaborated in the literature. One major difference, however, is that they all relate to society's norm acceptance and adherence, and therefore might be a theoretical contribution that needs to be further polished. The provision of material incentives, awareness raising or normative persuasion, monitoring and capacity-building, for instance, are already established in the literature and have, at the same time, been inductively explored in this study. Hence, they seem to play a role in both state and society socialization. Only targeting and income-generation are not yet mentioned in any similar form in socialization and compliance research. Nevertheless, both seem to be important for norm adoption in societies in which rights are being denied to certain groups (targeting) and in which poverty impedes rule adoption and adherence (income-generation). The provision of material incentives in particular, but also monitoring and income-generation, follow a logic of consequences, whereas awareness raising and capacity-building pertain to a logic of appropriateness. Although strategies of society socialization and compliance have not yet been deeply explored, it is probably a combination of material and immaterial regulative mechanisms, i.e. an integrative approach that needs to be stressed. This book offers preliminary hypotheses about mechanisms relevant to children's rights socialization among societal actors. Whether these hold true as mechanisms fostering norm adoption and adherence among societal targets that must change their behavior in accordance with other human rights, requires further empirical testing.

7.4 Research limitations and open questions

The study conducted here is, of course, limited in several regards. It only considers a single case, namely children's rights implementation in Bangladesh. To make the project feasible, three major rights principles were selected for an in-depth analysis. International conventions embracing these principles, the CRC and the C138 belong to the so-called targeted treaties, meaning that they reflect civil, political, as well as economic, social, and cultural rights (Alston 2005: 789). These were selected to generate hypotheses on children's rights implementation that are neither limited to just civil and political nor to economic, social, and cultural rights, a division that is still upheld in the Spiral Model of Human Rights Change. Nevertheless, some differences between *protecting* children and *providing* them with rights-related services remain. Infrastructure, for instance, is mostly needed for providing education and health services. On the other hand, it might be exactly this infrastructure, the NFE center in an urban slum, which prevents a child from re-entering a hazardous occupation. This again highlights how human rights are indivisible, interdependent, and mutually reinforcing (Alston 2005: 789). Although the rights principles investigated here are of utmost importance, there are other – not less relevant ones – that were neglected in this book. Children's rights to benefit from social security (CRC Article 24, UN 1989), children's protection from sexual exploitation and abuse (CRC Article 34, UN 1989), children's protection from all forms of physical and mental violence (CRC Article 19, UN 1989), and children's rights to nutrition, clothing, and housing (CRC Article 27.3, UN 1989) at first sight seem to require similar implementation measures to the ones introduced here. For realizing these rights, a local infrastructure, managing institutions, regulative mechanisms, and actors reaching out to these children are most probably of relevance as well. Nevertheless, an in-depth investigation of further rights could possibly lead to slightly differing results or at least add conditions, such as further regulative mechanisms, not yet considered here. This also means that all generalized hypotheses developed here require further empirical testing.

In addition, there might be other possible methodical ways of tracing the process of global norms to the local level than via temporary transnational, national and local policy programs. Some of the projects investigated here were hardly comparable in their quantitative scope and differed in their objectives. Whereas a few simply focused on pushing enrollment figures towards new records, others concentrated explicitly on the elimination of the worst forms of child labor in certain predetermined sectors. The success of these projects, according to the research objective pursued here, was measured against their outcome relating to children protected from hazardous child labor and children provided with education and health services. Output, outcome, and impact constitute analytical dimensions of effectiveness (Underdal 2004: 34). This study, however, refrained from making strong statements about a program's impact mainly due to the temporal character of the projects. A – more or less successful – outcome could be observed in every single case. This means the protection measures and services offered through the projects (output) were extensively used by the beneficiaries, who were protected from the worst forms of child labor and provided with education and health services (outcome). Nevertheless, there was usually not enough evidence for a clear statement about whether the problem at hand could be significantly reduced, i.e. an impact according to Underdal (2004: 34). Hence, reflections "beyond outcome" could be collected, particularly from the interview partners in the field, but the impact dimension that appeared to be strong in the face of weak evidence and limited data at hand, could only be indicated.

Some projects, from their initial stages on, aimed at tackling several of the three rights considered here at once, whereas others solely concentrated on fostering education. The latter, of course, were discounted by the definition of implementation success used in this work, which focused on three interdependent rights at once. In particular, the FFE and its successor, the PESP, had a wide outreach and became internationally prominent for enhancing primary school enrollment, attendance rates, and considerably fostering gender parity in Bangladesh's elementary schools. Nevertheless, their success pertinent to the definition utilized here was fairly limited, since only one of the three rights had been fostered. The ILO projects, in contrast, were considered the most successful at implementing the combination of rights principles investigated here. This was most probably due to ILO/IPEC's overall concept of providing viable social and economic alternatives for child laborers, including education, after their withdrawal from hazardous occupations. In the end, the results obtained have to be viewed in light of this definition focusing on children's rights' interdependency, and are limited to the rights principles chosen for this analysis, i.e. protecting children from the worst forms of labor, and providing primary education and basic health services to them.

7.5 Political implications

Although each of the seven programs considered here contributed to an implementation outcome – either by reducing the number of children occupied under hazardous conditions, fostering the number of children enrolling in schools or increasing the number of children provided with health services – their impact remains limited, far too limited. An impact, in the sense of Underdal's (2004: 34) dimension of effectiveness, can only be achieved if the problem at hand is being reduced. However, with these policy activities, problems are only temporarily reduced. Most of the projects operate with external funding and deliver services within a very limited time frame, often not longer than four or five years. If the government does not take over the infrastructure by then and keeps running the services and awareness-raising activities, progress towards eliminating child labor and providing education and health care will not be sustainable. In Bangladesh, this leads to a situation in which infrastructure is set up to be in place for about five years – the time period a project might be running – and is then dismantled again. The same proves to be true for the delivery of social services. After their initiation has been shouldered with the help of external investments granted by donor countries or private associations, it is the government that has to take over their maintenance. In Bangladesh, however, this was usually not the case. Refraining from doing so is not only a waste of donor money, it also leaves the rights-holders in a situation in which they were made aware of how to claim their rights but, again, are denied the required social services. This was highlighted by an ILO/IPEC Chief Technical Advisor who had to manage a process of dismantling and then rebuilding multi-purpose centers between a project's pilot phase and its next stage:

> So that's why I was so incredibly disappointed that we had to cut down our infrastructure, that we had to dismantle it because we had raised expectation levels, we had raised value levels, we had raised et cetera which will sustain and then you can't provide it. It's like making people aware and then you can't do anything with it.[2]

This statement highlights how problematic it is to simply abolish the entire infrastructure and the services delivered, even though the rights-holders have been made aware that receiving protection and social services belong to their entitlements. To prevent such an outcome and help achieve a sustainable impact in Bangladesh, it is the donors' responsibility to invest their money purposefully and to insist on continuity in what was initiated through such projects. If Bangladesh's government is assured that new externally funded projects will repeatedly be launched with a continuously re-established infrastructure and re-installed services, it will refrain from making any efforts to take over costly responsibilities. In contrast, it will try to maintain a procedure like this, which also means that local NGOs are constantly contracted by IOs and, therefore, provided with rare employment opportunities. But not only NGOs and the government keep profiting; whoever is hired to build up and then dismantle the infrastructure at stake will be paid with money channeled through IOs. This cycle of project building and re-building not only leads to an incremental growth of NGOs in Bangladesh through contracting in transnational development projects, it also ensures continuous financial

2 Interview Ronald E. Berghuys, ILO/IPEC Chief Technical Advisor, 19 May 2008.

flows from external grant givers for internal disposal in Bangladesh. This is money that is not effectively used; it helps to marginally reduce child labor and enhance enrollment figures without creating a sustainable social system and without leading to a real impact.

Apart from expounding these problems relating to sustainability, the results of this study also contribute to another significant debate in development research, a debate pertinent to questions of conditionality. The IMF and World Bank's political programs have often been criticized for granting access to loans under certain conditions subsumed under the framework of "structural adjustment policies" requiring measures of "fiscal stability" with the aim of reducing governmental spending and enhancing privatization (compare Arat 2002: 190–1). In the early 2000s, new discussions on conditionality arose relating to demand-side interventions called conditional cash transfers (CCT). In Latin America, many countries had successfully adopted the CCT concept of social assistance programs from a Brazilian role model. It embraces the idea of paying stipends to families for their compliance with certain conditions (Schapper 2006a; for a literature overview see Schapper 2006b). These conditions, among others, entailed that children attended school and were sent to health checks and medical care on a regular basis (Rawlings 2005: 133). This, of course, implied a behavioral change among parents and families whose children were illiterate and used to work to contribute to the household income. Compared to supply-side interventions that concentrate solely on setting up required infrastructure – a school or a health clinic, these demand-side interventions fostered synergies in human development pertinent to health, nutrition, and education (Schapper 2006a: 3; Tabatabai 2006: vii). Clear evidence of success demonstrated through independent impact evaluations of the first generation of these programs in Brazil, Mexico, Nicaragua, and Colombia raised expectations of replicability in other Latin American countries and world regions (Rawlings 2005: 133). United Nations agencies and development banks intensively studied these programs (e.g. ILO/UNCTAD 2001; Das, Do and Özler 2004; Palma and Urzúa 2005), also in relation to particular development problems, such as child labor (Tabatabai 2006; Schapper 2006a). One issue at stake was to find out what exactly made these programs so successful. The debate circled around particular program mechanisms such as their demand-side character, the conditionality involved, the targeting procedure to identify the poorest children according to certain community and household income criteria, and providing grants and not loans (compare Tabatabai 2006: 11–15).

In this case study on the implementation of children's rights in Bangladesh, a set of conditional transfer programs was part of the empirical analysis: the FFE and its successive PESP. Whereas the FFE functioned with an in-kind transfer in the form of rice or wheat, the PESP is a classical CCT program providing stipends upon certain conditions. A comparison of regulative project mechanisms pertinent to the programs investigated here indicates that it is not conditionality that leads to a successful outcome. In contrast, the results of the QCA in Chapter 4 explicitly reveal that conditions should be absent in the implementation of children's rights. This, of course, can also be explained with the fact that only one CCT program was compared to six others pursuing a different project approach. A second alternative explanation would be that Bangladesh's conditional transfer programs concentrated exclusively on promoting primary education and left out child labor and health aspects that played a significant role in this book's definition of children's rights implementation. Nevertheless, project activities excluding any conditionality could be evaluated to be more successful in rights realization. Relevant examples are the ILO/IPEC projects concentrating on the elimination of the worst forms of child labor funded by the Government of the Netherlands and the US Department of Labor. What seems to be much more relevant, and contributes to the current CCT debate, is the issue of targeting. Identifying the poorest children with the help of household survey data played a dominant role in CCT programs throughout the world. Targeting also turned out to be a necessary condition for realizing children's rights. Before any policy activities could commence, those children and families whose rights had been denied and who were the neediest for social protection had to be identified. This related to children working in the worst forms of child labor, not attending school at all, and children who were deprived of any kind of basic health care services. Hence, a limited but not irrelevant contribution to the CCT debate is that targeting should be an essential project feature. The results of this study suggest that conditionalities can be successful for promoting the right to education and possibly also the right to health, but should be completely absent when children have to be protected from the worst forms of labor. Protection does not require a behavioral change of the rights-holders and cannot be achieved by a demand-side intervention. It has to be provided by the government and children's social environment, including their employers, parents, and the entire community.

Examining relations between the global, the national, and the local, of course, raises questions of the universality of human rights and children's rights. This discussion has been largely ignored in this book and an emphasis has been placed on a "global consensus" of children's rights in the sense of basic principles any world government could more or less agree to (Reynolds, Nieuwenhuys and Hanson 2006: 298). It is unquestioned that hazardous child labor has to be abolished, and that children need basic education and primary health services. This consensus, however, requires further local handling, it needs "local emphasis, refurbishing and interpretation" (Reynolds, Nieuwenhuys and Hanson 2006: 298). Bangladesh's case has illustrated extensively how context-specific some solutions to the problem of children's rights implementation were, such as the establishment of NFE centers in Dhaka's slums and the integration of religious leaders in CMCs. The political context of the Harkin Bill, a legislative draft introduced to the

US Senate which led to an inconsiderate dismissal of all under-age workers from Bangladesh's garment factories, reminds us that standards are not universal, and that coercive imposition of a Western understanding of norms can lead to devastating and counterproductive effects (compare Myers 2001: 42) in developing countries. In this sense, the Harkin Bill is an interesting two-sided example. As an extra-national instrument, it had a significant impact on Bangladesh, an impact that – at first sight – might be even more significant than that of international conventions. On the other hand, the Harkin Bill only triggered a development, the dismissal of tens of thousands of children that needed an appropriate policy response. But it was the policy response, i.e. the Bangladesh *Garment Sector Projects*, which finally resulted in a viable change for under-age factory workers. This, again, highlights the need for local and context-specific answers to transnational problems at stake.

7.6 Where to go from here?

This book concludes with suggestions for two future research paths that can be developed from the results of this empirical study. First of all, the hypotheses summarized in the model advocating a reconsidered understanding of human rights implementation (Table 7.1) need to be fed with additional empirical material, and require systematic testing. It is important to find out whether these hypotheses hold true in the case of other children's and human rights, and whether they are applicable to other world regions. Second, the findings of this in-depth research on children's rights in Bangladesh imply a strong call for reconsidering the role of non-state actors in realizing human rights change. The comparative analysis of seven norm-promoting projects in Bangladesh delivered substantial evidence that non-state actors at the local level take a crucial role in realizing children's rights. They act as internal and active participants in the local implementation process. In most of the programs considered here, NGOs were contracted to establish infrastructure, create institutions, and deliver services to the local rights-holders. This means that domestic and local NGOs take responsibilities as both policy advocates who remain external to the implementation process, and service providers who are integral participants in implementing rights at the same time. Such insights have already been discussed in development scholarship (e.g. Deacon 2007: 94–5) but are not yet to be found in IR studies that focus on the realization of human rights.

Service-providing NGOs are usually contracted by IOs or the government in the framework of transnational development projects. This contracting of NGOs is an ambiguous phenomenon requiring further exploration. To do so, Bangladesh constitutes an excellent study object displaying some wondrous trends. According to statistics published by the Government of Bangladesh, both the number of approved externally funded development projects and the number of local NGOs have increased significantly over the last 20 years. Whereas in June 1990, eight projects financed through foreign grants had been approved and 267 local NGOs existed,.ten years later, in 2000, the numbers were 776 projects and 1,347 NGOs. The latest figures from June 2010 show another major expansion, with 1,172 development projects and 2,305 local NGOs (NGO Affairs Bureau, Prime Minister's Office Bangladesh 2010).[3] These calculations, however, only relate to officially registered organizations. Unpublished reports point to a situation in which more than 20,000 organizations have already been working as social welfare agencies for a whole decade (Chowdhury 2000: 4). What exactly the defining features of a social welfare organization are, and how they can be distinguished from those of other local NGOs, remains blurry and requires a clear demarcation. Nevertheless, and regardless of what figures are the correct ones, questions relating to a link between the growing numbers of transnational development projects initiated in Bangladesh on the one hand and the rapid increase of local NGOs on the other hand need to be raised. Is there a demand for more NGOs that can be contracted in even more development projects? And do more and more NGOs emerge because they know that they will be contracted and that they can secure scarce employment opportunities through external donor money?

The process of contracting between IOs and NGOs itself should also be subject to further investigation. In Bangladesh, IOs or the government regularly publish bids in bigger daily newspapers in order to search for capable NGOs with local expertise, community contacts, and issue-related knowledge as implementers in transnational or national development projects. Sometimes, however, it remains unclear what exactly the contracting criteria are and how they are weighted. What precisely is it that matters for gathering a lucrative, well-paid project contract? Is it solely expertise pertinent to a particular policy field, is it about access to certain local elites or religious leaders in hard-to-reach communities in the urban slums or poor rural areas, or is it available capacities, material and immaterial resources, that matter? And what follows as a result of these criteria and the process of contracting itself? Doesn't it generate a competition among NGOs who apply for it? And if this is the case, doesn't competition for lucrative development contracts contradict NGOs' initial mandate that might possibly be focused on reducing child labor, fostering education, and promoting children's health? Competition and commercialization, at least, would explain why more and more organizations come into existence in the face of increasing development projects and contracts that secure work places in Bangladesh's NGO landscape. To feed this hypothesis of commercialization with empirical evidence, a much more systematic exploration of the issue would be

3 Flow of Foreign Grant Fund Through NGO Affairs Bureau: At A Glance: http://www.ngoab.gov.bd/Files/statistics.pdf.

required. The phenomenon of contracting in transnational development projects is of relevance to the discipline; answers to the questions raised above would contribute largely to scholarship on global policy networks, PPPs, the cooperative state in global governance, and shared responsibilities in transnational relations.

Bibliography

Legislative texts and policy documents

Bangladesh Labour Code, 2006: Translated English Version, Dhaka, Bangladesh: CCB Foundation.

Constitution of the People's Republic of Bangladesh 1971 (modified 2004), <http://www.pmo.gov.bd/constitution/index.htm> [retrieved 27 August 2009].

ILO 1973a: Minimum Age Convention C138, Adopted by the General Conference of the International Labour Organization, 58th Session, 26 June 1973, Geneva: International Labour Organization.

ILO 1973b: Minimum Age Recommendation R146, Adopted by the General Conference of the International Labour Organization, 58th Session, 26 June 1973, Geneva: International Labour Organization.

ILO 1999a: Worst Forms of Child Labour Convention C182, Adopted by the General Conference of the International Labour Organization, 87th Session, 17 June 1999, Geneva: International Labour Organization.

ILO 1999b: Worst Forms of Child Labour Recommendation R190, Adopted by the General Conference of the International Labour Organization, 87th Session, 17 June 1999, Geneva: International Labour Organization.

IMF 2005: Bangladesh: Poverty Reduction Strategy Paper, Washington, DC: International Monetary Fund.

IMF 2012: Bangladesh: Poverty Reduction Strategy Paper, Washington, DC: International Monetary Fund.

MFDM 2006: National Food Policy 2006. Ministry of Food and Disaster Management, Dhaka: Government of Bangladesh.

MoE 2010: National Education Policy, Ministry of Education, Dhaka: Government of Bangladesh.

MoLE 2010: National Child Labour Elimination Policy 2010, Ministry of Labour and Employment, Dhaka: Government of Bangladesh.

MoPME (without publication date): Learning for Change. Education for All: National Plan of Action (NPA II) 2003–2015. Dhaka: Government of Bangladesh.

MWCA 2005: National Plan of Action for Children Bangladesh 2004–2009. Ministry of Women and Children Affairs, Dhaka: Government of Bangladesh.

National Child Labor Policy (Draft) 2007: Unpublished document. Dhaka, Bangladesh.

Primary Education Compulsory Act 1990, Part V – Acts, Bills, etc, of the Bangladesh Parliament, Act No. 27 of 1990, http://www.mopme.gov.bd/ [retrieved 27 August 2009], Dhaka: Bangladesh Parliament.

UN 1948: Universal Declaration of Human Rights. Adopted by the United Nations General Assembly G.A. res. 217A (III), U.N. Doc A/810 at 71 (1948), United Nations General Assembly: Paris.

UN 1989: Convention on the Rights of the Child, Adopted and opened for signature, ratification and accession by General Assembly resolution 44/25 of 20 November 1989, United Nations: New York.

UN 1990: World Declaration on Education For All. Adopted at the World Conference on Education For All, Jomtien, Thailand, 5–9 March 1990.

UN 2006a: The International Bill of Human Rights. Fact Sheet No. 2 (Rev.1), Centre for Human Rights, United Nations, New York and Geneva.

UN Treaty Collection [a]: Covenant on Economic, Social and Cultural Rights, <http://treaties.un.org/Pages/ViewDetails.aspx?src=TREATY&mtdsg_no=IV-3&chapter=4&lang=en> [retrieved 27 August 2009].

UN Treaty Collection [b]: Covenant on Civil and Political Rights, <http://treaties.un.org/Pages/ViewDetails.aspx?src=TREATY&mtdsg_no=IV-4&chapter=4&lang=en> [retrieved 27 August 2009].

UN Treaty Collection [c]: Convention on the Rights of the Child, <http://treaties.un.org/Pages/ViewDetails.aspx?src=TREATY&mtdsg_no=IV-11&chapter=4&lang=en> [retrieved 27 August 2009].

Evaluation reports

Ahmed, Akhter U. and del Ninno, Carlo 2002: The Food for Education Program in Bangladesh: An Evaluation of its Impact on Educational Attainment and Food Security, FCND Discussion Paper No. 138, International Food Policy Research Institute, Washington, DC, Food Consumption and Nutrition Division.

Ahmed, Akhter U. and Babu, Suresh C. 2007: The Impact of Food for Education Programs in Bangladesh, Case Study # 3-8 of the Program: "Food Policy for Developing Countries: The Role of Government in the Global Food System", Ithaca: Cornell University.

Børnearbejde, Lotte 2003: Growing hope, Qualitative study, 1st batch, BST, Tongi, Bangladesh Institute of Labour Studies: Unpublished project document.

GoB/DNFE 2002: Non-formal Education Project-3 (Hard to Reach), Mid-term Evaluation Report, Dhaka: Eusuf and Associates in association with Center on Social Research and Human Development (unpublished project document).

GoB/BNFE 2008: Draft Mid-Term Evaluation Report of The Basic Education for Hard To Reach Urban Working Children's Project (unedited and unpublished project document).

Hossain, Sajjad 2008: Child Labour Situation, Major Responses in Bangladesh and BILS Activities. Bangladesh Institute for Labour Studies: Unpublished Project Document.

ILO/IPEC 2003a: Prevention and Elimination of the Worst Forms of Child Labour in the Urban Informal Sector in Bangladesh BGD/00/P01/NET, An Independent Mid-term Project Evaluation by An Independent Evaluation Team, ILO/IPEC Design, Evaluation and Documentation Section.

ILO/IPEC 2003b: Preventing and Eliminating the Worst Forms of Child Labour in Selected Formal and Informal Sectors in Bangladesh BGD/00/P50/USA, An Independent Mid-term Project Evaluation by An Independent Evaluation Team, ILO/IPEC Design, Evaluation and Documentation Section.

ILO/IPEC 2004a: Combined Evaluation of ILO/IPEC garment sector projects as part of the "Memorandum of Understanding" framework with the Bangladesh Garment Manufacturers and Exporters Association, A Final Project Evaluation by An Independent Evaluation Team, ILO-IPEC Design, Evaluation and Documentation Section.

ILO/IPEC 2004b: Manual for Child Labour Monitoring and Verification – Vol. I, A BGMEA/ILO/UNICEF MOU Project, International Labour Organization, International Programme on the Elimination of Child Labour (IPEC): Dhaka.

ILO/IPEC 2004c: ILO/IPEC BGMEA Phase III – Continuing the Child Labour Monitoring and Education Components and Prepare for the Integration Into a Broader Project in the Garment Export Industry in Bangladesh BGD/00/52/USA, A Final Evaluation by An Independent Evaluation Team, ILO-IPEC Design, Evaluation and Documentation Section.

ILO/IPEC 2004d: BGMEA Income and Employment Generation Project of the Extended Component of the BGMEA-UNICEF-ILO MOU Project BGD/98/M01/ITA, A Final Evaluation by An Independent Evaluation Team, ILO-IPEC Design, Evaluation and Documentation Section.

ILO/IPEC 2004e: BGMEA Integrated Child Labour Rehabilitation Project Extended Component of the BGMEA-UNICEF-ILO Project BGD/99/M02/NAD, A Final Evaluation by An Independent Evaluation Team, ILO-IPEC Design, Evaluation and Documentation Section.

ILO/IPEC 2006: Prevention and Elimination of Selected Worst Forms of Child Labour in the Informal Economy in Dhaka City BGD/00/P01/NET, An independent final evaluation by a team of external consultants, Unedited and unpublished project document.

ILO/IPEC 2007: Urban Informal Economy (UIE) Programme of the Project of Support to the Time Bound Programme towards the Elimination of the Worst Forms of Child Labour in Bangladesh, International Labour Organisation (ILO), Multi-Bilateral Programme of Technical Cooperation (unpublished project document).

ILO/UNICEF 2004: Addressing Child Labour in the Bangladesh Garment Industry 1995–2001: A synthesis of UNICEF and ILO evaluation studies of the Bangladesh garment sector projects, New York and Geneva, ILO and UNICEF.

Meng, Xin and Ryan, Jim 2003: Evaluating the Food for Education Program in Bangladesh, Preliminary draft, Department of Economics Research School of Pacific and Asian Studies, Canberra: Australian National University.

Meng, Xin and Ryan, Jim 2007: Does a Food for Education Program Affect School Outcomes? The Bangladesh Case. Discussion Paper No. 2557, Bonn: Forschungsinstitut zur Zukunft der Arbeit.

Mostofa, Golam Md. 2008: Eradication of Hazardous Child Labour in Bangladesh (Phase-2) Project, Annual Report (July 2007–June 2008) (unpublished project document), Dhaka: Eco-Social Development Organization (ESDO).

Ravallion, Martin and Wodon, Quentin 1998: Evaluating a Targeted Social Program When Placement Is Decentralized, Policy Research Working Paper 1945, Washington, DC: The World Bank, Development Research Group.

Literature

Abbott, Kenneth and Snidal, Duncan 2009: Strengthening International Regulation Through Transnational New Governance: Overcoming the Orchestration Deficit, in: *Vanderbilt Journal of Transnational Law*, Vol. 42: 501, 501–78.

Abels, Gabriele and Behrens, Maria 2005: ExpertInnen-Interviews in der Politikwissenschaft: Geschlechtertheoretische und politikfeldanalytische Reflexion einer Methode, in: Bogner, Alexander, Littig, Beate and Menz, Wolfgang (eds.): Das Experteninterview: Theorie, Methode, Anwendung, Wiesbaden: VS Sozialwissenschaften, 173–90.

ADB 2009: Asian Development Outlook 2009: Rebalancing Asia's Growth, South Asia, Mandaluyong City: Asian Development Bank, 184–221.

Ahmed, Akhter U. and del Ninno, Carlo 2002: The Food for Education Program in Bangladesh: An Evaluation of its Impact on Educational Attainment and Food Security, FCND Discussion Paper No. 138, Washington, DC: International Food Policy Research Institute, Food Consumption and Nutrition Division.

Ahmed, Akhter U. and Babu, Suresh C. 2007: The Impact of Food for Education Programs in Bangladesh, Case Study # 3-8 of the Program: "Food Policy for Developing Countries: The Role of Government in the Global Food System", Ithaca, NY: Cornell University.

Ahmed, Iqbal 2011: Statement by the Permanent Mission of Bangladesh to the UN, New York at the General Debate of the Third Committee of the 66th Session of the UNGA on "Promotion and protection of the rights of children", New York, 14 October 2011.

Alston, Philip 2005: Ships Passing in the Night: The Current State of the Human Rights and Development Debate Seen Through the Lens of Millennium Development Goals, in: *Human Rights Quarterly*, Vol. 27: 755–829.

Arat, Zehra F. 2002: Analyzing Child Labor as a Human Rights Issue: Its Causes, Aggravating Policies, and Alternative Proposals, in: *Human Rights Quarterly*, Vol. 24, 177–204.

Atkinson, Paul and Coffey, Amanda 1997: Analysing Documentary Realities, in: David Silverman (ed.): Qualitative Research: Theory, Method and Practice, London/Thousand Oaks/New Delhi: SAGE, 45–62.

Axelrod, Robert and Keohane, Robert 1985: Achieving Cooperation Under Anarchy: Strategies and Institutions, in: *World Politics*, Vol. 38, No. 1: 226–54.

Bache, Ian 2012: Multi-Level Governance in the European Union, in: Levi-Faur, David (ed.): Oxford Handbook of Governance, Oxford: Oxford University Press, 628–41.

Bache, Ian and Flinders, Matthew 2004: Multi-Level Governance and the Study of the British State, in: *Public Policy and Administration*, Vol. 19: 31, 31–51.

Bailey, Kenneth D. 1994: Typologies and Taxonomies: An Introduction to Classification Techniques. SAGE University Papers Series: Quantitative Applications in the Social Sciences, Thousand Oaks/London/New Delhi: SAGE.

BANBEIS 2006a: Bangladesh Bureau of Educational Information and Statistics: Primary Education, <http://www.banbeis.gov.bd/db_bb/primary_education_1.html> [retrieved 26 April 2009].

BANBEIS 2006b: Bangladesh Bureau of Educational Information and Statistics: Secondary Education, <http://www.banbeis.gov.bd/db_bb/secondary_education_1.htm> [retrieved 30 April 2009].

BANBEIS 2008: Bangladesh Bureau of Educational Information and Statistics: Primary Education, <http://www.banbeis.gov.bd/db_bb/primary_education_1.html> [retrieved 21 March 2013].

Bangladesh Development Gateway: Health Policy of Bangladesh, <http://www.bangladeshgateway.org/healthpolicy.php> [retrieved 27 August 2009].

Bannerman, Mathew J. and Berghuys, Ronald E. 2008: Breaking the Cycle: Key Learning from an ILO-IPEC Project in Bangladesh, Dhaka, Bangladesh: International Labour Office.

Basu, Kaushik 2003: International Labour Standards and Child Labour, in: Kabeer, Naila, Nambissan, Geetha B. and Subrahmanian, Ramya: Child Labour and the Right to Education in South Asia: Needs versus Rights? New Delhi/Thousand Oaks/London: Sage, 95–106.

BBS 2003: Report on National Child Labour Survey, Bangladesh Bureau of Statistics, Planning Division, Ministry of Planning, Dhaka: Government of the People's Republic of Bangladesh.

BBS 2009: Statistical Pocket Book, Bangladesh Bureau of Statistics, Ministry of Planning, Dhaka: Government of the People's Republic of Bangladesh.

BBS 2011: Population and Housing Census 2011: Bangladesh at a Glance, Bangladesh Bureau of Statistics, Statistics and Informatics Division, Ministry of Planning, Dhaka: Government of the People's Republic of Bangladesh.

Bedford, Kate 2008: Governing Intimacy in the World Bank, in: Rai, Shirin M. and Waylen, Georgina (eds.): Global Governance. Feminist Perspectives, Houndmills/New York: Palgrave Macmillan, 84–106.

Beer, Raphael and Bittlingmayer, Uwe 2008: Die normative Verwobenheit der Sozialisationsforschung, in: Hurrelmann, Klaus, Grundmann, Matthias and Walper, Sabine (eds.): Handbuch Sozialisationsforschung, 7. Auflage, Weinheim and Basel: Beltz Verlag, 56–69.

Begum, Shahin Ara 2008: Child Protection in Natural Disasters, in: BSAF: State of Child Rights in Bangladesh, Dhaka: Bangladesh Shishu Adhikar Forum (BSAF), 44–51.

Beisheim, Marianne, Dreher, Sabine, Walter, Gregor, Zangl, Bernhard and Zürn, Michael 1999: Im Zeitalter der Globalisierung? Thesen und Daten zur gesellschaftlichen und politischen Denationalisierung, Baden-Baden: Nomos.

Beisheim, Marianne, Liese, Andrea and Ulbert, Cornelia 2007: Erfolgsbedingungen transnationaler Partnerschaften: Hypothesen und erste Ergebnisse, in: Risse, Thomas and Lehmkuhl, Ursula (eds.): Regieren ohne Staat? Governance in Räumen begrenzter Staatlichkeit, Baden-Baden: Nomos, 247–71.

Benz, Arthur (ed.) 2004: Governance – Regieren in komplexen Regelsystemen: Eine Einführung, Wiesbaden: VS Verlag für Sozialwissenschaften.

Benz, Arthur 2009: Politik in Mehrebenensystemen, Wiesbaden: VS Verlag für Sozialwissenschaften.

Berger, Peter L. and Luckmann, Thomas 1991: The Social Construction of Reality: A Treatise in the Sociology of Knowledge, London: Penguin Books.

Bissell, Susan 2003: The Social Construction of Childhood, in: Kabeer, Naila, Nambissan, Geetha B. and Subrahmanian, Ramya: Child Labour and the Right to Education in South Asia: Needs versus Rights?, SAGE: New Delhi/Thousand Oaks/London, 53.

Blanchet, Thérèse 1996: Lost Innocence, Stolen Childhoods, Dhaka: University Press Limited.

Bogner, Alexander and Menz, Wolfgang 2005a: Expertenwissen und Forschungspraxis: Die modernisierungstheoretische und die methodische Debatte um die Experten. Zur Einführung in ein unübersichtliches Problemfeld, in: Bogner, Alexander, Littig, Beate and Menz, Wolfgang (eds.): Das Experteninterview: Theorie, Methode, Anwendung, Wiesbaden: VS Sozialwissenschaften, 7–30.

Bogner, Alexander and Menz, Wolfgang 2005b: Das theoriegeleitete Experteninterview: Erkenntnisinteress, Wissensformen, Interaktion, in: Bogner, Alexander, Littig, Beate and Menz, Wolfgang (eds.): Das Experteninterview: Theorie, Methode, Anwendung, Wiesbaden: VS Sozialwissenschaften, 33–70.

Børnearbejde, Lotte 2003: Growing hope, Qualitative study, 1st batch, BST, Tongi, Dhaka: Bangladesh Institute of Labour Studies (unpublished project document).

Börzel, Tanja A. 2005: European Governance – nicht neu, aber anders, in: Schuppert, Gunnar Folke (ed.): Governance Forschung: Vergewisserung über Stand und Entwicklungslinien, Baden-Baden: Nomos, 72–94.

Börzel, Tanja 2012: The European Union – A Unique Governance Mix, in: Levi-Faur, David (ed.): Oxford Handbook of Governance, Oxford: Oxford University Press, 613–27.

Börzel Tanja A. and Risse, Thomas 2001: Die Wirkung internationaler Institutionen: Von der Normanerkennung zur Normeinhaltung, Bonn: Preprints aus der Max-Planck-Projektgruppe Recht der Gemeinschaftsgüter, 2001/15.

Börzel, Tanja A. and Risse, Thomas 2005: Public-Private Partnerships: Effective and Legitimate Tools of Transnational Governance?, in: Grande, Edgar and Pauly, Luis W. (eds.): Complex Sovereignty: On the Reconstitution of Political Authority in the 21st Century, Toronto: University of Toronto Press, 195–216.

Boyden, Jo, Ling, Birgitta and Myers, William 1998: What Works for Working Children, Stockholm: Rädda Barnen.

Boyden, Jo and Mann, Gillian 2005: Children's Risk, Resilience, and Coping in Extreme Situations, in: Ungar, Michael (ed.): Pathways to Resilience Across Cultures and Contexts: Handbook for Working with Children and Youth, SAGE: Thousand Oaks, 3–25.

BpB 2004: Menschenrechte: Dokumente und Deklarationen, 4. aktualisierte und erweiterte Auflage, Band 397, Bundeszentrale für politische Bildung: Bonn.

Breitmeier, Helmut, Young, Oran R. and Zürn, Michael 2006: Analyzing International Environmental Regimes: From Case Study to Database, Cambridge, MA: MIT Press.

Brühl, Tanja and Liese, Andrea 2004: Grenzen der Partnerschaft. Zur Beteiligung privater Akteure an internationaler Steuerung, in: Albert, Mathias, Moltmann, Bernhard and Schoch, Bruno (eds.): Die Entgrenzung der Politik. Internationale Beziehungen und Friedensforschung, Frankfurt am Main: Campus, 162–90.

BSAF 2007: BSAF's Alternative Report on the Implementation of UNCRC in Bangladesh 2001–2006, Dhaka: Bangladesh Shishu Adhikar Forum (BSAF).

BSAF 2008: State of Child Rights in Bangladesh, Dhaka: Bangladesh Shishu Adhikar Forum (BSAF).

Bull, Hedley 1977: The Anarchical Society, London: Macmillan.

Burr, Rachel 2002: Global and Local Approaches to Children's Rights in Vietnam, in: *Childhood*, Vol. 9: 49–61.

Caparaso, James A. 2000: Changes in the Westphalian Order: Territory, Public Authority, and Sovereignty, in: *International Studies Review*: Continuity and Change in the Westphalian Order (Special Issue, edited by James A. Caparaso): 1–28.

CDPS 1997: Child Labour Situation in Nepal (Report from Migration and Employment Survey, 1995/96, Central Department of Population Studies (CDPS), Kathmandu, Nepal: Tribhuvan University and International Labour Organization (ILO), International Programme on the Elimination of Child Labour (IPEC).

Chayes, Abram and Chayes, Handler Antonia 1998: The New Sovereignty. Compliance with International Regulatory Agreements, Cambridge, MA: Harvard University Press.

Chayes, Abram, Chayes, Handler Antonia and Mitchell, Ronald B. 1998: Managing Compliance: A Comparative Perspective, in: Jacobsen, Harold K. and Brown Weiss, E. (eds.): Engaging Countries: Strengthening Compliance with International Environmental Accords, Cambridge, MA: MIT Press, 39–62.

Checkel, Jeffrey T. 1999: Why Comply? Constructivism, Social Norms and the Study of International Institutions. Centre for European Studies, University of Oslo: ARENA Working Paper.

Checkel, Jeffrey T. 2000: Compliance and Conditionality. Centre for European Studies, University of Oslo: ARENA Working Paper.

Checkel, Jeffrey T. 2005a: International Institutions and Socialization in Europe: Introduction and Framework, in: *International Organization*, Vol. 59: 801–26.

Checkel, Jeffrey T. 2005b: It's the Process Stupid! Process Tracing in the Study of European and International Politics, Centre for European Studies, University of Oslo: ARENA Working Paper.

Checkel, Jeffrey T. 2007: Constructivism and EU Politics, in: Jørgensen, Knud Erik, Pollack Mark A. and Rosamond, Ben (eds.): Handbook of European Union Politics, London: SAGE, 57–76.

Checkel, Jeffrey T. and Zürn, Michael 2005: Getting Socialized to Build Bridges: Constructivism and Rationalism, Europe and the Nation State, in: *International Organization*, Vol. 59, Fall: 1045–79.

Chowdhury, A. J. M. Ifjalul Haque 2000: History of Genesis – Growth of Development NGOs and their Networks with Special Reference to NGO-NGO Collaboration in Bangladesh, Dhaka: CORDAID – The Netherlands.

Christiansen, Thomas 1997: Reconstructing European Space: From Territorial Politics to Multilevel Governance, in: Jørgensen, Knud Erik (ed.): Reflective Approaches to European Governance, London: Macmillan, 51–68.

Das, Jishnu, Do, Q.-T. and Özler, B. 2004: Conditional Cash Transfers and the Equity-efficiency Debate, Washington, DC: World Bank.

DCS 1999: Child Activity Survey Sri Lanka, Department of Census and Statistics (DCS), Colombo, Sri Lanka: Ministry of Finance and Planning Sri Lanka and International Programme on the Elimination of Child Labour (IPEC).

Deacon, Bob 2007: Global Social Policy and Governance. London, Thousand Oaks/New Delhi/Singapore: SAGE.

Del Rosso, Joy Miller and Marek, Tonia 1996: Class action: Improving school performance in the developing world through better health and nutrition, Washington, DC: World Bank.

Dingwerth, Klaus 2004: Effektivität und Legitimität globaler Politiknetzwerke, in: Brühl, Tanja, Feldt, Heid, Hamm, Brigitte, Hummel, Hartwig and Martens, Jens (eds.) 2004: Unternehmen in der Weltpolitik: Politiknetzwerke, Unternehmensregeln und die Zukunft des Multilateralismus, Bonn: Dietz Verlag, 74–95.

Dingwerth, Klaus and Pattberg, Philipp 2006: Global Governance as a Perspective on World Politics, in: *Global Governance*, Vol. 12, No. 2: 185–203.

Dobusch, Leonhard and Quack, Sigrid 2009: Internationale und nichtstaatliche Organisationen im Wettbewerb um Regulierung: Schauplatz Urheberrecht, in: Dingwerth, Klaus, Kerwer, Dieter and Nölke, Andreas (eds.): Die Organisierte Welt: Internationale Beziehungen und Organisationsforschung, Baden-Baden: Nomos, 235–61.

Dorman, Peter 2008: Child labour, education and health: A review of the literature, International Programme on the Elimination of Child Labour (IPEC), Statistical Information and Monitoring Programme on Child Labour (SIMPOC), Geneva: International Labour Office.

Ebbinghaus, Bernhard 2005: When Less is More: Selection Problems in Large-N and Small-N Cross-national Comparisons, in: *International Sociology*, Vol. 20, No. 2: 133–52.

Ehsan, Khaled 2001: Chapter Seven: Children and Education, in: Child Rights: Reality and Challenges, Dhaka: The British Council, 147–56.

Ensing, Anna (2009): Hazardous Child Labour in the Leather Sector of Dhaka, Bangladesh, Amsterdam: Foundation for International Research on Working Children (IREWOC).

FBS 1996: Summary Results of Child Labour Survey in Pakistan (1996), Islamabad, Pakistan: Federal Bureau of Statistics (FBS), Statistics Division Ministry of Labour, Manpower and Overseas Pakistanis, International Labour Organization (ILO) and International Programme on the Elimination of Child Labour (IPEC).

Fearon, John and Wendt, Alexander 2002: Rationalism vs. Constructivism: A Skeptical View, in: Carlnaes, Walter, Risse, Thomas and Simmons, Beth A. (eds.): Handbook of International Relations, London: SAGE, 52–72.

Feldman, Shelley and Larson, Desi 2004: Bangladesh, in: Schmitz, Cathryne L., Traver, Elizabeth KimJin, Larson, Desi (eds.): Child Labor. A Global View, Westport/London: Greenwood Press, 13–25.

Finkelstein, Lawrence S. 1995: What is Global Governance? in: *Global Governance*, Vol. 1, No. 3: 367–71.

Finnemore, Martha and Sikkink, Kathryn 1998: Norm Dynamics and Political Change, in: *International Organization*, Vol. 52, No. 4: 887–917.

Flick, Uwe 2007: Designing Qualitative Research, Los Angeles: SAGE.

Flockhart, Trine 2004: "Master and Novices": Socialization and Social Learning through the NATO Parliamentary Assembly, in: *International Relations*, Vol. 18, No. 3: 361–80.

Flockhart, Trine 2006: "Complex Socialization": A Framework for the Study of State Socialization, in: *European Journal of International Relations*, Vol. 12, No. 1: 89–118.

Ganghof, Steffen 2005: Vergleichen in qualitativer und quantitativer Politikwissenschaft: X-zentrierte versus Y-zentrierte Forschungsstrategien, in: Sabine Kropp and Michael Minkenberg (eds.): Vergleichen in der Politikwissenschaft, Wiesbaden: VS Verlag, 76–93.

Genschel, Philipp and Zangl, Bernhard 2008: Metamorphosen des Staates: Vom Herrschaftsmonopolisten zum Herrschaftsmanager, in: *Leviathan*, Vol. 36: 430–54.
George, Alexander L. and Bennett, Andrew 2005: Case Studies and Theory Development in the Social Sciences, Cambridge, MA: MIT Press.
Gerring, John 2007: Case Study Research: Principles and Practices: Cambridge: Cambridge University Press.
Ghuznavi, Ruby and Ghuznavi, Farah 2001: Chapter One: Introduction, in: Child Rights: Reality and Challenges, Dhaka, Bangladesh: The British Council, 21–32.
Gurowitz, Amy 2006: The Diffusion of International Norms: Why Identity Matters, in: *International Politics*, Vol. 43: 305–41.
Habermas, Jürgen 1998: Die postnationale Konstellation und die Zukunft der Demokratie, in: Die postnationale Konstellation. Politische Essays, Frankfurt am Main: Suhrkamp, 91–169.
Halim, Abdul and Rahman, Masum Saifur 2007: The Bangladesh Labour Code, 2006: Translated English Version, Dhaka: CCB Foundation.
Hamm, Brigitte and Kocks, Alexander 2006: 40 Jahre UN Sozialpakt: Bilanz und Perspektiven, in: *Die Friedenswarte, Journal of International Peace and Organization*, Vol. 81, No. 1: 87–106.
Hasan, Jesmul 2007: Chapter 6: An Assessment of Child Labour Laws, Prevention Strategies and their Effectiveness in Bangladesh, in: Herath, Gamini and Sharma, Kishor 2007: Child Labour in South Asia, Aldershot/Burlington: Ashgate, 81–98.
Hasenclever, Andreas and Mayer, Peter 2007: Einleitung: Macht und Ohnmacht internationaler Institutionen, in: Hasenclever, Andreas, Wolf, Klaus Dieter and Zürn, Michael: Macht und Ohnmacht internationaler Institutionen. Festschrift für Volker Rittberger, Frankfurt/New York: Campus, 9–37.
Hooghe, Liesbet and Marks, Gary 1997: The Making of a Polity: The Struggle Over European Integration, in: European Integration online Papers (EIoP), Vol. 1, No. 4, <http://eiop.or.at/eiop/texte/1997-004a.htm> [retrieved 7 October 2002].
Hossain, Syeda Rubbaiyat 2007: Women's Rights, in: Ain o Salish Kendra (ASK) 2007: Human Rights in Bangladesh 2006, Dhaka: Ain o Salish Kendra (ASK), 139–52.
Hossain, Sajjad 2008: Child Labour Situation, Major Responses in Bangladesh and BILS Activities, Dhaka: Bangladesh Institute for Labour Studies (unpublished project document).
Huckel, Carmen, Rieth, Lothar and Zimmer, Melanie 2007: Die Effektivität von Public-Private Partnerships, in: Hasenclever, Andreas, Wolf, Klaus Dieter and Zürn, Michael: Macht und Ohnmacht internationaler Institutionen. Festschrift für Volker Rittberger, Frankfurt/New York: Campus, 115–44.
Hurrelmann, Klaus 2002: Einführung in die Sozialisationstheorien, 8. Auflage, Weinheim and Basel: Beltz Verlag.
Ikenberry, G. John and Kupchan, Charles A. 1990: Socialization and Hegemonic Power, in: *International Organization*, Vol. 44, No. 3: 283–315.
ILO 2000: Child Labour Convention achieves fastest ratification pace in ILO history. Press release, 7 June 2000, International Labour Organization: Geneva, <http://www.ilo.org/global/About_the_ILO/Media_and_public_information/Press_releases/lang--en/WCMS_007896/index.htm> [retrieved 27 August 2009].
ILO 2001: Eliminating the Worst Forms of Child Labour: An Integrated and Time-Bound Approach. A Guide for Governments, Employers, Workers, Donors and other Stakeholders, International Labour Office: Kathmandu, Nepal.

ILO 2002a: Every Child Counts. New Global Estimates on Child Labour. International Programme on the Elimination of Child Labour (IPEC), Statistical Information and Monitoring Programme on Child Labour (SIMPOC), International Labour Office, International Labour Organization: Geneva.

ILO 2002b: Decent work and the informal economy, International Labour Conference, 90th Session 2002, Report VI, Sixth item on the agenda, International Labour Office: Geneva.

ILO 2004a: IPEC Action against Child Labour 2002–2003. Progress and future priorities, International Programme on the Elimination of Child Labour (IPEC): Geneva.

ILO 2004b: Child Labour and Responses: Overview Note – Bangladesh, International Programme on the Elimination of Child Labour (IPEC), International Labour Office: Geneva.

ILO 2006: The end of child labour: Within reach. Global Report under the Follow-up to the ILO Declaration on Fundamental Principles and Rights at Work 2006, International Labour Conference, 95th Session 2006, Report I (B), International Labour Office: Geneva.

ILO 2007: Child Labour Facts and Figures: An Analysis of Census 2001, International Labour Office: Geneva.

ILO 2009: National Legislation and Policies Against Child Labour in Bangladesh, ILO Subregional Office for South Asia, International Labour Organization: <http://www.ilo.org/public/english/region/asro/newdelhi/ipec/responses/bangladesh/national.htm> [retrieved 16 April 2010].

ILO 2010: New global report on child labour as effort to end child labour slow, ILO calls for "re-energized" global action, Press release ROAP/10/11, Bangkok: ILO Regional Office for Asia and the Pacific.

ILOLEX [a]: Database of International Labour Standards, C182 Worst Forms of Child Labour Convention, <http://www.ilo.org/ilolex/english/convdisp1.htm> [retrieved 27 August 2009].

ILOLEX [b]: Database of International Labour Standards, Convention No. C182, <http://www.ilo.org/ilolex/english/convdisp1.htm> [retrieved 27 August 2009].

ILO NATLEX: Bangladesh, (Database, country profiles, International Labour Organization) <http://www.ilo.org/dyn/natlex/natlex_browse.details?p_lang=en&p_country=BGD&p_classification=00&p_origin=COUNTRY&p_sortby=SORTBY_COUNTRY> [retrieved 27 August 2009].

ILO/UNCTAD 2001: The Minimum Income for School Attendance Initiative (MISA): Achieving International Development Goals in African Least Developed Countries, Geneva: ILO/UNCTAD Advisory Group.

IMF 2005: Bangladesh: Poverty Reduction Strategy Paper, Washington, DC: International Monetary Fund.

IRIN 2008: Integrated Regional Information Networks (IRIN), Bangladesh: Skills education for working children, 17 June 2008, available at: <http://www.unhcr.org/refworld/docid/4858bfe1c.html> [retrieved 27 April 2010].

Jacobsen, Harold K. and Brown Weiss, E. (eds.) 2000: Engaging Countries: Strengthening Compliance with International Environmental Accords, Cambridge, MA: MIT Press.

James, Allison 2008: Giving Voice to Children's Voices: Practices and Problems, Pitfalls and Potentials, in: *American Anthropologist*, Vol. 109, No. 2: 261–72.

Jenichen, Anne 2012: Politische Innovation in internationalisierten Nachkriegskontexten: Bosnische Frauenrechtspolitik in vergleichender Perspektive, Wiesbaden: VS Verlag für Sozialwissenschaften.

Jepperson, Ronald L., Wendt, Alexander and Katzenstein, Peter J. 1996: Norms, Identity and Culture in National Security, in: Katzenstein, Peter J. (ed.): The Culture of National Security: Norms and Identity in World Politics, New York: Columbia University Press, 33–75.

Jetschke, Anja and Liese, Andrea 2013: The power of human rights a decade after: from euphoria to contestation? in: Risse, Thomas, Ropp, Stephen C. and Sikkink, Kathryn (eds.): The Persistent Power of Human Rights: From Commitment to Compliance, 26–42.

Joachim, Jutta 2001: NGOs, die Vereinten Nationen und Gewalt gegen Frauen. Agenda-Setting, Framing, Gelegenheits- und Mobilisierungsstrukturen, in: *Zeitschrift für Internationale Beziehungen*, Vol. 2: 209–41.

Jones, Gareth A. 2005: Children and Development: Rights, Globalization and Poverty, in: *Progress in Development Studies*, Vol. 5, No. 4: 336–42.

Judge, Anthony 1995: NGOs and Civil Society: Some Realities and Distortions: The Challenge of Necessary to Governance Organizations, in: *Transnational Associations*, Vol. 47, No. 3: 156–80.

Kabir, FHM Humayan 2009: Govt may re-introduce "five-year dev plan", in: The Financial Express, Internet Edition: http://www.thefinancialexpress-bd.com/more.php?news_id=62660 [retrieved 6 May 2010].

Kaufmann, Daniel 2004: Human Rights and Development: Towards Mutual Reinforcement, Paper prepared for a conference co-sponsored by the Ethical Globalization Initiative and the NYU for Human Rights and Global Justice, New York: New York University School of Law.

Keck, Margaret E. and Sikkink, Kathryn 1998: Activists Beyond Borders. Ithaca, NY: Cornell University Press.

Kelman, Herbert C. 2006: Interests, Relationships, Identities: Three Central Issues for Individuals and Groups in Negotiating their Social Environment, in: *Annual Review of Psychology*, Vol. 57: 1–26.

Keohane, Robert O. and Nye, Joseph S. 1977: Power and Interdependence. World Politics in Transition, Boston, MA: Little, Brown.

Khair, Sumaiya 2001: Chapter Four: Child Labour, in: Child Rights: Reality and Challenges, Dhaka: The British Council, 79–92.

Khair, Sumaiya 2004: Bangladesh Child Domestic Workers in Dhaka City: Situation Analysis, Dhaka: International Programme on the Elimination of Child Labour (IPEC), International Labour Office.

Khair, Sumaiya 2005: Child Labour in Bangladesh: A Forward Looking Policy Study, Centre for Policy Dialogue, Geneva: International Programme on the Elimination of Child Labour, International Labour Office.

Khan, Mahub Husain 2008: Primary Education in the New Millennium, in: BSAF: State of Child Rights in Bangladesh, Dhaka: Bangladesh Shishu Adhikar Forum (BSAF), 36–42.

Khan, Mohammad Ali 2001: Child Labour in Dhaka City, Dhaka: Hakkani Publishers.

Khan, Shamsul I., Islam, S. Aminul and Haque, M. Imdadul 2008: Political Culture, Political Parties and the Democratic Transition in Bangladesh, Dhaka: The University Press Limited.

Khondker, Rokhsana 1993: Bangladesh, in: ICJ: Rights of the Child: Report of a Training Programme in Asia, Geneva: International Commission of Jurists.

Khundker, Nasreen 2005: Situation of Child Labour in Bangladesh. Highlights from the National Child Labour Survey 2002–03, Dhaka: International Labour Office.

King, Gary, Keohane, Robert O. and Verba, Sidney 1994: Designing Social Inquiry: Scientific Inference in Qualitative Research, Princeton, NJ: Princeton University Press.

Koenig-Archibugi, Mathias 2006: Introduction: Institutional Diversity in Global Governance, in: Koenig-Archibugi, Mathias and Zürn, Michael (eds.): New Modes of Governance in the Global System. Exploring Publicness, Delegation and Inclusiveness, Houndmills and New York: Palgrave Macmillan, 1–30.

Kohler-Koch, Beate and Rittberger, Berthold 2009: A Futile Quest for Coherence: The Many Frames of EU Governance, in: Kohler-Koch, Beate and Larat, Fabrice: European Multi-Level Governance, Cheltenham/Northampton, MA: Edward Elgar, 3–18.

Kooiman, Jan 1994: Social-Political Governance: Introduction, in: Kooiman, Jan (ed.): Modern Governance: New Government – Society Interactions, London/ Thousand Oaks/New Delhi: SAGE, 1–6.

Krasner, Stephen D. (ed.) 1983: International Regimes, Ithaca, NY: Cornell University Press.

Krasner, Stephen D. 1993: Sovereignty, Regimes and Human Rights, in: Rittberger, Volker (ed.): Regime Theory and International Relations, Oxford: Clarendon, 139–67.

Krennerich, Michael 2010: Menschenrechte – ein Einstieg, in: Utz, Britta (ed.): Handbuch der Menschenrechtsarbeit, Edition 2010/2011, Berlin: Friedrich-Ebert-Stiftung, Forum Menschenrechte, 5–14.

Kumar, Anand 2007: Bangladesh: Care Taker Government on the Offensive – Bangladesh Monitor – Paper No. 7, Paper no. 2143, South Asia Analysis Group, <http://www.southasiaanalysis.org/%5Cpapers22%5Cpaper2143.html> [retrieved 26 August 2009].

Lansky, Mark 1997: Perspectives. Child labour: How the challenge is being met, in: *International Labour Review*, Vol. 136, No. 2: 233–57.

Leibfried, Stephan and Zürn, Michael 2006: Von der nationalen zur postnationalen Konstellation, in: Leibfried, Stephan and Zürn, Michael (eds.): Transformation des Staates? Frankfurt am Main: Suhrkamp, 19–65.

Levy, Marc A., Young, Oran R. and Zürn, Michael 1995: The Study of International Regimes, in: *European Journal of International Relations*, Vol. 1, No. 3: 267–330.

Lieberson, Stanley 1985: Making it Count: The Improvement of Social Research and Theory, Berkeley: University of California Press.

Liese, Andrea 2003: Internationale Regulierung im Politikfeld Kinderarbeit, in: Senghaas-Knobloch, Eva, Dirks, Jan and Liese, Andrea: Internationale Arbeitsregulierung in Zeiten der Globalisierung. Politisch-organisatorisches Lernen in der Internationalen Arbeitsorganisation (IAO), Münster: LIT Verlag, 39–102.

Liese, Andrea 2005: „Capacity Building" als Strategie zur Förderung der Regeleinhaltung. Erfahrungen der ILO bei der Abschaffung von Kinderarbeit, zur Veröffentlichung in: Senghaas-Knobloch, Eva (ed.): Weltweit geltende Arbeitsstandards trotz Globalisierung. Analysen, Diagnosen, Einblicke, Münster: LIT Verlag.

Liese, Andrea 2006: Staaten am Pranger. Zur Wirkung internationaler Regime auf innerstaatliche Menschenrechtspolitik, Wiesbaden: VS Verlag für Sozialwissenschaften.
Liese, Andrea 2009: Die unterschiedlich starke Öffnung internationaler Organisationen gegenüber nichtstaatlichen Akteuren. Erklärungen der Institutionen- und Organisationstheorie, in: Dingwerth, Klaus, Kerwer, Dieter and Nölke, Andreas (eds.): Die Organisierte Welt: Internationale Beziehungen und Organisationsforschung, Baden-Baden: Nomos, 189–207.
Littig, Beate 2005: Interviews mit Experten und Expertinnen: Überlegungen aus geschlechtertheoretischer Sicht, in: Bogner, Alexander, Littig, Beate and Menz, Wolfgang (eds.): Das Experteninterview: Theorie, Methode, Anwendung, Wiesbaden: VS Sozialwissenschaften, 191–206.
Maloney, Clarence, Aziz, K. M. Ashraful and Sarker, Profulla C. 1981: Beliefs and Fertility in Bangladesh, Dhaka: International Centre for Diarrhoeal Disease Research.
March, James G. and Olsen, Johan P. 1998: The Institutional Dynamics of International Political Orders, Oslo: ARENA Working Papers.
Marcus, George 1998: Ethnography through Thick and Thin, Princeton, NJ: Princeton University Press.
Masud, M.A. Kashem 2011: Selection of NGOs for Survey, Non-Formal Education and Skill Development Training, Dhaka: Government of the People's Republic of Bangladesh, Ministry of Labour and Employment.
Mayntz, Renate 2009a: Über Governance: Institutionen und Prozesse politischer Regelung. Schriften aus dem Max-Planck-Institut für Gesellschaftsforschung, Frankfurt/New York: Campus.
Mayntz, Renate 2009b: Governancetheorie: Erkenntnisinteresse und offene Fragen, in: Grande, Edgar and May, Stefan (eds.): Perspektiven der Governance-Forschung, Baden-Baden: Nomos, 9–19.
Mayring, Philipp 2000: Qualitative Content Analysis, in: *Forum Qualitative Social Research*, Vol. 1: 2.
McNicoll, Geoffrey and Cain, Mead 1990: Institutional Effects on Rural Economic and Demographic Change, Working Papers No.14, Research Division, New York: The Population Council.
Meng, Xin and Ryan, Jim 2007: Does a Food for Education Program Affect School Outcomes? The Bangladesh Case. Discussion Paper No. 2557, Bonn: Forschungsinstitut zur Zukunft der Arbeit.
Merry, Sally E. 2006a: Human Rights and Gender Violence: Translating International Law into Local Justice, Chicago/London: Chicago University Press.
Merry, Sally E. 2006b: Transnational Human Rights and Local Activism: Mapping the Middle, in: *American Anthropologist*, Vol. 108: 38–51.
Merry, Sally E., Levitt, Peggy, Rosen, Mihaela S. and Yoon, Diana H. 2010: Law From Below: Women's Human Rights and Social Movements in New York City, in: *Law & Society Review*, Vol. 44, No. 1: 101–28.
Merry, Sally E. and Stern, Rachel E. 2005: The Female Inheritance Movement in Hong Kong: Theorizing the Local/Global Interface, in: *Current Anthropology*, Vol. 46: 387–409.
Meuser, Michael and Nagel, Ulrike 2005: ExpertInneninterviews – vielfach erprobt, wenig bedacht: Ein Beitrag zur qualitativen Methodendiskussion, in: Bogner,

Alexander, Littig, Beate and Menz, Wolfgang (eds.): Das Experteninterview: Theorie, Methode, Anwendung, Wiesbaden: VS Sozialwissenschaften, 71–94.

MFDM 2006: National Food Policy 2006. Ministry of Food and Disaster Management, Government of Bangladesh: Dhaka.

Mitchell, Ronald B. 2005: Flexibility, Compliance and Norm Development in the Climate Regime, in: Schram Stokke, Olav, Hovi, John and Ulfstein, Geir (eds.): Implementing the Climate Regime: International Compliance, UK: Earthscan Press, 65–83.

Mitchell, Ronald B. 2007: Compliance Theory: Compliance, Effectiveness, and Behaviour Change in International Environmental Law, in: Brunee, Jutta, Bodansky, Daniel and Hey, Ellen (eds.): Oxford Handbook for International Environmental Law, Oxford: Oxford University Press, 894–921.

MoPME: Ministry of Primary and Mass Education, Government of the People's Republic of Bangladesh, <http://www.mopme.gov.bd/> [retrieved 26 August 2009].

Morgenthau, Hans J. 1973: Politics Among Nations: The Struggle for Power and Peace, New York: Alfred A. Knopf.

Myers, William E. 2001: The Right Rights? Child Labor in a Globalizing World, in: *The Annals of the American Academy of Political and Social Science*, Vol. 575, May: 38–55.

National Institute of Population Research and Training/Mitra and Associates/Macro International 2009: Bangladesh Demographic and Health Survey 2007, Dhaka and Calverton: National Institute of Population Research and Training, Mitra and Associates, and Macro International: Dhaka and Calverton.

Neyer, Jürgen 2005: Domestic Limits of Supranational Law: Comparing Compliance with European and International Foodstuff Regulations, in: Zürn, Michael and Joerges, Christian (eds.): Law and Governance in Postnational Europe: Compliance Beyond the Nation State, Cambridge: Cambridge University Press, 118–48.

NGO Affairs Bureau, Prime Minister's Office Bangladesh 2010: Flow of Foreign Grant Fund Through NGO Affairs Bureau: At A Glance, <http://www.ngoab.gov.bd/Files/statistics.pdf> [retrieved: 19 December 2010].

OHCHR 2006a: Annual Report 2006, Geneva: United Nations, Office of the United Nations High Commissioner for Human Rights.

OHCHR 2006b: Frequently Asked Questions on a Human Rights-Based Approach to Development Cooperation, New York and Geneva: United Nations, Office of the United Nations High Commissioner for Human Rights.

Olsen, Johan P. 2009: EU Governance: Where Do We Go From Here?, in: Kohler-Koch, Beate and Larat, Fabrice: European Multi-Level Governance, Cheltenham/Northampton, MA: Edward Elgar, 191–209.

Palma, Julieta and Urzúa, Raúl 2005: Anti-poverty Policies and Citizenry: The Chile Solidario Experience, UNESCO Policy Paper 12, Paris: UNESCO.

Park, Susan 2006: Theorizing Norm Diffusion Within International Organizations, in: *International Politics*, Vol. 43: 342–61.

Phillips, Douglas A. and Gritzner, Charles F. 2007: Bangladesh, New York: Infobase Publishing.

Preuss, Ulrich K. 1996: Prospects of a Constitution for Europe, in: *Constellations*, Vol. 3, No. 2: 209–24.

Prior, Lindsey 2004: Documents, in: Seale, Clive, Gobo, G., Gubrium, J. F. and Silverman, D. (eds): Qualitative Research Practice, London: SAGE, 375–90.

Prügl, Elisabeth 2008: Gender and the Making of Global Markets: An Exploration of the Agricultural Sector, in: Rai, Shirin M. and Waylen, Georgina 2008: Global Governance. Feminist Perspectives, Houndmills/New York: Palgrave Macmillan, 43–63.

Prügl, Elisabeth and Meyer, Mary K. 1999: Introduction. Gender Politics in Global Governance, in: Prügl, Elisabeth and Meyer, Mary K.: Gender Politics in Global Governance, Rowman and Littlefield Publishers: Lanham, MD/Oxford, 3–16.

Ragin, Charles C. 1987: The Comparative Method: Moving Beyond Qualitative and Quantitative Strategies, Berkeley/Los Angeles/London: University of California Press.

Ragin, Charles C. 1989: The Comparative Method: Moving Beyond Qualitative and Quantitative Strategies, Berkeley/Los Angeles/London: University of California Press.

Ragin, Charles C. 2004: Turning the Tables: How Case-Oriented Research Challenges Variable-Oriented Research, in: Brady, Henry E. and Collier, David 2004 (eds.): Rethinking Social Inquiry. Lanham, MD: Rowman & Littlefield, 123–38.

Rahman, Atiur, Kabir, Mahfuz and Alam, AKM Muksudul 2005: Public Expenditure in Primary Education in Bangladesh: An Analysis, Working Paper No. 1/2005, Shamunnay: Dhaka.

Raustiala, Kal and Slaughter, Anne-Marie 2002: International Law, International Relations and Compliance, in: Carlsnaes, Walter, Risse, Thomas and Simmons, Beth A. (eds.): Handbook of International Relations. London: SAGE, 538–58.

Rawlings, Laura B. 2005: A New Approach to Social Assistance: Latin America's Experience with Conditional Cash Transfer Programmes, in: *International Social Security Review*, Vol. 58, Nos. 2–3: 133–61.

Raynor, Janet 2005: Educating girls in Bangladesh: watering a neighbour's tree?, in: Aikman, Sheila and Unterhalter, Elaine: Beyond Access: Transforming Policy and Practice for Gender Equality in Education, London: Oxfam Publishing, 83–105.

Reinicke, Wolfgang H. and Deng, Francis M. 1999: Critical Choices: The United Nations, networks, and the future of global governance. UN Vision Project on Global Public Policy Networks, Washington, DC: The Global Public Policy Project.

Reynolds, Pamela, Nieuwenhuys, Olga and Hanson, Karl 2006: Refractions of Children's Rights in Development Practice: A View from Anthropology, in: *Childhood*, Vol. 13: 291–302.

Riedel, Eibe 2004: Der internationale Menschenrechtsschutz. Eine Einführung, in: BpB Menschenrechte: Dokumente und Deklarationen, Bonn: Bundeszentrale für politische Bildung, 11–40.

Rihoux, Benoît and Ragin, Charles C. 2009: Configurational Comparative Methods: Qualitative Comparative Analysis (QCA) and Related Techniques. Applied Social Research Methods Series, Vol. 51, Thousand Oaks/London/Delhi/Singapore: SAGE.

Risse, Thomas 2003: Konstruktivismus, Rationalismus und Theorien Internationaler Beziehungen – Warum empirisch nichts so heiß gegessen wird, wie es theoretisch gekocht wurde, in: Hellmann, Gunther, Wolf, Klaus Dieter and Zürn, Michael (eds.): Die neuen Internationalen Beziehungen. Forschungsstand und Perspektiven in Deutschland, Baden-Baden: Nomos, 99–132.

Risse, Thomas 2007: Menschenrechte als Grundlage der Weltvergemeinschaftung? Die Diskrepanz zwischen Normanerkennung und Normeinhaltung, in: Janz, Nicole and Risse, Thomas (eds.): Menschenrechte – Globale Dimensionen eines universellen Anspruchs, Baden-Baden: Nomos, 17–37.

Risse, Thomas, Jetschke, Anja and Schmitz, Hans Peter (eds.) 2002: Die Macht der Menschenrechte. Internationale Normen, Kommunikatives Handeln und politischer Wandel in den Ländern des Südens, Baden-Baden: Nomos.

Risse, Thomas, Ropp, Stephen C. and Sikkink, Kathryn (eds.) 1999: The Power of Human Rights. International Norms and Domestic Change, Cambridge: Cambridge University Press.

Risse, Thomas and Sikkink, Kathryn 1999: The Socialization of International Human Rights Norms into Domestic Practices, in: Risse, Thomas, Ropp, Stephen C. and Sikkink, Kathryn (eds.): The Power of Human Rights. International Norms and Domestic Change, Cambridge: Cambridge University Press, 1–38.

Rittberger, Volker 1994: Internationale Organisationen – Politik und Geschichte, Opladen: Leske und Budrich.

Rittberger, Volker 2009: Legitimes Weltregieren durch inklusive, multipartistische Institutionen?, in: Rittberger, Volker (ed.): Wer regiert die Welt und mit welchem Recht? Baden-Baden: Nomos, 261–82.

Rittberger, Volker and Zangl, Bernhard 2006: International Organization. Polity, Politics and Policies, Basingstoke: Palgrave Macmillan.

Robinson, Mary 2002: "Making Human Rights Matter", speech at the ARCO Forum of Public Affairs, 30 September 2002, <http://www.ksg.harvard.edu/news/news/2002/robinson_100102.htm> [retrieved 26 January 2007].

Rosenau, James N. 1992: Governance, Order, and Change in World Politics, in: Rosenau, James N. and Czempiel, Ernst-Otto (eds.): Governance without Government: Order and Change in World Politics, Cambridge: Cambridge University Press, 1–29.

Rosenau, James N. 1995: Governance in the Twenty-first Century, in: *Global Governance*, Vol. 1, No. 1: 13–43.

Rosenau, James N. and Czempiel, Ernst-Otto (eds.) 1992: Governance without Government: Order and Change in World Politics, Cambridge: Cambridge University Press.

Ruggie, John G. 1998: What Makes the World Hang Together? Neo-utilitarianism and the Social Constructivist Change, in: *International Organization*, Vol. 52, No. 4: 855–85.

Save the Children UK 2008: The Child Development Index: Holding governments accountable for children's wellbeing, London: The Save the Children Fund.

Save the Children UK 2012: The Child Development Index 2012: Progress, Challenges and Inequality, London: The Save the Children Fund.

Schäferhoff, Marco 2009: Kooperation oder Konkurrenz? Zur Kooperationsbereitschaft internationaler Verwaltungsstäbe in transnationalen öffentlich-privaten Partnerschaften, in: Dingwerth, Klaus, Kerwer, Dieter and Nölke, Andreas (eds.): Die Organisierte Welt: Internationale Beziehungen und Organisationsforschung, Baden-Baden: Nomos, 211–31.

Schapper, Andrea 2006a: Reviewing Conditional Cash Transfers from a Child Labor Perspective: Evidence from Brazil and Mexico. ILO/IPEC Working Paper, Geneva: International Labour Organization (ILO).

Schapper, Andrea 2006b: Conditional Cash Transfers: An Annotated Bibliography. ILO/IPEC, Child Labour Research Network, Geneva: International Labour Organization (ILO).

Schapper, Andrea 2009: From the Global to the Local: How International Children's Rights in Bangladesh Reach the Grassroots' Level, in: *Consilience: The Journal for Sustainable Development*, 1:2.

Schapper, Andrea 2010: Global Child Rights and Local Change: Evidence from Bangladesh, in: *Journal of Human Security*, 6:1, 3–21.

Schimmelfennig, Frank 2000: International Socialization in the New Europe: Rational Action in an Institutional Environment, in: *European Journal of International Relations*, Vol. 6, No. 1: 109–39.

Schimmelfennig, Frank 2002: Internationale Sozialisation: Von einem "erschöpften" zu einem produktiven Forschungsprogramm?, in: Hellmann, Gunther, Wolf, Klaus Dieter and Zürn, Michael (eds.): Die neuen Internationalen Beziehungen. Forschungsstand und Perspektiven in Deutschland. Baden-Baden: Nomos, 401–27.

Schimmelfennig, Frank 2003: Strategic Action in a Community Environment: The Decision to Enlarge the European Union to the East, in: *Comparative Political Studies*, Vol. 36, Nos. 1/2; 156–83.

Schmitz, Hans Peter and Sikkink, Kathryn 2002: International Human Rights, in: Carlsnaes, Walter, Risse Thomas and Simmons, Beth A. (eds.): Handbook of International Relations, Thousand Oaks/London/New Delhi: SAGE, 517–37.

Schmitz, Hans Peter and Sikkink, Kathryn 2013: International Human Rights, in: Carlsnaes, Walter, Risse Thomas and Simmons, Beth A. (eds.): Handbook of International Relations, Thousand Oaks/London/New Delhi: SAGE, 827–51.

Schneckener, Ulrich 2007: Fragile Staatlichkeit und State-building: Begriffe, Konzepte und Analyserahmen in: Beisheim, Marianne and Schuppert, Gunnar Folke (eds.): Staatszerfall und Governance, Baden-Baden: Nomos, 98–120.

Schuppert, Gunnar Folke (2008): Governance – auf der Suche nach Konturen eines „anerkannt uneindeutigen Begriffs", in: Schuppert, Gunnar Folke and Zürn, Michael (eds.): Governance in einer sich wandelnden Welt, Wiesbaden: VS Verlag für Sozialwissenschaften, 13–20.

Seifer, Kerstin 2009: Governance als Einfluss-System: Der politische Einfluss von NGOs in asymmetrisch strukturierten Interaktionsarrangements. Wiesbaden: VS Verlag für Sozialwissenschaften.

Sengupta, Sumun and Hossain, Deloar 2007: Child Protection and Child Rights: Current Status and Challenges, in: Ain o Salish Kendra (ASK): Human Rights in Bangladesh, Dhaka: Ain o Salish Kendra, 183–200.

Shishu Adhikar Sangjog 2001: Executive Summary, in: Child Rights: Reality and Challenges, Dhaka: The British Council, 5–20.

Shrestha, Nanda R. 2002: Nepal and Bangladesh: A Global Studies Handbook, Santa Barbara, CA: ABC-CLIO.

Siddiky, Chowdhury Irad Ahmed 2003: The Compromised Republic: An Inquiry into the Development of Underdevelopment, Dhaka: Oriental KAS Publishers.

Siddiqui, Kamal 2003: Better Days, Better Lives: Towards a Strategy for Implementing the Convention on the Rights of the Child in Bangladesh, Dhaka: The University Press Limited.

Snidal, Duncan 1985: The Game Theory of International Politics, in: *World Politics*, Vol. 38, No. 1: 25–57.

Snow, David A. 2004: Framing Processes, Ideology, and Discursive Fields, in: Snow, David A., Soule, Sarah A. and Kriesi, Hanspeter (eds.): The Blackwell Companion to Social Movements, Malden, MA: Blackwell, 380–412.

Steffek, Jens and Nanz, Patrizia (eds.) 2008: Emergent Patterns of Civil Society Participation in Global and European Governance, in: Steffek, Jens, Kissling, Claudia and Nanz, Patrizia 2008: Civil Society Participation in European and Global Governance, Houndmills/New York: Palgrave Macmillan, 1–29.

Strange, Susan 1996: The Retreat of the State: The Diffusion of Power in the World Economy, Cambridge: Cambridge University Press, 3–15.

Stryker, Sheldon and Burke, Peter J. 2000: The Past, Present, and Future of an Identity Theory, in: *Social Psychology Quarterly*, Vol. 63, No. 4: 284–97.

Sultana, Fadia and Ahmed, Mohiuddin 2001: Chapter Two: Child Health and Nutrition, in: Child Rights: Reality and Challenges, Dhaka: The British Council, 33–50.

Tabatabai, Hamid 2006: Eliminating Child Labour: The Promise of Conditional Cash Transfers, Geneva: International Labour Office.

Tallberg, Jonas 2002: Paths to Compliance. Enforcement, Management and the European Union, in: *International Organization*, Vol. 56, No. 3: 609–43.

Thanki, Mridu Shailaj and Dhingra, Jyoti 2006: Our Lives and Hopes: Beyond Statistics and Reports, Dhaka: The University Press Limited.

The Daily Star (2008a, 30 December): Landslide mandate, The Daily Star, Internet Edition, <http://www.thedailystar.net/newDesign/news-details.php?nid=69338> [retrieved 26 August 2009].

The Daily Star (2008b, 6 December): Freed Hasina asks for quick election, The Daily Star, Internet Edition, <http://www.thedailystar.net/story.php?nid=40807> [retrieved 26 August 2009].

The Daily Star (2008c, 13 June): Pilot project on primary schools. Brac's role is focused on improving quality, The Daily Star, 10.

The Daily Star (2008d, 14 June): Resistance to BRAC-run teachers training project spreads, The Daily Star, 3.

The Daily Star (2008e, 14 June): Pilot Project to Supervise Pry Schools. Teachers' protest programs begin tomorrow, The Daily Star, 5.

The Daily Star (2009, 9 April): National Education Policy: 16-member body formed to make recommendations, The Daily Star, Internet Edition: <http://www.thedailystar.net/story.php?nid=83392> [retrieved 27 August 2009].

Tietjen, Karen 2003: The Bangladesh Primary Education Stipend Project: A Descriptive Analysis, Partnership for Sustainable Strategies on Girls' Education: World Bank, British Department for International Development, The Netherlands, The Nike Foundation, UNESCO and UNICEF.

Tillmann, Klaus-Jürgen 2000: Sozialisationstheorien: Eine Einführung in den Zusammenhang von Gesellschaft, Institution und Subjektwerdung, 10. Auflage, Reinbek: Rowohlt.

Transparency International 2012: 2012 Corruption Perceptions Index, <http://cpi.transparency.org/cpi2012/results/> [retrieved 18 March 2013].

UIA 2010: Union of International Associations. What is a non-governmental organization (NGO)?, http://www.uia.be/node/163573, [retrieved 24 June 2010].

UN 1968: Arrangements for consultation with non-governmental organizations, ECOSOC Resolution 1296 (XLIV), Adopted at the 1520th plenary meeting, 23 May 1968, 21–6.

UN 2004: Basic Facts: About the United Nations, Department of Public Information, New York: United Nations.

UN 2005: Civil and Political Rights: The Human Rights Committee, Office of the High Commissioner for Human Rights, New York and Geneva: United Nations.

UN 2006b: The Committee on Economic, Social and Cultural Rights, Centre for Human Rights, New York and Geneva: United Nations.

UN 2006c: The Rights of the Child, Fact Sheet No. 10 (Rev1), Centre for Human Rights, New York and Geneva: United Nations.

Underdal, Arild 2004: Methodological Challenges in the Study of Regime Effectiveness, in: Underdal, Arild and Young, Oran R. (eds.): Regime Consequences: Methodological Challenges and Research Strategies, Dordrecht: Kluwer Academic Publ., 27–48.

UNDP: United Nations Development Programme Bangladesh: MDGs and Bangladesh, <http://www.undp.org.bd/mdgs.php> [retrieved 30 April 2009].

UNDP 2008: Human Development Reports. 2008 Statistical Update. The Human Development Index – going beyond income, <http://hdrstats.undp.org/2008/countries/country_fact_sheets/cty_fs_BGD.html> [retrieved 26 August 2009].

UNDP 2009a: Human Development Report 2009: Bangladesh. The Human Development Index – going beyond income, <http://hdrstats.undp.org/en/countries/country_fact_sheets/cty_fs_BGD.html> [retrieved 15 April 2010].

UNDP 2009b: Human Development Report 2009: Nepal. The Human Development Index – going beyond income, <http://hdrstats.undp.org/en/countries/country_fact_sheets/cty_fs_NPL.html> [retrieved 15 April 2010].

UNDP 2009c: Human Development Report 2009: Myanmar. The Human Development Index – going beyond income. <http://hdrstats.undp.org/en/countries/country_fact_sheets/cty_fs_MMR.html> [retrieved 15 April 2010].

UNDP 2011: Human Development Report 2011: Sustainability and Equity: A Better Future for All: Bangladesh: HDI values and rank changes in the 2011 Human Development Report, http://hdrstats.undp.org/images/explanations/BGD.pdf [retrieved 18 March 2013].

Ungar, Michael 2004: Nurturing Hidden Resilience in Troubled Youth, Toronto: Toronto University Press.

UNICEF 2008: The State of the World's Children 2009, New York: United Nations Children's Fund (UNICEF).

UNICEF 2012: The State of the World's Children 2012, New York: United Nations Children's Fund (UNICEF).

UNICEF: UNICEF South Asia: Meena Communication Initiative, <http://www.unicef.org/rosa/media_2479.htm> [retrieved 17 November 2009].

USDoL: United States Department of Labor, Bureau of International Affairs, Bangladesh, <http://www.dol.gov/ilab/media/reports/iclp/sweat/bangladesh.htm> [retrieved 27 August 2009].

USDoL 2006: United States Department of Labor: 2006 Findings on the Worst Forms of Child Labor. Country Profile: Bangladesh, Washington, DC: U.S. Department of Labor, Bureau of International Labor Affairs.

USDoL 2009: United States Department of Labor: 2009 Findings on the Worst Forms of Child Labor. Country Profile: Bangladesh, Washington, DC: U.S. Department of Labor, Bureau of International Labor Affairs.

USDoL 2011: United States Department of Labor: 2011 Findings on the Worst Forms of Child Labor. Country Profile: Bangladesh, Washington, DC: U.S. Department of Labor, Bureau of International Labor Affairs.

Uvin, Peter 2004: Human Rights and Development, Bloomfield: Kumarian Press.

Van Aaken, Anne 2005: Making International Human Rights Protection More Effective: A Rational Choice Approach to the Effectiveness of Ius Standi Provisions, Bonn: Reprints of the Max Planck Institute for Research on Collective Goods, 16.

Van Evera, Stephen 1997: Guide to Methods for Students of Political Science, Ithaca, NY: Cornell University Press.

Van Schendel, Willem 2009: A History of Bangladesh, Cambridge: Cambridge University Press.

Vogel, David and Kessler, Timothy 2000: How Compliance Happens and Doesn't Happen Domestically, in: Jacobsen, Harold K. and Brown Weiss, E. (eds.): Engaging Countries: Strengthening Compliance with International Environmental Accords, Cambridge, MA: MIT Press, 19–38.

Waltz, Kenneth N. 1979: Theory of International Politics, New York: McGraw-Hill.

Weiler, Joseph H.H. 1997: The Reformation of European Constitutionalism, in: *Journal of Common Market Review*, Vol. 35, No. 1: 97–131.

Wendt, Alexander 1992: Anarchy is what states make of it: the social construction of power politics, in: *International Organization*, Vol. 46, No. 2: 391–425.

White, Sarah T. 2002: Being, Becoming and Relationship: Conceptual Challenges of a Child Rights Approach in Development, in: *Journal of International Development*, Vol. 14: 1095–104.

Whyte, William F. 1984: Learning from the Field: A Guide from Experience, Beverly Hills, CA: SAGE.

Wiener, Antje 2007: Making Normative Meaning Accountable in International Politics, Discussion Paper SP IV 2007-305, Wissenschaftszentrum Berlin für Sozialforschung 2007.

Witzel, Andreas 2000: Das problem-zentrierte Interview, in: *Forum Qualitative Sozialforschung* 1:1, <http://www.qualitative-research.net/index.php/fqs/article/viewArticle/1132/2519> [retrieved 19 December 2010].

Woodhead, Martin 1996: In Search of the Rainbow: Pathways to Quality in Large Scale Programmes for Young Disadvantaged Children, The Hague: Bernard Van Leer Foundation.

Woodhead, Martin 2006: Changing Perspectives on Early Childhood: Theory, Research and Policy, Background paper prepared for the Education for All Global Monitoring Report 2007, UNESCO.

Young, Oran R. 1982: Regime Dynamics: The Rise and Fall of International Regimes, in: *International Organization*, Vol. 36, No. 2: 277–97.

Zürn, Michael 1997: Vom Nutzen internationaler Regime für eine Friedensordnung, in: Senghaas, Dieter (ed.) 1997: Frieden machen, Frankfurt am Main: Suhrkamp, 465–81.

Zürn, Michael 2002: From Interdependence to Globalization, in: Walter Carlsnaes, Thomas Risse and Beth A. Simmons (eds.): Handbook of International Relations, London: SAGE, 235–54.

Zürn, Michael 2005: Introduction: Law and Compliance at Different Levels, in: Zürn, Michael and Joerges, Christian (eds.): Law and Governance in Postnational Europe: Compliance Beyond the Nation State, Cambridge: Cambridge University Press, 1–39.

Zürn, Michael 2012: Global Governance as Multi-Level Governance in: Levi-Faur, David (ed.): Oxford Handbook of Governance, Oxford: Oxford University Press, 730–44.

Zürn, Michael and Joerges, Christian (eds.) 2005: Law and Governance in Postnational Europe: Compliance Beyond the Nation State, Cambridge University Press, Cambridge.

Zürn, Michael and Koenig-Archibugi, Mathias 2006: Conclusion II: The Modes and Dynamics of Global Governance, in: Koenig-Archibugi, Mathias and Zürn, Michael (eds.): New Modes of Governance in the Global System: Exploring Publicness, Delegation and Inclusiveness, Houndmills/New York: Palgrave Macmillan, 236–54.

Zürn, Michael and Leibfried, Stephan 2005: A New Perspective on the State: Reconfiguring the National Constellation, in: Zürn, Michael and Leibfried, Stephan (eds.): Transformations of the State, Cambridge: Cambridge University Press, 1–36.

Zürn, Michael and Neyer, Jürgen 2005: Conclusions: The Conditions of Compliance, in: Law and Governance in Postnational Europe: Compliance Beyond the Nation State, Cambridge: Cambridge University Press, 183–217.

Zwingel, Susanne 2005: How do international women's rights norms become effective in domestic contexts? An analysis of the Convention on the Elimination of all Forms of Discrimination against Women (CEDAW), Inauguraldissertation zur Erlangung des akademischen Grades eines Doktors der Sozialwissenschaft, Bochum: Ruhr Universität Bochum, Fakultät für Sozialwissenschaft.

Interviews

Interview *Aftab Uddin Ahmad*, Underprivileged Children's Educational Programs, Executive Director, 25 June 2008.

Interview *Rafique Uddin Ahmed*, ILO/IPEC/UNICEF/BGMEA garment sector projects; former ILO National Project Coordinator, 18 June 2008.

Interview *Shahida Akther*, Project Officer, World Food Program, 23 June 2008.

Interview *Musbah Alim*, CATALYST, Executive Director, 19 June 2008.

Interview *Profulla Chandra Barman*, Bangladesh Rural Advancement Committee, former Project Coordinator, 17 July 2008.

Interview *Ronald E. Berghuys*, ILO/IPEC Chief Technical Advisor, 19 May 2008.

Interview *Shafiqur Rahman Bhuian*, former Ministry of Labour and Employment, Deputy Chief Planning and Project Director Eradication of Hazardous Child Labour in Bangladesh, 18 June 2008.

Interview *Tapan Kumar Chakravorty*, Deputy Director, Primary Education and Stipend Program, Ministry of Primary and Mass Education, 17 July 2008.

Interview *A.N.M. Shamsuddin Dewan*, Jano Seba Kendra, Director, 26 June 2008.

Interview *Hasina Habib*, Gono Shahajja Sangstha, Coordinator Field Education Programme, 9 June 2008.
Interview *Sajjad Hossain*, BILS, Child Labour Elimination Project Coordinator, 21 May 2008.
Interview *Md. Hamidul Islam*, Bangladesh Development Service Center, Assistant Director, 24 May 2008.
Interview *Khandaker Asraful Islam*, Bangladesh Development Service Center, Deputy Director, 24 May 2008.
Interview *Abul Haseeb Khan*, Resource Integration Centre, Director, 26 May 2008.
Informal Interview *Sumaiya Khair*, Professor, Department of Law, University of Dhaka, 23 June 2008.
Interview *Md. Monwer Hossain Khandker*, Bangladesh Rural Advancement Committee; Programme Manager, Field Operations BRAC Education Programme, 8 June 2008.
Interview *Mohammad Golam Kibria*, UNICEF, Education Section, Education Officer, 4 June 2008.
Interview *Nazrul Islam Miah*, ILO, Administrative and Finance Assistant, 24 June 2008.
Interview *M. Mohiuzzaman*, Underprivileged Children's Educational Programs, Manager Technical Education, 2 June 2008.
Interview *Sanwar Moni*, Padakhep, Coordinator Executive Director's Secretariat, 1 July 2008.
Interview *Rezaul Quader*, Ministry of Primary and Mass Education, Project Director, 8 July 2008.
Interview *M. Ehsanur Rahman*, Dhaka Ahsania Mission, Deputy Executive Director, 25 May 2008.
Interview *Md. Harun-or Rashid*, Lighthouse, Executive Director, 20 May 2008.
Interview *Ali Hossain Sarder*, Regional Coordinator Monitoring and Evaluation, Education Programme, Gono Shahajjo Sangstha, 22 June 2008.
Interview *Shahid Uz Zaman*, Eco-Social Development Organization, Executive Director, 6 July 2008.

Index

For Product Safety Concerns and Information please contact our EU representative GPSR@taylorandfrancis.com
Taylor & Francis Verlag GmbH, Kaufingerstraße 24, 80331 München, Germany

www.ingramcontent.com/pod-product-compliance
Ingram Content Group UK Ltd.
Pitfield, Milton Keynes, MK11 3LW, UK
UKHW022026061126
477531UK00002B/65